THE FIGHTING QUAKER:
NATHANAEL GREENE

Books by Elswyth Thane

FICTION
Riders of the Wind
Echo Answers
Cloth of Gold
His Elizabeth
Bound to Happen
Queen's Folly
Tryst
Remember Today
From This Day Forward
Melody
Letter to a Stranger

THE WILLIAMSBURG NOVELS
Dawn's Early Light
Yankee Stranger
Ever After
The Light Heart
Kissing Kin
This Was Tomorrow
Homing

NONFICTION
The Tudor Wench
Young Mr. Disraeli
England Was an Island Once
The Bird Who Made Good
Reluctant Farmer
The Family Quarrel
Washington's Lady
Potomac Squire
Mount Vernon Is Ours
Mount Vernon: The Legacy
Mount Vernon Family
The Virginia Colony
Dolley Madison

PLAYS
The Tudor Wench
Young Mr. Disraeli

THE FIGHTING QUAKER:
Nathanael Greene

by ELSWYTH THANE

Hawthorn Books, Inc.
PUBLISHERS / New York

THE FIGHTING QUAKER

DESIGN BY STANLEY S. DRATE

1 2 3 4 5 6 7 8 9 10

The maps and illustrations on pages 88, 96, 109, 113, 114, 119, 205, 238, and 248 are reproduced from *Pictorial Fieldbook of the Revolution*, by Benson Lossing, published by Harper in 1850.

The map on page 143 is reproduced by permission of Alfred A. Knopf, Inc., from *Portrait of a General*, by William Willcox, copyright © 1964.

The map on page 195 is reproduced from *History of South Carolina in the Revolution*, by Edward McCrady, published by The MacMillan Company in 1901.

FOR

HOWARD GOTLIEB

Preface

In the present state of this country, and with the observance of the Bicentennial of the Revolution approaching in 1976, the story of the stormy and precarious beginnings of these United States cannot be too often told. George Washington and Nathanael Greene were the only two generals who served *continuously* throughout the eight years of the conflict, until the final evacuation of American soil by the British in 1783. For the last three years of that weary time, while Washington was pinned down on the Hudson by Clinton's occupation of New York City, Greene carried an independent command in the Carolina swamps, where he was sent to confront England's most energetic and competent general, Lord Cornwallis—after two American armies, under Horatio Gates and Benjamin Lincoln, had already been swallowed up in the South.

There is no question among informed scholars of the period that Washington had no peer and no accredited rival in the American army. The most detailed examination of his character and behavior by *qualified* researchers has uncovered nothing that could be called self-interest, vanity, weakness, or scandal. Standing next to Washington and still in his shadow is the man equally remarkable in many ways, whose early death robbed him and his country of further service that might have raised him higher in history—the Quaker general from Rhode Island,

Nathanael Greene. It was Greene's campaign in the Carolinas during 1780 and 1781 that sent Cornwallis reeling northward into Virginia in such bad shape that after another running fight there with Lafayette, Wayne, and Steuben he went to ground at Yorktown and could be brought to surrender by the combined forces of Washington and his French ally, Rochambeau.

Without Greene's stubborn, selfless expenditure of himself and eventually of his own private funds which represented the future security of his family, it is possible that the British army under Cornwallis, or later under Alexander Leslie, might have been able to overrun the Carolinas and Virginia from the south and by combining with Clinton from New York to compel the surrender of the whole American force—an end to the war which could have seen the American commander in chief transported to London to be tried and executed for treason.

Yet Greene was a book-soldier, without any experience in the field before he was pitched into the war at its beginning as a colonial brigadier. Except for the random bombardment of the Cambridge camp in the winter of 1775, he had never been under fire till the New York campaign of 1776. Many of his fellow officers in the colonial army, though relatively young men, still were veterans, like Washington, of the old frontier wars with the French and the Indians. But Greene had had a quiet Quaker boyhood working at his father's forge and mills in the Rhode Island countryside, building up his small personal library and reading military memoirs and Latin classics despite his Quaker father's disapproval.

He was expelled from Meeting for taking an un-Quaker interest in the "independent companies" of volunteers that formed and drilled everywhere in the colonies after the Boston Port Bill in 1774 sparked the rebellion in New England, and he soon joined the local Kentish Guards as a private in the ranks. When he marched with them to join the colonial army besieging the British regulars in Boston after Lexington and Concord, he left a bride of less than a year. He was ten years younger than Washington, who was forty-three when the war began. His normal life expectancy would have carried him beyond Washington's, perhaps even to the War of 1812, when there were very few ranking veterans of the Revolution left.

A born student and a self-educated soldier, even in the field Greene maintained the habit of reading a few pages of some favorite book to relax his mind before the scant hours of sleep he allowed himself. His letters were as well composed and as legibly written as Washington's own, and his General Orders written on a little portable desk in his tent were literate and forceful. At a time when such ideas seemed novel if not dangerous in America, he believed in the necessity of an armed force enlisted for the duration of the war, uniformly equipped and disciplined, and subject to the orders of a single commander in chief. If these beliefs had been realized, without the interference of an ill-informed and muddle-headed Congress at Philadelphia, the war might have been appreciably shortened.

He was an instinctive tactician rather than an experienced strategist, with an eye for terrain like Washington's. He had the ability to make quick decisions and act on them promptly, and he had the personal magnetism—the word is now "charisma"—which drew men to him and held their loyalty and confidence in the face of discouragement and failure.

After the battle of Eutaw Springs during the Southern campaign, a British officer complained that Greene was "indefatigable in collecting troops and leading them to be defeated," and then added, "The more he is beaten, the farther he advances in the end." Like Washington, Greene had a quick temper and great self-control. Above all, he could believe in and support a cause that often seemed lost, and he could inspire in others the same steadfast conviction.

The sheer physical misery of the ill-provided men in the ranks was fully shared by their officers—the untended wounds which took a hideous toll, the grinding hunger and the blistering thirst, the unsheltered wet and cold of the endless marches where the famous bloody footprints on frozen ground were attested to by the men who were there and saw them, and the hateful, humid heat of the Low Country swamps, alive with snakes and leeches, where to fall was often to drown. We must contemplate these ordeals again and again, in the light of our present comforts and privileges—not with indifference because it was all so long ago, not with a skepticism which only reveals willful ignorance of the written record, but with a grateful awareness of the agonies our simple, great-hearted forefathers were able to endure in order to realize their dream of a new nation, conceived in liberty. Some pride in our country and our heritage must be revived and sustained. They were giants in those days. We can still learn from them.

                                                    E. T.

Acknowledgments

As always, the prompt and efficient service of the New York Society Library has been of enormous assistance. Thanks are also rendered to the library staff of the Mount Vernon Ladies' Association; to Dr. Howard Gotlieb, archivist of the Mugar Memorial Library at Boston University; to Raymond Pisney, of the North Carolina Department of Archives; to John Reed, of the Valley Forge Historical Society; to Mrs. T. C. Greene, of East Greenwich, Rhode Island; to Mr. Lloyd Nourse, of the Nathanael Greene Homestead, Coventry, Rhode Island; to Mrs. Albert Harkness, Vice-Regent for Rhode Island of the Mount Vernon Ladies' Association; and to Miss Marguerite Steedman, of Charleston, South Carolina. Correspondence with Lieutenant-Colonel W. E. G. Ord-Statter, British Army, retired, yielded much useful information on the British regiments in America during the Revolution.

E. T.

Contents

xiii

p. 269
269-270
p 278

Chapter 1

There are certain years in the life of a man or of a nation which appear as milestones, marking the end of one phase of the journey through time and the beginning of another. Often they are not recognized at once as the swift, crowded days slip by, and it is only later that one can say: It happened here; the change came here. The year 1774 stands bright and clear as a turning point in the life of everyone who lived it, significant also for generations to come—the year the first Continental Congress met at Philadelphia.

It found Nathanael Greene on the threshold of marriage and at the opening of an unforeseen, unlikely career as the right-hand man of the commander in chief in a war everyone then still hoped might never start. The Greene family were substantial Quaker citizens, established in Rhode Island for five generations. They were the prosperous owners of grist and saw mills and a forge that was famous for its anchors. Nathanael was born on the seventh of August, 1742, the third of that name in his family. He had seven brothers, two of them by his father's first wife, Phoebe Greene, and five by his own mother, Mary Mott. Nathanael was the second child of his father's second marriage, and his two half-brothers died in the same year, when he was nineteen. He and his brother Jacob then became his father's chief heirs in the business of the forge and the mills.

At Boston citizens disguised as Indians had dumped the over-taxed tea into the harbor in December of 1773, and reprisals by the government in London were anticipated. The slow communications of the period involved a delay of several months before the certain wrath of George III's Parliament could descend upon Massachusetts. In the early months of 1774 its form could only be guessed at, and in the uneasy interim the colonies pursued their daily lives with apparent unconcern. Red-coated British regulars swarmed in Boston—overbearing men, professionals at intimidation, and bored with overseas duty among the stiff-necked inhabitants.

In Rhode Island the flame of freedom burned as brightly as in Massachusetts, but perhaps less noisily. It must be remembered that Rhode Island is half water and that Narragansett Bay is full of smaller islands, on one of which is Newport town, while Providence, Warwick, East Greenwich, and Narragansett town may be considered mainland. The bay was crisscrossed by an organized packet, or ferry service, of small, sloop-rigged boats carrying both freight and passengers. To reach Providence, at the head of the bay, it was necessary to run the gauntlet of British revenue vessels stationed in the sheltered waters at the entrance to Newport.

Newport in the 1760's was one of the most elegant and prosperous cities in the New World, notable for its accomplished social atmosphere, the beauty of its fashionable women, and the wealth of its merchant citizens. It lay only a short sail from the point on shore nearest to Nathanael Greene's roomy white house at Coventry.

In 1770, when he was twenty-seven, he had been chosen by his father to supervise the new forge established there, a few miles from the family home and the parent forge at Potowomut, where his brother Jacob and the younger boys worked at their father's side. Though he was still unmarried, Nathanael built a comfortable house on a hillside looking toward the bay. From nearby East Greenwich he made frequent trips to Newport, where he had a host of young friends who appreciated his cheerful, vigorous though thoughtful presence among them. He was high-spirited for a Quaker lad and always enjoyed the country dances and informal sports of the neighborhood.

When he still lived under the parental roof, Nathanael had often broken the family curfew by climbing out an upper window for an evening with his friends, accepting the inevitable discipline on his return with fortitude. Another weakness, in his father's opinion, was his passion for learning and his stubborn love of books. An itinerant teacher had been hired during the winter months of his childhood to teach the Greene boys to read, write, and cypher, which apparently satisfied his brothers. His father was convinced that if a man was able to read his Bible and keep his accounts, that was all anyone needed to know.

At the age of fourteen Nathanael had wanted more education than his father thought right or needful. By his industry at the forge and the mills the boy earned reluctant indulgence and was allowed to attend a little school in East Greenwich where a Scot named Maxwell introduced him to Latin and geometry. Under Maxwell's guidance he read Horace and Euclid and Caesar, often keeping a book in his hand during his attendance on the forge fires and the hopper at the grist mill. His brother has recorded that in the winter evenings after the day's work was done, his mother would sit down in her favorite fireside corner with her knitting and mending, while his father settled opposite her with a mug of homemade cider spiced with ginger against the cold. But Nat would leave the cozy family circle and retire to an unheated little room above the kitchen where he could study his books without distractions.

Although there was no lack of money, none could be spent to satisfy Nathanael's craving to read. There is a legend that as a boy he earned his spending money by fashioning miniature anchors and other toys while he worked at the forge. These he sold as a sideline during his excursions to Newport and Warwick and invested in books to extend his education and augment his little library.

As the 1770's began, it was plain that Newport had much to lose if a rupture occurred between the colonies and England. Nevertheless, it soon became the scene of growing dissatisfaction and rebellion as a result of the trade restrictions imposed by the government in London. The arbitrary behavior of the commanding officers of the small fleet of armed vessels sent out by Parliament to enforce its navigation acts in Rhode Island waters created great resentment among the inhabitants. The persistent interference with local commerce caused several lively incidents in which the British revenue sloops were fired on and threatened after they had seized cargoes bound for Rhode Island ports or had attempted to impress seamen captured from incoming colonial ships for service in the British navy.

Rhode Islanders were an independent aquatic breed long accustomed to their own "legitimate" form of piracy known as privateering—a system by which small, fast, privately owned vessels were armed and sent out to prey on foreign cargo ships, carrying off the captured goods for sale in home ports at a substantial profit to the owners. Many Rhode Island fortunes had been founded and maintained by this questionable practice, which the governors usually winked at in their own interest when the adventurers returned from the Spanish Main or the Madeiras with such exotic spoils as periwigs, looking glasses, cocoa, woven birdcages, lace, indigo, flutes, wineglasses, and gold-headed canes.

Rhode Island naturally objected when its high-handed conduct at sea was perpetrated off its own coast by the British vessels assigned to watch and harass American shipping subject to British import duty and carrying taxable commodities. By 1772, when Nathanael had been two years at Coventry, the atmosphere on Narragansett Bay was so volatile that it needed only a spark to cause an explosion.

Provocation was repeatedly provided by the British naval lieutenant commanding the revenue schooner *Gaspée* of eight guns, stationed in the bay. Lieutenant Duddington exceeded his authority in all directions, apparently just for the fun of molesting the local shipowners and sea captains. He detained even market boats for search and seized produce and cargoes, delaying and frightening ferry passengers on their lawful occasions and even plundering ashore. Providence complained to Governor Wanton, who sent a sheriff aboard the *Gaspée* to remonstrate with Duddington. The lieutenant returned an insolent reply and called on John Montagu, the British admiral at Boston, to back him up. This the admiral was delighted to do, expressing his opinion of Rhode Island as "a set of lawless piratical people." Wanton responded sharply to Montagu's reprimand, pointing out that the governor of Rhode Island did not require instructions from the King's admiral at Boston. Duddington continued to harass local enterprise.

In June 1772 the American packet *Hannah* arrived at Newport from New York, reported herself properly at customs, and proceeded up the bay toward Providence. Lieutenant Duddington pursued her, intending to intercept her with the usual trumped-up charge of smuggling. Led on by the *Hannah*, with an ebbing tide, the *Gaspée* made a reckless change of course and ran aground below Pawtucket on a sandbar that still bears her name. The *Hannah* escaped and reached Providence about sunset in a state of indignation. Her captain reported the *Gaspée*'s pursuit and resulting mishap to Mr. John Brown, one of the foremost merchants and shipowners of Providence. Knowing the tides as he did, Brown was aware that the *Gaspée* could not be floated off the sandbar till the small hours of the morning, and he promptly went into action.

Drums beat in the streets of the town, calling volunteers to a meeting at Sabin's Tavern on the waterfront, where it was proposed to board and destroy the *Gaspée* while she lay stranded. Brown ordered his own shipmasters to collect eight large longboats, with their oars and rowlocks muffled, at Fenner's wharf opposite the tavern. Veteran sea captains, notably Abraham Whipple of the West Indies trade, acted as steersmen of the boats, and before midnight the party was under way.

Arriving within sixty yards of the motionless *Gaspée*, they approached on the bows to avoid her guns and were twice hailed by the single sentinel on watch without returning an answer. Pistols were fired toward the boats, and Lieutenant Duddington, roused from bed, suddenly appeared on the starboard gunwale in his shirt, hailed twice more, and fired a pistol himself. According to the account of young Ephraim Bowen, who was present as one of the volunteers in Whipple's longboat, the doughty Captain Whipple replied as follows: "I am the sheriff of the county of Kent, God damn you! I have got a warrant to apprehend you, God damn you! So *surrender*, God damn you!"

The young man on the narrator's right in Whipple's boat said to Bowen: "Eph, reach me your gun, I can kill that fellow."

Eph obliged, and his friend fired the musket, and Duddington fell. More shots were promptly fired from the *Gaspée* and were returned by the men in the longboats, which were then alongside.

An attacking party boarded the *Gaspée* at the bow, drove the half-dressed crew below, and made themselves masters of the deck. The bleeding commander was assisted to the cabin of his ship, and a student of medicine who had accompanied Whipple as surgeon was ordered to dress his wound, which was in the groin. Duddington so appreciated his services that he offered a gold stock-buckle in payment. It was refused as being too valuable, but a silver one was accepted in its place, no doubt as a souvenir.

Having surrendered, the *Gaspée*'s crew were ordered to collect their belongings and at daylight were put into their own boats with a guard and set ashore at Pawtucket wharf, where Duddington was received into the house of Joseph Rhodes. His wound was not fatal, but it was the first shedding of British blood in the shooting war which became more inevitable every day.

Whipple and his volunteers set a fire on the *Gaspée* that burned her to the water's edge and returned in triumph to Providence. The British Admiralty was of course incensed and offered large rewards for the identification of the colonials who had taken part in the expedition which ended the *Gaspée*'s career, the offenders, if caught, to be transported to England and tried for treason. No disguises had been worn, and all the members of the raiding party were well known at Providence. Even while the *Gaspée*'s hulk was still smoking, some of the younger ones were openly boasting of having been in Brown's longboats that night. There is a tradition that on the following morning a young man named Justin Jacobs paraded down the main streets of the town wearing Duddington's gold-laced beaver hat and entertaining a delighted following with a colorful eyewitness account of the affair.

But despite the rewards in pounds sterling, the court of inquiry could obtain no satisfactory evidence on which to base an arrest. In some chagrin they sent a report to London announcing their failure and expressing their belief that "the whole was conducted suddenly and secretly," and then they adjourned with a vague censure of all concerned. By the time the Boston Tea Party became history, in December of the following year, the funeral pyre of the *Gaspée* was almost forgotten.

Nat Greene missed taking part in the *Gaspée* affair by being at his Coventry home that night—a fact he was able to prove when one of the *Gaspée* officers at the hearing mentioned Nathanael Greene as a suspected ringleader of the boarding party. Journeying to Providence the following day with a party of friends from Coventry, Greene saw the smoke still rising from the smoldering hull and heard with envy the vainglorious stories of those who had seen it ablaze. His rage at the unfounded charge of participation may have stemmed from his own youthful chagrin at having accidentally missed the fun. It caused him to make the un-Quaker threat that if ever he met up with his accuser he would "put a hole in him big enough to let the sun shine through."

Nothing came of the attempt to link him with Whipple's young men in the longboats, and he considered the futile court of inquiry a ridiculous threat to American liberties. Later that year he served on a committee to revise the militia laws of the colony. A resolution was passed by that committee to form a public magazine, to conserve powder by forbidding its use for sports shooting, and to recommend monthly "exercises in martial discipline."

Everywhere little groups of ardent patriots, or Whigs, began to prepare for the worst—forming local "independent companies" of volunteers to drill on the village greens in imitation of the parade-trained, seasoned British regulars strutting about the Boston streets; collecting and hiding away in the provincial countryside the tools of war, muskets, powder, and shot; raising contributions to buy drums and colors and uniforms; and studying military manuals and memoirs of old campaigns and stratagems.

The crucial year of 1774 began ominously with the Boston Port Bill, which was Parliament's inevitable reprisal for the Tea Party. The intention at Whitehall was to isolate the rebellious city of Boston from commerce by a tight blockade and starve it into submission and apology. The sister colonies rallied angrily to its defense. A Congress was called to meet in Philadelphia in

September, and delegates were chosen in each of the colonies, except Georgia, to attend it. Nathanael Greene was acquainted with the Rhode Island representatives—his friend Sam Ward's father, who had been three times elected governor of Rhode Island, and Ward's political rival, Stephen Hopkins, who had also served as governor. These two old opponents now buried the hatchet in a common interest.

Massachusetts was sending the Adams brothers to Philadelphia. From Connecticut there would be Roger Sherman and from New Hampshire John Sullivan. From Virginia, the nursery of America, there was a battery of names already becoming familiar throughout the colonies—Patrick Henry, Peyton Randolph, Benjamin Harrison, and the picturesque Indian fighter who had survived the British General Braddock's disastrous campaign against the French and the Indians on the Monongahela River twenty years before—George Washington.

What the Philadelphia Congress could accomplish, beyond another lengthy and futile letter of protest to the King, no one seemed to know. But it was being said that Patrick Henry wanted to declare the American colonies independent of the London government, and Hopkins of Rhode Island was expected to support him. England might then send an army to uphold her authority in America. And that would mean civil war.

During that tense summer of 1774 one of the more famous of the independent volunteer companies, calling themselves the Kentish Guards after their home county, was formed in the East Greenwich district of Rhode Island, and one of its first volunteers was young Nathanael Greene from nearby Coventry. All the members were his neighbors, and some, like James Varnum and Sam Ward, Jr., were his close friends since boyhood.

Living a bachelor life in his comfortable Coventry house, he pursued his studies doggedly and enjoyed a social life free from his father's daily censure. The little northeast room which served as a country store and dispensed the miscellaneous goods and fishing gear required by his neighbors and employees also provided shelf space for his growing library. The desk where he labored over his accounts made room for his evening sessions with his beloved books. He was wrestling meanwhile with a great decision which was not only painful to contemplate but represented a personal Rubicon that was to alter the whole course of his life. It had become imperative for responsible men to choose sides, and he recognized unwillingly that an appeal to arms would claim his support for the colonial cause—with the predictable result that if he chose the sword he would be cast out from the Quaker society in which he had been reared.

The tempo of the amateur drills and parades was quickening, and Nathanael made public profession of his convictions by attending with his cousin Griffin a military rally and exhibition at Plainfield in Connecticut. As he had expected, this unseemly interest in martial display was promptly taken notice of "in Meeting" at East Greenwich, where he had attended for worship since childhood. A committee was appointed to inquire into the conduct of the two Greenes, and in June the clerk recorded sadly that "as they had not given this Meeting any satisfaction for their outgoing and misconduct, therefore this Meeting doth put them from under the care of the Meeting."

His lonely decision once taken, Nathanael stood by it firmly. When he put down his name for membership as a private in the Kentish Guards he had no thought of looking higher or taking a commission. His friends insisted on bringing him forward for a lieutenancy, and this raised an unexpected embarrassment. He had had from boyhood a stiff knee, of unknown origin, which although it caused a slight hitch in his daily gait had never handicapped him in riding, dancing, or the more vigorous sports in which he had always excelled. But the enthusiastic amateurs of the drill ground found it a blemish on their marching ranks and objected to his presence in the company at all, even as a private.

Nathanael was hurt and incredulous. It was the first public setback he had ever received, either in personal popularity or his prestige in the community. His friends were indignant, and Varnum threatened to withdraw from the Guards himself if Greene were barred from membership. Such an action would have been a serious loss to the company, since Varnum had been chosen as one of its first officers. Nathanael refused to allow any such demonstration of loyalty, and a letter from him to Varnum testifies to his dignity and self-command:

"Let me entreat you, sir, if you have any regard for me, not to forsake the company at this critical season, for I fear the consequences; if you mean to oblige me by it, I assure you it will not. I would not have the company break and disband for fifty dollars; it would be a disgrace upon the country, and upon the town in particular. I feel more mortification than resentment, but I think it would manifest a more generous temper to have given me their opinions in private than to make a proclamation of it in public as a capital objection; for nobody loves to be the subject of ridicule, however true the cause. . . ."

Some arrangement was arrived at, doubtless to the discomfiture of the overzealous objectors, and he remained in the Guards as a private. A more legitimate difficulty was his lack of a musket, for firearms had now disappeared from the market and were not supposed to be transported by the colonials, under a heavy penalty. He therefore resolved on a trip to Boston, for which his business affairs provided an excuse, with the secret purpose of procuring a weapon there and smuggling it home.

He had been to Boston before and had made the acquaintance there of the bookseller Henry Knox, whose shop was a magnet Greene could never resist. Knox was a hearty man with a brawny build and a resounding voice who had adopted the genteel manners and dress of his British customers. His shop had become a sort of club, frequented by British officers and their Tory friends, as well as the Boston Whigs, or Patriots. It was also a gathering place for the local bluestocking ladies, who were accustomed to meet their friends and suitors there for informal conversation not always confined to books.

Knox had been for some time a lieutenant in the Boston Grenadier Corps, a militia outfit which wore a splendid uniform and had been complimented by the British Governor Gage for their martial bearing and drill precision. It was an offshoot of the Ancient and Honorable Artillery Company of Boston, formed and drilled by British officers, as was the custom for militia companies since the early days of Indian warfare. These local organizations furnished their own arms and equipment, met for regular training periods, and learned from their British sponsors something of the tactics that were soon to be turned against the soldiers of the King. The study of military memoirs had become Knox's hobby, and he had a wide theoretical knowledge of the art of war, reinforced by his ability to pick the brains of the convivial British veterans who visited his shop to indulge in flirtations as well as in reminiscences with their fellow officers.

At the time of Greene's visit in 1774 Knox was only recently married to Lucy Flucker, a buxom, vivacious young lady of twenty who had defied the disapproval of her Tory family to marry the big militia lieutenant, after a courtship conducted under the very noses of the British officers who were rival admirers of the lively Lucy. Her only brother was a lieutenant in the British army occupying Boston, and through his influence Knox had been offered a British commission—an attempt to bribe him away from his growing Whiggish tendencies which, to the Flucker family's indignation, was unsuccessful.

Greene found his own patriotic convictions matched and strengthened by those of Knox. The smart daily parades of the British troops stationed in Boston stirred his blood and delighted his eyes and made him ambitious for the future accomplishments of the Kentish Guards at East Greenwich. Military books now had a place on his own shelves, and a study of the memoirs of Saxe and Turenne had lately occupied much of his time in the little storeroom library at home in Coventry.

It was from Boston in that July, 1774, that he made an announcement which may or may not have been a surprise to his friend Sam Ward. "On the 20th, this instant, I expect to be married to Miss Kitty Littlefield, at your uncle Greene's," he wrote. "As a relation of hers, and a friend of mine, your company will be required on that occasion."

Miss Kitty was not a Quaker, and the marriage completed his severance from the Meeting. She was a pretty and charming young woman just turning eighteen, and he was nearly fourteen years older. The ceremony which took place at William Greene's mansion in East Greenwich was the beginning of an unusually happy marriage, which would weather in domestic serenity all the storms and tragedies of the war so soon to begin.

When Greene returned to Rhode Island for his wedding, the newly purchased musket traveled hidden in the straw of a farmer's cart, followed at a discreet distance by its owner. A man named Ditson had recently been tarred and feathered for buying a gun. Greene was accompanied on his homeward journey by a new acquaintance he had made in Boston—a British deserter whom he had persuaded to become drillmaster to the Kentish Guards.

When he appeared on parade with his new musket and his drillmaster, nothing more was heard about his limp. But not even Varnum would have entertained any idea then that within a year Nat Greene would be wearing the epaulets of a brigadier.

Chapter 2

Military enthusiasm in the colonies soared during the winter of 1774–75, and more Rhode Island volunteer companies were chartered. Dress parades, company dinners, and meetings to raise subscriptions for the relief of Boston multiplied. British customs officers were threatened in the performance of their duties. Tea was proscribed and publicly burned, and the word itself was painted out on the shop signs.

Early in 1775 a general muster was held, and the independent companies were reviewed. The Provincial Congress of Massachusetts resolved to raise a colonial army and requested the other New England colonies to furnish their quotas for the common defense. Anticipating a violent reaction from Governor Gage as a result of the Massachusetts resolution, and fearing arrest and transportation for treason, the radical leaders of the Boston Whigs (better called Patriots), Sam Adams and his political protégé and figurehead, the wealthy and aristocratic John Hancock, fled to the house of Hancock's kinsman, Jonas Clark, at Lexington, sixteen miles from Boston. They intended to remain there, in prudent seclusion, until their departure for the second Continental Congress convening at Philadelphia in May. Another leading Massachusetts Patriot, Dr. Joseph Warren, courageously ignored his own personal risk to remain in his fashionable Hanover Street home in order to report to Lexington on events in Boston.

There was a fourth man who, like Warren, had blacked his face and joined the silent company which in Indian disguise had dumped the East India Company's tea into Boston harbor late in 1773—the substantial silversmith, Paul Revere. It had been his choice to do the "outdoor work" of the rebel committees—which meant riding courier from Boston as far as Philadelphia to maintain communications and report on British activities in Boston. On the night of April 15 it was plain to Warren and Revere that something was afoot in the town. Rowboats belonging to the British transports were launched and moored under the sterns of the British ships in the harbor. Light infantry companies were detached from their regiments on mysterious special duty. Men billeted in the private houses were readying their equipment as though for a sudden move.

The alert Dr. Warren at once thought of the precious stores collected by the Patriots and stockpiled at Concord, twenty-two miles in the countryside west of Boston—muskets, musket balls, cartridge paper by the ream, gunpowder, spades, axes, hogsheads of flour, salt, pork, candles, canteens, etc. Governor Gage might be even more interested in seizing this valuable cache before it could be used against him than in capturing the two Patriot ringleaders hiding at Lexington, which stood on the road to Concord. They might of course be taken along with the stores, in a single British foray.

On Sunday the sixteenth, Boston was full of rumor and apprehension as the redcoats mustered on the Common with field equipment. The elaborate if amateur Patriot intelligence system was watching, and Warren dispatched Revere to Lexington to warn Adams and Hancock to be ready to flee at a moment's notice. Riding back to Boston the same day, Revere arranged with his friends at Charlestown for code signals to identify the alternate routes the British might take to reach Concord—one lantern in the steeple of the North Church if they marched by land over Boston Neck and through Roxbury and Watertown, two lanterns if they crossed the Back Bay by boat and took the country lanes through Cambridge and Lexington.

Shortly before midnight on Tuesday, April 18, an unknown messenger summoned Revere to Warren's home in Hanover Street. It was time. Revere wrote down his own account: "I left Dr. Warren, called upon a friend and desired him to make the signals. [Two lanterns.] I then went home, took my boots and surtout, and went to the north part of the town, where I kept a boat. Two friends rowed me across the Charles River, a little to the eastward where the *Somerset* man-of-war lay. They landed me on the Charlestown side. When I got into the town I met Colonel Conant and several others. They said they had seen our signals. I told them what was acting, and went to get me a horse. While the horse was preparing, Richard Devens (of the Committee of Safety) told me that he came down the road from Lexington after sundown that evening; and that he met ten British officers, all well mounted and armed, going up the road."

On his borrowed horse Revere spurred out across Charlestown Neck under a bright cold moon, to Medford, where he woke the captain of the Minute Men, and from there on he "alarmed almost every house till I got to Lexington." The barnlike meetinghouse at Lexington stood on the little triangular village green, with a tavern and pleasant dwellings clustered round it. At Clark's house on the Bedford road he found a militia guard posted, for Devens had sent back a warning. The distinguished refugees had retired for the night, requesting the militia sergeant to see that they were not disturbed by noise from his men.

"Noise!" Revere exploded. "You'll have noise enough! The regulars are coming!"

Inside the house, Hancock heard and recognized the lusty tones, and Revere was admitted at once. There was instant domestic uproar, while the womenfolk begged their guests to flee at once, and Hancock (whose pretty fiancée was present on a visit) declared his heroic intention to arm himself and join the

Minute Men. Hardheaded Adams protested that as delegates-elect to the Philadelphia Congress it was their immediate duty to save themselves for more important work than midnight alarums and excursions.

While they argued, William Dawes, a second messenger from Warren traveling by way of Boston Neck, arrived. With no more time for Hancock's theatricals, he and Revere partook of hasty refreshment and cantered off to arouse the countryside toward Concord. They were soon joined on the road by Dr. Prescott, a Concord resident late abroad on his courtship of a Lexington lady, and "a high Son of Liberty" well known to the local Patriots. He offered to ride along with them, to lend credence to their tidings. These three were soon accosted by a patrol of British officers, who attempted to turn them aside into a pasture. Prescott jumped his horse over a stone wall and galloped for Concord. Dawes attempted a similar action, but fell off his horse and escaped through the dark woods on foot.

Revere's bridle had been seized and held, and with pistols pointed at his breast he was forced to dismount. Roughly questioned by his captors, he manufactured a tall tale of British boats run aground at Boston and pointed out that such a mishap would delay the march until by the time the regulars could reach Lexington there would be five hundred armed Americans waiting to confront them, all roused by his warnings on the way up. At this point four Minute Men carrying arms were brought in captive by the patrol, who cut the girths on their prisoners' horses and ordered them to disperse on foot. Revere himself was left to make his way back on foot to Clark's house, regretting that the gallant little borrowed horse which had carried him as far as Lexington now disappeared forever into the British army. Adams and Hancock accepted his escort from Clark's to greater safety at Woburn, and, accompanied by Hancock's secretary, he then returned to Clark's to see what was going on.

The alarm bells were ringing at Lexington, signal guns were firing, and drums were beating to arms across the moonlit countryside. The tavern windows were all alight, and Minute Men were collecting on the village green under the eye of their captain, John Parker. The British were indeed late. As time passed,

Revere's report began to be discounted as just another false alarm, and Parker's men straggled home to bed or convened in the tavern for comfort, although still "within drumbeat."

Everything had gone wrong for Gage at Boston as his secret plans for the Concord expedition leaked out into the streets. The British detail of about seven hundred men was led by the senior field officer, elderly Colonel Smith, with Major Pitcairn of the Marines as second in command. It finally embarked in pitch-darkness at the bottom of the Common and was landed on the Cambridge side knee-deep in marshland about two in the morning. Here another delay concerned with rations occurred. By now the whole countryside around Boston was awake in a rural din of alarm guns and bells, and rebel scouts and messengers hurrying to their various appointed rendezvous were picked up all along the British line of march. Since the stockpile at Concord was their main objective, Smith sent Pitcairn ahead with six companies to secure the bridges there. When Pitcairn met the patrol that had taken Revere, he heard from them Revere's story that five hundred men would be gathered at Lexington to oppose him, and he sent back to Boston for reinforcements.

During the lull at Clark's house, Revere had engaged with Hancock's secretary to remove a trunkful of incriminating papers that had been left at the tavern. From a window he saw Pitcairn's column approaching in the early light and "hastened away" with his precious burden. Captain Parker of the Minute Men stood his ground on the usual place of parade, near the road leading on to Concord, as Pitcairn came up with his regulars. Parker's assemblage probably numbered less than one hundred. "Don't fire unless fired upon! But if they want a war, let it begin here!" Parker's grandson heard him say.

The mounted British officer "swung his sword and said, 'You damned rebels, lay down your arms and disperse!'" a contemporary account runs. And then, as nobody moved, "'Fire! By God, *fire!*'" The first British platoon fired, too high, and there were no casualties, as the militia dashed for the protection of trees and stone walls, without, the eyewitness maintained, returning the fire. When the second platoon fired, four Minute Men fell, and then the American guns replied without waiting for orders. The regulars promptly charged into them with bayonets and more gunfire.

When the smoke haze lifted on a scene now lit by the sunrise it revealed the green in wild confusion, the regulars being entirely out of hand so that Pitcairn's cease-fire order could not be heard. Parker's cousin was shot and bayoneted to death where he stood trying to reload his piece. Jonathan Harrington, shot through the body, managed to drag himself from the green almost to the doorstep of his fine house just accross the road and died there as his anguished wife ran out of the house to clasp him in her arms.

By the time Pitcairn was able to re-form his ranks the main body of the British force arrived under Colonel Smith. A victory volley was fired, the blood-curdling British huzzah was given, and the redcoats marched off briskly for Concord, leaving eight Massachusetts men dead on the green and ten wounded. On the British side, there was one man with a leg wound, and Pitcairn's horse was bleeding.

Concord, six miles away, had been alerted by Prescott and sent out a scout who witnessed the shooting at Lexington and sped back to confirm the warning. Summoned by the alarm bell, the Minute Men were assembling there too. About three hundred in all, they gathered on the little height beyond the North Bridge, which was at once possessed by a British detachment when the reinforced column swept into the town. The rest of the regulars, under Smith and Pitcairn, destroyed property, set the courthouse afire, and threw what ammunition they could find into the wells and mill pond. At the same time there was a fight for the bridge, and the British were driven back from it, leaving three killed and eight wounded and rejoining the main army in the town.

The reinforcements from Boston requested by Pitcairn arrived too late. Led by Lord Percy, they had been harassed all the way by an aroused countryside and finally encountered their punished comrades stumbling back along the road to Boston, in retreat from a steadily growing Patriot force. There was another skirmish at Lexington when Percy's men attempted to make a stand while Pitcairn's troops threw themselves on the ground "with their tongues hanging out like dogs." The woods on either side of the road were now filled with sharpshooters, and the weary withdrawal of the regulars toward the shelter of Boston was soon resumed.

Dr. Warren had reached Lexington with the old-timer militia officer William Heath, and they accompanied the pursuit of the disorganized British. During another little skirmish at West Cambridge a British bullet nicked Warren's ear curl, and the vengeful regulars committed some plundering and abuse of the population. Because the Cambridge bridge had been taken up, the retreat had to go round by way of Charlestown, and Heath called off the pursuit when the British gained Charlestown Neck, where there was little cover for the American riflemen.

Charlestown was in a state of terror, but Percy controlled his angry and exhausted men, formed a line across the neck, and occupied unfinished fortifications at Bunker Hill while awaiting the boats to be sent out from Boston to convey his crestfallen troops and their wounded back to their quarters in Boston. The Minute Men retired in weary triumph to Cambridge to establish a makeshift camp there.

It was April, 1775, and the war had begun.

Chapter 3

The news reached Providence the same night, and the Rhode Island volunteer companies assembled to their beaten drums. It was nightfall when Nathanael Greene at Coventry heard what had happened in Massachusetts. He at once rode off to the alarm post of the Kentish Guards at East Greenwich, and they all set out for Providence at dawn, with Varnum as their colonel mounted at the head of the column. They had passed through the town on their way to the Massachusetts border when a messenger from Governor Wanton overtook them with orders to turn back. The British had been driven into Boston and were there besieged by a growing army of farmers and tradesmen encamped roundabout Cambridge.

The Rhode Island Assembly convened at Providence on the twenty-second of April, when a day of fasting and prayer was appointed, and a committee was chosen to consult with the Connecticut Assembly on the common defense of the New England colonies. Because Samuel Ward, Sr., was absent on his duties with the Congress in Philadelphia, Nathanael Greene was named to the committee in his place. The King's ships, with headquarters at Newport, continued to annoy the commerce in the bay, and one of John Brown's vessels loaded with flour and the owner aboard was seized and sent as a prize to Boston. Governor Gage soon released Brown and he returned home.

The Rhode Island "army of observation," which consisted of some 1,500 men, was formed into a brigade and divided into three regiments of eight companies each. The choice of its commanding officer may have caused surprise, even at that time. For some still inexplicable but fortunate reason, the Assembly passed over the major general of the militia and Colonel Varnum of the Kentish Guards and named Nathanael Greene as brigadier general of the Rhode Island forces. Baffled historians have since ascribed the choice to "the direct interposition of Providence." Others have fostered a perhaps more likely legend that the first choice was an Episcopalian, who declined; the second choice was a Congregationalist, who declined also; and the third vote having fallen on Nat Greene, he remarked, "Since the Episcopalian and the Congregationalist won't, I suppose the Quaker must."

His private affairs, including the welfare of his wife of less than a year, he consigned to the care of his brothers. Details of organization and preparation at once absorbed him, but he remembered to order a uniform to be sent to him at Cambridge "by Wednesday," from the same tailor who had made him many a suit of Quaker drab. On the second of June he sat down in Providence to compose a letter to Kitty at Coventry:

"My dear wife—I am at this moment going to set off for camp, having been detained by the Committee of Safety till now. I have not so much in my mind that wounds my peace, as the separation from you. My bosom is knitted to yours by all the gentle feelings that inspire the softest sentiments of conjugal love. It had been happy for me if I could have lived a private life in peace and plenty, enjoying all the happiness that results from a well-tempered society founded on mutual esteem.

"But the injury done my country, and the chains of slavery forging for posterity, calls me forth to defend our common rights, and repel the bold invaders of the sons of freedom. I hope the righteous God that rules the world will bless the armies of America, and receive the spirits of those whose lot it is to fall in action into the paradise of God, and into whose protection I commend you and myself; and am, with truest regard, your loving husband, N. GREENE."

Two weeks later in Philadelphia the tall, grave Virginian who had been chosen commander in chief by the Continental Congress was confronted with the necessity to write a remarkably similar letter to his Martha at Mount Vernon, who had been sixteen years his wife. Washington was ten years older than Nat Greene, who was thirty-three.

The situation around Boston before the battle of Bunker Hill must be understood. George Washington was still in Philadelphia. Governor Gage had received reinforcements from England in the summer of 1774, and these were first quartered in tents on the Common, while building their own barracks for the winter. Gage had withdrawn from overcrowded Boston and established himself more comfortably at Salem, to the north—from where he proclaimed martial law, declaring the Patriot volunteers already under arms "rebels" guilty of treason.

Late in May the British frigate *Cerberus* had arrived at Boston with no less than three experienced generals aboard, which gave rise to the famous derisive rhyme:

Behold the *Cerberus* the Atlantic plough,
Her precious cargo, Burgoyne, Clinton, Howe—
Bow, wow, wow!

When this distinguished company learned that 5,000 British regulars were jammed up in Boston by a disorganized but determined mob of armed provincials, Burgoyne, the wit, remarked, "Well, let *us* get in, and we'll soon find elbow-room!" Which premature jest when it got out caused him to be referred to thereafter, to his chagrin, as "General Elbow-room."

The American forces had gathered themselves in a camp forming a rough semicircle west of Boston, reaching from the Mystic River in the north to Roxbury in the south, with Cambridge about midway. It should be remembered that Boston at that time was almost an island in the bay, reached by a narrow neck of land linking it to the shore between Roxbury and Dorchester, while Charlestown lay at the lower end of a peninsula at the mouth of the Mystic River opposite the north side of Boston and facing it. Behind Charlestown on the same small peninsula rose two hills called Bunker and Breed's, which the British through carelessness or overconfidence had only recently thought of fortifying.

The command in the colonial camp at Cambridge was not as yet united or organized on any military basis. Artemus Ward, revered for his record in the French and Indian wars, had set up a sort of headquarters in the Hastings house and had been named general of the Massachusetts forces. But each colony was still operating as an independent unit, with its own elected officers, separate pay scale, and commissary.

There was lack of heavy ordnance outside Boston, the nearest supply being at Fort Ticonderoga, where Lake Champlain narrows to a funnel connecting with Lake George. The British had held this fort with a small garrison ever since they took it from the French in 1759. Now, nearly twenty years later, they lost it to a small American raiding party of Ethan Allen's "Green Mountain Boys," who had been joined by a Connecticut contingent led by Benedict Arnold. This brilliantly executed coup prevented the British from removing the cannon and powder from

Ticonderoga for their own use, though most of it was allowed to remain at the fort after the raid instead of being brought into the American camps at once.

The affair at Ticonderoga, remote as it was, extended the rebellion beyond Boston, even beyond New England, so that it became a colonial matter involving the whole transatlantic settlement. The word "Continental" was born, as applied to the motley army congregated at Cambridge, and to the Congress convening for the second time at Philadelphia. There was even a project, fostered by Allen, to invade Canada, where a British governor ruled at Montreal.

True enough, the rebel forces were somewhat overinflated by their initial successes at Concord and Ticonderoga. But the British too were surprised, if unpleasantly so. With the arrival of the imposing trio of generals aboard the *Cerberus*, their self-confidence returned, and they never doubted their ability to break through the straggling ring of untrained farmer-soldiers around their Boston stronghold whenever the word of command was given.

The triumphant mob outside the town lacked leadership and discipline and sanitation and an organized commissary system. The Congress at Philadelphia recognized its obligation to remedy this situation and on June 15, 1775, named George Washington as commander in chief of the American forces. As a colonel in the First Virginia Regiment at twenty-three, he had already fought on the side of the British against the French and Indians on the western frontier. Since 1759 he had retired from the army, married a widow with two small children, and had been living quietly at his handsome Potomac estate as a country squire and family man. Serving as Burgess in the Virginia Assembly at Williamsburg, he had twice been named delegate to the Philadelphia Congress, where his distinguished presence and untalkative good sense had commanded respect and admiration. He was unwilling, and considered himself incompetent, to assume the supreme command for the colonies in a war with the mother country. But even to him it was pretty plain that he was the best the colonies had, and his stern sense of duty compelled him to try. Congress then named four major generals and eight brigadiers to assist him.

Among these were Artemus Ward, already established with his Massachusetts command at Cambridge; Israel Putnam, veteran of a long and lurid career as an Indian fighter, who had recently arrived at Cambridge like a landslide at the head of 6,000 Connecticut volunteers; and Philip Schuyler, a New York veteran of the frontier fighting who had retired into the Assembly at Albany and was living at his Saratoga estate much as Washington had settled down at Mount Vernon.

It soon became apparent that the fourth major general's commission granted at Philadelphia was an unfortunate choice. Charles Lee, a British adventurer claiming the rank of colonel in the British army, after a colorful career in Turkey, Poland, and Portugal, had come to America in the autumn of 1773 as a soldier of fortune looking for a cause. He had purchased an estate in the Shenandoah Valley of Virginia with money borrowed from the Philadelphia banker Robert Morris. There he had set up an odd bachelor household consisting of slaves and a pack of untrained, devoted dogs of very untidy habits. Lee was so loud in his support of the colonial stand against British taxation that he impressed his hearers, and Congress took him at his own high evaluation. He was consulted and flattered as an expert in military matters by the gullible amateurs at Philadelphia, and even Washington was taken in by Lee's self-advertisement and was glad to have him assigned to the military "family" which was forming around him. Lee, who coveted the supreme command for himself, was dissatisfied and jealous from the beginning, though at first he contrived to conceal it well enough.

The eight brigadiers, all holding colonial commissions already, were Pomeroy, Heath, and Thomas of Massachusetts; Wooster and Spencer of Connecticut; Greene of Rhode Island; Sullivan of New Hampshire; and Montgomery of New York. Additionally, Horatio Gates, who had been born in England and accompanied Braddock to America in 1755, was named adjutant general with the rank of brigadier. After undistinguished service in the same campaign on the western frontier which had made George Washington's name known and admired throughout the colonies, Gates had retired, married, and bought a plantation near the one where Lee had come to roost in the Virginia hills.

Thomas Mifflin of Philadelphia, a wealthy young Quaker

with a charming wife, was appointed quartermaster general, and another Philadelphian, Joseph Reed, became Washington's confidential military secretary and aide as a volunteer without rank or pay, and he remained in that position off and on for several years.

These were the men with whom Greene was to learn his new trade of soldiering and receive his baptism of fire during the first long winter of the war at Cambridge. Surrounded by his aides and field officers, Washington left Philadelphia on June 23, 1775, and arrived at Cambridge on July 2. In the meantime, the battle of Bunker Hill had been fought.

Chapter 4

Greene's time since arriving at Cambridge early in June had been devoted to bringing order out of the chaos in the encampment of the Rhode Island contingent at Jamaica Plain. He had been summoned at once to a council with other officers at Ward's headquarters in the Hastings house. He found there, besides Artemus Ward, Heath of Massachusetts and Putnam of Connecticut. All of them were his seniors in years and firmly entrenched in their local commands. Ward, as the accepted commanding officer of all the New England forces, was held in great esteem and by general consent had been looked on as commander in chief before the appointment of Washington by Congress to that rank was known.

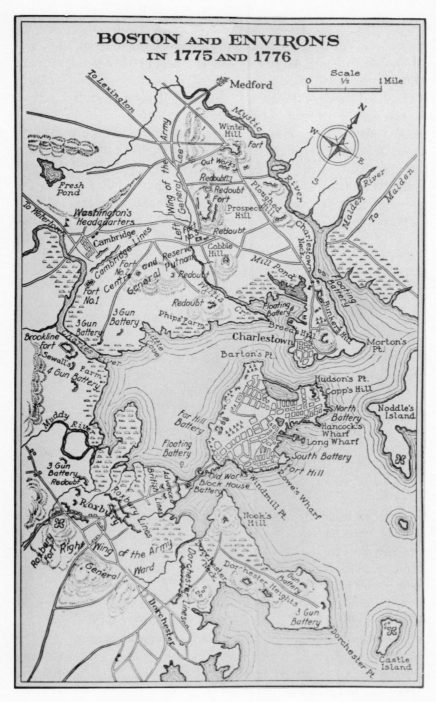

BOSTON AND ENVIRONS
IN 1775 AND 1776

Scale
0   ½   1 Mile

To Lexington

Medford

Mystic River

Winter Hill
Fort

Out Works

Redoubt

Redoubt Fort

Prospect Hill

Ploughed Hill

Charlestown Neck

Malden River

To Malden

Left Wing of the Army

General Lee

Fort No. 2

Redoubt

Cobble Hill

Fresh Pond

To Watertown

Washington's Headquarters

Cambridge

Cambridge Lines

Fort No. 2

General Centre and Reserve Putnam

Redoubt

Willis Creek

Fort No. 1

3 Gun Battery

Redoubt

Phips' Farm

Little Cove

Floating Battery

Breed's Hill

Bunker's Hill

Footing

Charlestown

Barton's Pt.

Morton's Pt.

Brookline Fort

Charles River

Sewall's Farm

4 Gun Battery

Hudson's Pt.

Copp's Hill

North Battery

Noddle's Island

Muddy River

Far Hill Battery

Hancock's Wharf

Long Wharf

Floating Battery

South Battery

Fort Hill

3 Gun Battery Redoubt

Roxbury Lines

Advance British Lines

Old Works
Block House
Battery

Windmill Pt.

Rowe's Wharf

Roxbury

Nook's Hill

Roxbury Fort

Right Wing of the Army

General Ward

Dorchester Neck

Dorchester Heights

Gun Battery

Dorchester Lines

3 Gun Battery

Dorchester

Dorchester Pt.

Castle Island

2 5

Among the officers who had accompanied Greene to Cambridge were several who had had the benefit of training by the British deserter drillmaster imported from Boston to Coventry by Greene. A daily "exercise" and parade soon shaped Greene's brigade into a uniformity of discipline which most of the others lacked. At the daily exercise military etiquette as understood by the amateur officers is illustrated by the regimental Order of the Day just before the battle of Bunker Hill took place in mid-June: "The colonel expects that every officer will appear in his uniform, and that care is taken by the officers that every soldier be clean, and as neatly dressed as possible; and that no one who has breeches be permitted to wear trousers, nor to parade without having on his stockings and shoes; and that during the march no soldier be permitted to talk. . . ."

Whatever was loftily designated in Orders as "uniform," there was great variety in how the men had got themselves up for the campaign. Many still wore the clothes in which they had left home, often hastily, at the beat of the drum. These might be homemade working clothes or hunting outfits made of rough tow cloth or home-dressed leather, the tunics belted at the waist and worn outside the breeches. Some had dug out old military coats left from the French and Indian War twenty years before, and these were British red now turned brownish with butternut stain; or they might be militia blue with red facings and pewter buttons. Some of the volunteer companies sported their own well-worn local parade dress and at least matched each other. As time went on, some of the officers went into their own small funds to buy outfits for their companies. Most of the officers were able to provide themselves, at least, with a suit in the military fashion, and the majority rode good horses of their own, brought from home. But the traditional "Continental" uniform, blue with buff facings and underdress as worn by Washington and his staff, was never standardized for the ranks, largely because the army always lacked funds and materials to supply all the troops.

There were many obstacles to the establishment of military discipline in this rough and unready army. There was the natural obstinacy and independent spirit of pioneer men accustomed to think and act individually and not at the command of some fellow they considered no better than themselves, even if he wore epaulets. There was normal human laziness, not yet awake to crisis. And there was drunkenness, as evidenced by the court-martial of one Peter Young, who when confined after "being found in liquor behaved himself in a very indecent and contemptuous manner; damning the man that confined him, and also the man that kept him in confinement, and throwing his hat about the guard-house."

Greene felt the abrupt change from his quiet domestic life at Coventry and his studious habits, when war had been still only a theory with him. He did not lack old friends to uphold him in his heavy responsibilities as brigadier. Varnum was colonel of the Rhode Island Regiment, and young Sam Ward was a captain. There was a happy reunion with Knox, who had had to escape with his wife at night through the British lines at Boston, his cherished militia sword quilted into the lining of the ample Lucy's cloak. Reporting to Ward's headquarters, Knox was assigned to the fortifications at Roxbury and sent Lucy to friends at Worcester for safekeeping. Posted at the southern end of the Cambridge crescent, he was not to be involved in the Bunker Hill battle across the bay.

Neither was Greene present in the American lines at Bunker Hill, for he had taken a short leave to return to Rhode Island on his private business, so abruptly abandoned when the march to Cambridge began at the end of April. Word of the fighting at Bunker Hill reached him at his home on the evening after the battle, and he at once mounted his horse and rode all night, to arrive back at Cambridge the following morning. Charlestown was by then "all burnt to ashes," and his brigade had been divided to work on new entrenchments at Prospect Hill, north and east of Cambridge. But when he had heard the conflicting stories of what happened on June 17, he concluded in a letter to his brother Jacob that he "wished we could sell them another hill at the same price."

The British had won Bunker Hill, but they sacrificed more than one thousand men, including ninety-two officers, for the victory, such as it was. Gage was still in command at Boston, as the military governor, but he had sent Howe to lead the attack on unfinished American fortifications on Breed's Hill, which lay between Bunker Hill and Charlestown. The Charles River ran like a narrow strait between the Charlestown waterfront and the British battery on Copp's Hill on the north shore of Boston.

Burgoyne and Clinton together had watched from Copp's Hill while the battery there threw hot shot into the wooden buildings of Charlestown till the village was on fire. They saw Howe lead the British van up the slope of Breed's Hill toward the American redoubt, which held its fire till the red ranks were close enough to be swept by the first volley, mowing down whole platoons "like a scythe." They saw the disciplined red lines waver and break, then rally again behind Howe, who exposed himself recklessly and received a ball in his foot, which he ignored. A second advance up the hill recoiled again toward the shore, and Clinton, acting without orders, at that critical moment embarked a small reinforcement and took it across the strait in time to join the third assault and press the pursuit of the Americans, who were forced by lack of ammunition to fall back from their position on Breed's Hill to Bunker Hill, where hasty defenses were being constructed. After another fight there, they retreated across Charlestown Neck into the road which led past Prospect Hill to Cambridge.

In his long feud with Howe, which began that summer at Boston, Clinton always maintained that had the battle been fought according to his original plan—which Howe overruled in favor of the costly frontal assault—the Americans could have been cut off by troops landed on the neck in their rear, and the entire force taken prisoners, which might have ended the war before it began.

Howe's objective, and Gage's, was simply to drive the colonial force out of the fortifications behind Charlestown, which overlooked the Boston headquarters, and occupy the whole peninsula, as should have been done long since. This had now been accomplished by Howe, just barely, and at a terrible price. He had shown notable personal courage, and it was said that at one time during the battle his face was running with tears from the stinging powder smoke which blackened it and from grief over the appalling casualties which left not one of his staff officers alive and unwounded. His white buckskin breeches were splashed with the red blood of his slaughtered officers—the Americans were ordered to fire low, at the white crossbelts, and at the "epaulet men," or officers, while the British fire went high and caused a loss of less than five hundred among the Americans. Burgoyne, watching with a group of his helpless fellow officers from what amounted to a grandstand seat on Copp's Hill, described the scene on Breed's Hill as "a complication of horrors beyond anything it has ever been my lot to witness."

General Ward, a church warden who had not seen field service since 1758, was too stout and enfeebled to ride and remained at his Cambridge headquarters "in a posture of defense," keeping back a small army around him. Putnam, who was ten years older than Ward but still a vigorous "bear of a man," was everywhere among his men on the hill, commanding, pleading, "cursing and swearing like a madman," in his determination to rally and hold steady his green, embattled troops. When his men ran out of ammunition they fought the British bayonets with clubbed muskets, frail militia swords, and even rocks snatched up from the rough ground where they stood.

They did not win the battle. But they proved that raw provincial recruits would stand their ground and fight the disciplined British regulars, and they left the enemy so badly punished that Clinton's unsolicited advice was again vetoed by Howe. Instead of following up with an immediate attack on Cambridge, where there was not enough ammunition to defend it, Howe's battered regiments were permitted to lie down upon their arms that night on Bunker Hill, while the exhausted Americans did the same only a mile away at Prospect Hill.

A day of brilliant sunshine and summer heat ended under clear skies rendered sickly by the smoke of battle and the burning village of Charlestown. The citizens of Boston, many of whom had watched the carnage from the roofs and attic windows looking toward the Charles, saw Clinton and his officers picking their way back across the battlefield strewn with dead and dying and loud with the groans of men in agony with untended wounds. A boisterous wind rose at sunset, to carry smoke and cinders from the Charlestown embers into the streets of Boston.

The chief casualty among the Americans was the noble Dr. Warren, who was struck down by a musket ball through the head. Among the British who survived was young Lord Rawdon, a high-spirited, able Irish lieutenant in the 5th Foot, "tall, dark, and ugly," but with a compelling charm of manner. He had received in his arms the body of his captain as it fell from the parapet of the American redoubt, and thereafter led the company himself. He got two bullets through his cap but lived to become Greene's personal antagonist in the Carolina swamps six years later.

The excitement of the battle was still in the air when Greene arrived back at Cambridge. The British cannon in Boston were still firing at the American lines, to which the men who had fought at Bunker Hill had retreated when their powder gave out.

From the new fortifications being built on Prospect Hill the British could be seen with the naked eye working to convert the little redoubt behind Charlestown, which they had won at such sacrifice of life, into a miniature fortress, while they maintained their intermittent shelling of Roxbury to hamper the American operations there. Provisions were running short in the American camp, and the disgraceful record of peculation, profiteering, and bad faith among the purveyors of bread and beef had begun.

In the early afternoon of July 2, the man the Congress at Philadelphia had chosen to be commander in chief rode into Cambridge with his staff, accompanied by an escort of mounted citizens collected in Massachusetts along the way. He was at once conducted to the house that had been built by Harvard University for the use of its presidents, where its present tenant, Samuel Langdon, had been required to vacate all but one room, leaving the rest to be occupied by Washington and his military "family."

Washington's first tour of inspection was without formalities or fanfare. The troops were turned out, but powder was too scarce to waste on formal salutes honoring the arrival of the unknown commander from the South. With the showy, talkative Lee at his side, Washington rode in hot, sparkling summer weather to examine the lie of the land where his ragtag army was assembled in front of Boston. Lee, the professional soldier, was loud in his dissatisfaction with everything they saw. There were no army engineers, he pointed out; there was no artillery to speak of; there was no organized intelligence system; there was no military discipline, and the men did not show enough respect for their officers, who did not demand it.

Washington's first concern was the swift construction of a ring of fortifications from the Mystic River on the north to Roxbury on the south end of the crescent that cut off Boston from the rest of the country. An equal anxiety was the frightening shortage of powder and lead, which had already forced the Americans to abandon their defense of Bunker Hill, and the lack of adequate clothing, food, and arms for the men who had come to Cambridge to defend their liberties and who were seen at a glance to be guilty of scandalous inattention to military discipline. Courts-martial soon became frequent, and various unpopular and inept officers were relieved of duty and sent home.

Perhaps because the courteous Virginian felt an awkwardness about taking possession of President Langdon's house, Washington requested other lodgings and was invited to occupy the Vassall house in Brattle Street. This handsome dwelling belonged to a wealthy Tory, as the loyalists were called, who with his family had fled into Boston when the colonial forces descended upon Cambridge after Concord. Abandoned with all its furnishings by the owner, it served as Washington's headquarters till the spring of 1776 and was the scene of the first war Christmastide, when Mrs. Washington and some of the other officers' wives came to camp to spend the winter lull with their men.

The transfer of the supreme command from Ward to Washington was accomplished smoothly, with no hard feelings on Ward's part, and he gracefully accepted the command of the right wing at Roxbury. There is no record of the first meeting between Washington and Greene, who was to become one of the few close friends the lonely commander in chief would permit himself during the long, dreary war ahead of them. Greene was certainly present at the first council of war, held at the headquarters house in Brattle Street on July 9 and attended also by Ward, Lee, Gates, Knox, Putnam, and Heath. Greene had taken the appointment by Congress of a stranger from the South to the supreme command with more good will than some of the other New England officers, each of whom had a favorite candidate for the post if not aspiring to it himself, as John Hancock was known to do. Most of them were soon won over by Washington's quiet authority and honest desire to do his best in a difficult situation. And it did not take long for Washington to recognize in Greene a man whose steadfast character and integrity of purpose matched his own.

Chapter 5

Under Washington's command the army at Cambridge was divided roughly into three parts, with Ward on the right, Putnam in the center roundabout headquarters, and Lee on the left with his headquarters in a farmhouse on Prospect Hill. Greene was assigned to Lee's command with seven regiments, as was Sullivan of New Hampshire with six. The works at Prospect Hill were about two miles from Washington's house in Brattle Street. Greene's friends, Varnum and young Ward, were stationed with him.

By the time this reorganization was in effect, Washington had discovered with increasing dismay that if the British should come out of Boston and attack, the colonial army had barely enough powder to provide the men with nine cartridges apiece. Lead and flints would have been exhausted by a single engagement, rendering the whole army defenseless.

Appeals were sent out to the governors of the separate colonies to forward every pound of ammunition they could scrape together, and Washington reported grimly to Congress: "I need not enlarge upon our melancholy situation. It is sufficient to say that the existence of the Army and the salvation of the country depends on something being done for our relief both speedy and effectual, and that our situation be kept a profound secret."

Early in August he received the welcome news that Congress was forwarding six tons of powder, and he was able to estimate that the wagons would reach Cambridge by the sixteenth of that month. It would be enough to provide about thirty cartridges per man.

Gradually the siege tightened, as the American works were strengthened to form a semicircle of eight or nine miles, with the enemy in the center and still in command of the water but maintaining a mysterious inactivity. Every day as the summer waned there would be a skirmish or a cannonade with little resulting damage. The British shells fell short for lack of elevation, and the few that reached the American lines had little effect except "to inure the Americans to danger," as noted by Heath, who was to publish his memoirs in 1798. The casualties amounted to only twelve, and there were stories of the contempt which daily familiarity with the futile bombardment finally bred in the bored, homesick ranks of the colonials—the usual regimental clowns burned their fingers picking up fragments of exploded shells for souvenirs and ran to catch spent cannonballs to use as makeweights or bowling balls and other games devised to pass the time.

The "Tory hail," as Greene called the bombardments in a letter to his wife, brought his first sight of violent death, when Varnum's adjutant from East Greenwich was actually beheaded by a cannonball in flight. Fatalities were still so new that he sent Colonel Varnum himself to break the news to the man's wife, though the dispatch of a field officer on such a mission would soon become excessive.

After Washington's arrival the army at Cambridge was henceforth to be considered *Continental* and not colonial, and Greene noted that his Excellency had "a great desire to banish every idea of local attachments. For my own part," he wrote, "I would as soon go to Virginia as stay here. The interests of one colony are in no ways incompatible with the interests of another." Within six years he would be demonstrating to the South his conviction that the colonies were indeed one nation, indivisible, with a common cause which he served with entire devotion in districts much more remote than Virginia.

The necessity for conserving powder and for a daily check to prevent its waste or theft caused the officers much extra paper work. Firing at migratory birds or small game to add to the rations was prohibited. In November the arrangements for shorter days and severe weather required a nine o'clock curfew in camp. Sterner sentry work with passwords and countersigns resulted, as curious neighbors from the countryside made a fashion of coming in parties to the American lines to watch the building of breastworks and redoubts and the daily drill of the regiments on improvised parade grounds.

There was, as always in a war, perpetual anxiety about spies and military secrets. The discovery of a letter written in cypher and containing information useful to the enemy which was traced to a respected citizen with free access to the camp made the presence of visitors with possible Tory sympathies an increasing embarrassment at headquarters. The approach of winter brought another anxiety. The militia were enlisted for only a matter of months, and time was running out for most of them.

Before the end of the year confidence and friendship had been established between Washington and Greene that was to endure throughout Greene's life. Washington expressed to the canny Quaker his "uneasiness about the expenses" that were far exceeding the expectations of Congress—"but if you starve the cause you protract the dispute," Greene concluded.

The want of arms had forced Washington reluctantly to retain the weapons of men who insisted on leaving the army as soon as their term of enlistment was up, even though the guns had come to camp with their owners and were actually private property. "But," said Greene, "the great law of necessity must justify the expedient till we can be otherwise furnished." He had long envisioned an army well organized and disciplined, properly fed, clothed, and paid, and enlisted for the whole war. As the dreary days drew in toward winter, he began to contemplate the futility of hoping for redress from the King and Parliament in

London. And, as a logical corollary, he began to entertain the idea, not a new one any more, of colonial independence from the British government.

The councils of war and the closer association with the commander in chief had now taken the place of his solitary meditations in the little book-room at Coventry. His horizon was broadened, his acquaintance was enlarged, his experience was enriched by daily contact with other minds as keen as his own and of a wider cultivation. He spent hours in the saddle and perhaps as many with his pen; he listened, he thought deeply, he read, always calming his mind with a few pages from some favorite book before he settled to his belated night's rest.

Dinners at headquarters, to which the officers were invited in turn, were easy, friendly gatherings. "I am now going to dine with his Excellency General Washington," Greene wrote to his wife. "I wish you could fly to Cambridge and partake of a friendly repast." He would have been surprised at how soon that apparently farfetched wish for Kitty's presence at camp would come true.

Mrs. Washington had begun "that pleasant custom" of turning winter headquarters into some semblance of home life by arriving at the Vassall house before Christmas, accompanied by her son Jack Custis, his young wife, and Mrs. Gates, who had joined them along the way. Kitty Greene lost no time once the word went out that wives would be welcome at headquarters. She brought with her their first child, a son born since his father had ridden away to war. George Washington Greene was a baby still in the cradle when he first heard the guns at Boston, and his mother reported proudly that he showed no fear of the noise, adding that children "soon grew accustomed to anything." Kitty's youth and good looks and high spirits soon won the affection of Mrs. Washington, and she was always a favorite in the commander in chief's household.

By Christmas time headquarters had been considerably enlivened by the arrival of several other courageous wives, including Mrs. Knox, Mrs. Mifflin, and Mrs. Reed, the latter always in delicate health. General Lee, whose tongue was sharp and unguarded, habitually referred to Mrs. Gates as "the daemoness." He was himself none too popular with the headquarters ladies, owing to his bad manners, slovenly appearance, and his constant escort of noisy, socially unacceptable dogs.

As a result of his work on the Roxbury defenses Knox was commissioned colonel of the artillery regiment, to replace a veteran of the French war who had become too infirm for active service. Thanking Washington for the promotion, Knox inquired in his jolly way where the artillery was. Washington admitted wryly that there wasn't any to speak of, and Knox reminded him that Fort Ticonderoga must still be full of captured English ordnance left there at the time of the Allen–Arnold raid the previous spring. Knox was quite ready and willing to undertake to bring the heavy guns from New York State to Cambridge. By the middle of November he was on his way to Albany through a violent northeast storm.

Schuyler, as one of the first four major generals commissioned by Congress in June, had ridden out of Philadelphia with Washington, but, being assigned to the Northern Command, he was detached and sent to establish headquarters at Albany in his home district where he was well known and greatly respected. He was in Albany engaged in the hopeless task of recruiting an army to invade Canada when Knox arrived there en route for Ticonderoga. Before the end of the year Knox had begun his return journey, dragging his assorted arsenal through two feet of snow behind teams of oxen. He spent Christmas in a snowstorm at Saratoga on his way back. When he actually arrived at Cambridge with the guns in mid-January—after forty days—the camp cheered him till it echoed in the streets of Boston. From then on, the big guns were all named and cherished like horses, as Knox's particular care.

As the New England cold really set in, Washington's army suffered from lack of firewood to such an extent that some regiments had to eat their provisions raw, "notwithstanding that we have cut down all the trees for a mile around the camp." It was some consolation to learn that the British in Boston were even worse off, to the extent of burning doors and furniture for a little warmth. Early in February the cold even roused hopes in the Cambridge camp that a long-cherished scheme of attacking Boston across the ice in the bay would be practicable. But the weather changed before the risky attempt could be made, and

London. And, as a logical corollary, he began to entertain the idea, not a new one any more, of colonial independence from the British government.

The councils of war and the closer association with the commander in chief had now taken the place of his solitary meditations in the little book-room at Coventry. His horizon was broadened, his acquaintance was enlarged, his experience was enriched by daily contact with other minds as keen as his own and of a wider cultivation. He spent hours in the saddle and perhaps as many with his pen; he listened, he thought deeply, he read, always calming his mind with a few pages from some favorite book before he settled to his belated night's rest.

Dinners at headquarters, to which the officers were invited in turn, were easy, friendly gatherings. "I am now going to dine with his Excellency General Washington," Greene wrote to his wife. "I wish you could fly to Cambridge and partake of a friendly repast." He would have been surprised at how soon that apparently farfetched wish for Kitty's presence at camp would come true.

Mrs. Washington had begun "that pleasant custom" of turning winter headquarters into some semblance of home life by arriving at the Vassall house before Christmas, accompanied by her son Jack Custis, his young wife, and Mrs. Gates, who had joined them along the way. Kitty Greene lost no time once the word went out that wives would be welcome at headquarters. She brought with her their first child, a son born since his father had ridden away to war. George Washington Greene was a baby still in the cradle when he first heard the guns at Boston, and his mother reported proudly that he showed no fear of the noise, adding that children "soon grew accustomed to anything." Kitty's youth and good looks and high spirits soon won the affection of Mrs. Washington, and she was always a favorite in the commander in chief's household.

By Christmas time headquarters had been considerably enlivened by the arrival of several other courageous wives, including Mrs. Knox, Mrs. Mifflin, and Mrs. Reed, the latter always in delicate health. General Lee, whose tongue was sharp and unguarded, habitually referred to Mrs. Gates as "the daemoness." He was himself none too popular with the headquarters ladies, owing to his bad manners, slovenly appearance, and his constant escort of noisy, socially unacceptable dogs.

As a result of his work on the Roxbury defenses Knox was commissioned colonel of the artillery regiment, to replace a veteran of the French war who had become too infirm for active service. Thanking Washington for the promotion, Knox inquired in his jolly way where the artillery was. Washington admitted wryly that there wasn't any to speak of, and Knox reminded him that Fort Ticonderoga must still be full of captured English ordnance left there at the time of the Allen–Arnold raid the previous spring. Knox was quite ready and willing to undertake to bring the heavy guns from New York State to Cambridge. By the middle of November he was on his way to Albany through a violent northeast storm.

Schuyler, as one of the first four major generals commissioned by Congress in June, had ridden out of Philadelphia with Washington, but, being assigned to the Northern Command, he was detached and sent to establish headquarters at Albany in his home district where he was well known and greatly respected. He was in Albany engaged in the hopeless task of recruiting an army to invade Canada when Knox arrived there en route for Ticonderoga. Before the end of the year Knox had begun his return journey, dragging his assorted arsenal through two feet of snow behind teams of oxen. He spent Christmas in a snowstorm at Saratoga on his way back. When he actually arrived at Cambridge with the guns in mid-January—after forty days—the camp cheered him till it echoed in the streets of Boston. From then on, the big guns were all named and cherished like horses, as Knox's particular care.

As the New England cold really set in, Washington's army suffered from lack of firewood to such an extent that some regiments had to eat their provisions raw, "notwithstanding that we have cut down all the trees for a mile around the camp." It was some consolation to learn that the British in Boston were even worse off, to the extent of burning doors and furniture for a little warmth. Early in February the cold even roused hopes in the Cambridge camp that a long-cherished scheme of attacking Boston across the ice in the bay would be practicable. But the weather changed before the risky attempt could be made, and

Washington turned his attention to an alternate project—the seizure of Dorchester Heights south of Roxbury, a position that would command the city and the harbor traffic which was Howe's only means of supply or escape.

To divert the British attention Washington ordered the guns at Cobble Hill and Lechmore Point on the shore below Prospect Hill to start firing into Boston from the opposite end of the siege line. The British replied briskly, their backs to the stealthy operations at Dorchester. The guns on both sides shook the houses in Cambridge and set the windows rattling. On the night of March 4 there was an almost incessant roar of cannon and mortars, while the Americans at Dorchester cut down orchards to make an abatis—a defense of felled trees laid with the sharpened ends of the trunks projecting toward the enemy—and chained together barrels filled with rocks and earth, not just to strengthen the works but to be rolled down the hill into the ranks of an enemy attempting to storm the Heights.

It was anticipated that when the British discovered the Dorchester works in progress—which they did on the morning of the fifth—they would at once assemble boats for an attacking party across the bay. A defense unit was organized to create a diversion by attempting to force the British works at the neck, which would let the Roxbury troops into Boston by that route. Rough old Putnam, assisted by Sullivan, was in charge there. This expectant detachment was drawn up between the Cambridge lines and the shore of the Charles River, whose surface was now alive with floating batteries, small craft, and flatboats that would carry forty men each.

In full view of Boston they waited. Noon passed without the signal. Washington rode among them, calm and observant, so that each man straightened himself instinctively under his eye. The whole day passed, with a rising wind, which prevented the British from embarking. By nightfall it was a hurricane, and the cannon fell silent under a howling gale and battering rain, which continued through the following day. The British counterattack was called off.

On the night of the seventh a Captain Erving escaped from Boston with the intelligence that the British were preparing to leave the city by water. At a council held at Ward's Roxbury headquarters Washington, Ward, Lee, Putnam, Sullivan, Knox, Heath, and Greene debated the British intention, and a decision was taken to extend the Dorchester works by occupying Nook's Hill also, a point of land nearer to and overlooking the neck.

During the winter the British command in Boston had been transferred from Gage to Howe, and Gage returned to London, to be censured for inactivity and a lack of firmness in opposing the rebellion. Howe had since then proved to be no more aggressive, and the decision to evacuate Boston was his. On the seventh of March, having thrown over the whole idea of maintaining a hold on the city, he had given the order to load the transports in the harbor, which he still controlled. His secret destination was Halifax, where he could await supplies and reinforcements from England.

Indescribable confusion reigned in the city for ten days, while troops, stores, loot, and Tory refugees were embarked without regard for comfort or conveniences. The seizure of Nook's Hill by the Americans only hastened the British flight from Boston, though Washington did not take advantage of the opportunity to bombard and sink the overloaded transports at their moorings.

By sunset of March 19, 1776, though some of the British ships still lingered in the lower bay, Boston was again in the hands of its own people.

Chapter 6

As early as January, 1776, Congress had been made aware of the unwelcome possibility that a new British force from overseas might attack some Southern port, such as Charleston or Portsmouth. During the same month Washington at Cambridge had received word that Clinton, one of the three formidable *Cerberus* generals, had been smuggled out of Boston harbor with no one knew how many fighting men under his command. His destination was a mystery but could as well be New York as Charleston. Washington had at once dispatched the man he considered his most experienced general—Charles Lee—to organize fortifications at New York. Lee's arrival there, with a small force of volunteers accumulated during his march through Connecticut, caused consternation among the Tories, many of whom fled to Long Island or New Jersey with their families.

For his headquarters Lee took possession of a handsome house to be known as Number 1 Broadway, opposite the Bowling Green, and encamped his troops in "the fields" which became City Hall Park. He soon reported to Washington his opinion that since New York was surrounded by navigable waters it could not long be defended from an attack by a seaborne enemy but that its capture could be made very expensive to the victor by building a system of forts, redoubts, batteries and entrenchments to surround the island of Manhattan from King's Bridge on the north to Brooklyn Heights, across the East River on Long Island. Lee was also able to report that while Clinton had "looked in" at New York, without an army at his back, he had vanished again by sea in the probable direction of Norfolk, Virginia.

Before Lee could more than begin to lay out on paper his elaborate plans for New York's defenses, Congress took alarm at new rumors from the South and ordered Lee to Charleston to take command of the American forces rallying there to defend South Carolina against a possible seaborne invasion fleet.

Lee left Manhattan in the capable hands of General William Alexander, a New York veteran of the French war, newly commissioned brigadier of the New Jersey Continentals. Alexander's claim to an extinct Scottish earldom enabled him to call himself Lord Stirling, even while he acted as a field officer in the rebel army. He was a bluff, hard-drinking, courageous man, accused by a contemporary of "liking the table and the bottle full as much as became a lord, and more than becomes a general." But when fighting was to be done, Stirling proved himself sober and energetic, and his men followed him with confidence and devotion.

At Cambridge there remained considerable doubt as to Howe's intentions, when he finally sailed out of Boston harbor with his loaded transports. It was to be expected that he would try to compensate for his original mistake—which was really Gage's—of allowing himself to be cornered between the colonial army and the sea in a city that was of very little use strategically. He now had the opportunity to redeem this error by seizing New York, which could be a base of some value since from there he could command the Hudson River.

The score so far was about even, one year after Concord. The British had been forced to evacuate Boston, with enormous loss of prestige and self-confidence. But an ambitious American expedition to Canada under Gates, Schuyler, and Benedict Arnold was already proving to be an ill-planned disaster. Both sides could now race for New York, where a large Tory population might be expected to welcome Howe and present new difficulties to Washington.

In anticipation of Howe's next move, Washington set his army in motion southward, hoping to reach and fortify the New

York area before Howe could face about and seize the city from the sea. At Cambridge there was a general exodus homeward of the army wives, and the first regiment (some Pennsylvania rifles) left Boston for New York on March 18, followed in quick succession by Heath's, Putnam's, and Greene's brigades and a detachment of Knox's artillery accompanied by their colonel. Putnam was to be in general command at New York, over Stirling, until Washington, who was delayed at Boston by ceremonies of congratulation and arrangements for its repossession, could join his army on Manhattan. General Ward was left in command of Boston, with five regiments to hold it. By May of the same year his failing health obliged him to resign his commission.

Greene's marching orders from Cambridge were issued for April 1, at sunrise. His route took him through Providence to New London. From there transports would convey his troops across the Sound to New York. He turned aside briefly at Coventry, and hurried on along roads made soft and heavy by the spring thaw, causing artillery and baggage horses to give out, wagons to break down, and muddy, cursing men to drop beside the road to nurse their sodden, blistered feet. It was his first long march with troops, and he found it hard, dispiriting work, but the transports were waiting for him at New London and he pushed on doggedly.

He arrived in New York on April 17, to find Washington already there, engaged in carrying out, so far as was possible, Lee's interrupted plans for the city's defense. The north end of Manhattan Island was a wilderness of rocky cliffs running down steeply to the rivers on either side, the rough terrain dotted with baronial estates and little settlements at Bloomingdale and Harlem. Beyond Harlem Heights the land narrowed to permit the Hudson River to divide into the North River, flowing between Manhattan and Jersey, and the Harlem River, where a wooden bridge spanned Spuyten Duyvil from the eastern shore of Manhattan to the mainland called Westchester. Here Heath was posted to keep open a possible escape route from Manhattan to the Highlands. Below King's Bridge on the western shore of Manhattan the unfinished Fort Washington faced Fort Constitution (soon to be renamed Fort Lee) on the Jersey Palisades.

Greene, with fewer than 4,000 men, was made responsible for the Long Island defenses opposite the lower end of Manhattan, with orders to camp "on the spot marked out upon Long Island" —which was at Brooklyn Heights overlooking the East River and the little city of New York on the lower tip of Manhattan Island. It was a position very similar to the high ground at Dorchester that dominated Boston, and Lee had begun a redoubt there which remained unfinished at both ends. Greene was confronted now by much the same situation he had encountered on his arrival at Cambridge the previous year, but he was better qualified to handle it. His drilled and disciplined troops, distinguished for their good behavior during the first chaotic weeks of the siege of Boston, had been augmented by new men who needed patient training.

There was still a shortage of army engineers, and Greene's mathematical knowledge was useful in interpreting and carrying out Lee's plans. He was also better able than he had been to cope with the exhausting daily routine of an army in the field—the loss of privacy and adequate rest, the courts-martial, the perpetual daily problems of supply, sanitation, arms and ammunition, and the recurrent low spirits of the homesick, underfed, bored or frightened amateur soldiers in his command.

Mrs. Washington arrived at New York late in May, having traveled by coach from Cambridge via Hartford, and the headquarters house at Richmond Hill was illumined by her composed and gracious presence. Lucy Knox drove in from a visit at Fairfield, Connecticut, to display her first child, a daughter named Lucy, who had been born along the way. Kitty Greene sent word that she could be expected to join them all at New York at any time, and Greene wrote back urging her to leave their little son at home in brother Jacob's household at Potowomut. Howe's British fleet was still unaccounted for. If it appeared off New York the wives would have to scatter on very short notice from a city open to bombardment from the harbor.

With Knox beside him as their friendship ripened daily, Greene went reconnoitering on upper Manhattan and eastward from Brooklyn Heights on Long Island. Between them, they knew as much about creating defense works and marking gun emplacements as anyone at Washington's disposal. Time was what they needed, they told each other as they rode together through the summer landscape above the noble Hudson. Time and engineers. Time and an intelligence service. They set up a signal system on Staten Island of colored flags by day and lights by night to give warning if British sails were sighted off Sandy Hook. Express riders were kept in readiness to carry messages from Greene's post on Long Island to the commander in chief at New York and to summon the militia to their appointed rendezvous.

Espionage within the lines was more of a problem than it had been at Cambridge, because so many Tories and their sympathizers had taken refuge on Long Island and along the Jersey shore when the Patriot army occupied Manhattan. The officers had constantly to be on their guard against false reports from friendly-seeming people and a leakage of information through visitors pretending to notice nothing while memorizing vital facts. Patriot citizens were openly intimidated by Tories whenever the latter felt strong enough to reveal their true sentiments. It was plain that local Tory guides would be only too happy to lead the King's men to back roads, short cuts, and hiding places, once they landed. Lenience with these slippery gentry was regarded as a sign of weakness. Firmness and punishment were called violation of rights. Civil war, said Greene, did not permit neutrality.

At the end of his long, trying days he would sit at his little traveling desk and write his informal confidential letters to Kitty, to brother Jacob, and, when they were separated by the water running between Brooklyn Heights and lower Manhattan, to the commander in chief. He asked Washington for an officer to relieve him of the tedious duty of signing passes and other clerical work that wasted his time and energies and named Lieutenant Blodgett as his choice. This request was soon granted double, with both Blodgett and Major William Livingston being appointed his aides when he was promoted to major general in August. He asked that the incoming recruits be allowed to procure for themselves the milk, fruit, and vegetables which they craved instead of the steady diet of "animal food" provided by the commissary. He complained about the regimental hospitals, which were filling up with victims of a "putrid fever" from polluted drinking-water after heavy rains followed a severe drought.

Early in June a long-standing rumor was suddenly confirmed when some stolen British papers came into Washington's hands. Among these were copies of treaties dated the previous January arranging for the employment of almost 20,000 German mercenaries to be added to the regiments of British regulars sent to subdue George III's rebellious colonies in America. Knowing that such an action by Lord North's Ministry in London would give violent offense both to the Congress and to the population everywhere in America and forever close the door to negotiations for a peaceful settlement, Washington forwarded the papers to Congress.

A few days later, after drawing up careful instructions for Putnam's guidance in his absence, the commander in chief, accompanied by Mrs. Washington, set out for Philadelphia himself to confer. His situation had suddenly worsened. With all that additional manpower of European troops, the British attack when it came would be speedier and heavier and could fall on more than one objective at the same time. The general gloomy opinion in Congress was that these reinforcements could be expected to arrive off New York by the first of July.

Leaving his wife in Philadelphia to recover from an inoculation for smallpox, Washington hurried back to his army on Manhattan. The once social little city of New York was now grim and apprehensive under curfew, as preparations for its defense went forward everywhere, while the uneasy uncertainty lengthened. Where was Clinton? Where was Howe? Where would the first blow fall?

On the morning of June 29 it appeared that the answers would soon be known. Officers stationed at the Narrows to watch the high ground on Staten Island, where three flag staffs awaited the signal flags, saw through their field glasses a sudden glint of color as the signals flew—the British ships were sighted. Before evening nearly one hundred sail had been counted, "resembling a wood of pine trees trimmed," anchored in the Hook. "I declare I thought all London was afloat!" exclaimed a humble diarist on Staten Island.

Time was up, and headquarters, where Mrs. Washington had just returned, was abustle as the general officers met in council. At Fort Washington hulks and weighted barrels strung together with chains were sunk in the Hudson from shore to shore, except for a narrow unmarked channel, to block passage to the Highlands beyond. An urgent call for militia went out, and men began trickling in to enlist.

The next day Mrs. Washington was sent back to Philadelphia for safety, and Lucy Knox was suddenly "in distress and anxiety," her husband wrote his brother, "the city in an uproar, the alarm guns firing, the troops repairing to their posts, and everything in the height of bustle; I not being at liberty to attend her, as my country calls loudest. My God, may I never experience the like feelings again! They were too much; but I found a way to disguise them, for I scolded like a fury at her for not having gone before!"

This was one of the famous Knox rows, conducted at the top of their voices, which were to enliven the headquarters scene throughout the war and only testified to their mutual devotion— domestic fireworks which usually ended in tears, caresses, and hearty laughter. Lucy consented at last to take the baby back to Fairfield, where she was soon complaining of being unhappy apart from him and begging to return.

Greene's anxiety was silent but acute. So far as he knew, his Kitty was already on the road to New York, heading straight into the storm.

Chapter 7

Several days passed before the British ships anchored in Sandy Hook were known to be General Howe's, carrying his rested and refurbished Boston army back from their Halifax refuge. On the second of July they came up to Gravesend Bay and on the third began unloading troops on Staten Island, where they could be seen throwing up works on the low hills as though for a long stay. Young Rawdon was there and recorded in one of his racy letters to his uncle, the Earl of Huntington, that "The fair nymphs of this isle are in wonderful tribulation, as the fresh meat our men have got here has made them riotous as satyrs. A girl cannot step into the bushes to pluck a rose without running the risk of being ravished, and they are so little accustomed to these vigorous methods that they dont bear them with the proper resignation, and in consequence we have the most entertaining courts-martial every day."

The veteran James Grant was also there. He had fought in the same British army with Washington at Fort Duquesne in 1758 when the French were driven out and now professed the utmost professional contempt for the colonial troops.

Against the tide of the prudent exodus from New York, Kitty Greene arrived at headquarters as she had promised, and after a brief, affectionate reunion with her husband was bundled off toward home again, in the wake of all the other wives.

With the enemy disembarking on the doorstep, an exciting rumor for which Washington was scarcely prepared was running through the coffeehouses of New York. The Second Continental Congress at Philadelphia had declared the United Colonies of North America free and independent states, and the connection between this country and Great Britain was said to be dissolved. On the ninth of July copies of the Declaration of Independence were delivered to Washington at his New York headquarters, with instructions to have it read to the army. This was done at evening roll call, at the front of each brigade drawn up on their respective parades: "When in the course of human events . . ." straight through to its sobering conclusion: "And for the support of this Declaration, with a firm reliance on the protection of Divine Providence, we mutually pledge to each other our Lives, our Fortunes, and our Sacred Honor."

There was a silence in the ranks, then from somewhere came three cheers, which were drowned at once in a great spontaneous shout.

As the attack alarm might be sounded at any minute from the harbor, not all the troops could be dismissed at once. Those who were free to do so broke up into jubilant, talkative groups and milled about, exchanging views on what many of them were able to realize was the most tremendous news of their lives so far. It spread swiftly through the city, and the population took fire from it, and a cheering, exalted crowd gathered on the Bowling Green, where an equestrian statue of the King, a third larger than life, cast in lead and gilded, stood on a white marble pedestal fifteen feet high. The small grass plot that surrounded it was enclosed by an iron fence with a spiked top, which was soon scaled by the younger Sons of Liberty. With ropes and iron bars and tugging and hacking and shouting, they managed to pull down the statue of the King, and the head broke off in its fall. The dancing, singing, torchlight mob then went on to demolish the royal coat of arms wherever it could be found. The headless statue of the King wound up in Connecticut, where it was melted down to make bullets for the American army.

More British ships continued to arrive almost daily. It was learned that Howe had acquired by a new convoy from England some 9,000 Scots of a kilted Highland brigade under General

Alexander Leslie and that he was daily expecting the arrival of his brother, Admiral Viscount Richard Howe, with a fresh contingent, possibly including the hireling German soldiers to be collectively known as Hessians.

There could be no doubt about the arrival of the second Howe on July 12, for the tall ship which carried him flew a vice-admiral's flag and was saluted by every British ship of war already at anchor. Behind him were transports and smaller craft up to 150 sail. It was estimated that the reinforcements he brought would alone outnumber the whole American army under Washington's command. Joined to his brother's refitted troops from Halifax in an attack on any one of the several approaches to New York, they were supposed to be capable of inflicting an overwhelming defeat in the first full-dress confrontation of the war.

A desperate call went out for every Continental soldier available as far away as Connecticut. A bounty was offered for re-enlistments and to the troops already in service if they would sign on for another three years. Hot weather and bad drinking-water after the drought increased sickness and desertion in the American ranks, where suspense was also taking its toll. This present prospect was no longer just a matter of digging themselves in, as at Cambridge. This would be a fight—with musket-fire, gun-butts, bayonets, rocks, and fists, if New York was to be held. The odds could not be contemplated without sweating. As tension lengthened, little feuds and jealousies were rife among the men and even among the officers, where at least one challenge to a duel occurred. Even the tact and composure of the commander in chief were pressured into occasional sharp words to the harried aides and in his fruitless appeals to Congress for the wherewithal of war.

But still the British did not attack and did not disclose their intentions. In the camp on Staten Island and on the anchored transports, they, too, waited. The Hessians had not arrived with Admiral Howe.

On July 21 an old uncertainty was finally clarified by the news that Clinton, who had not been seen since his brief appearance at New York in February, had gone on to attack Charleston from the sea and had been beaten off by the South Carolina defenders under Charles Lee and an old Indian fighter named Moultrie. Speculation as to what Clinton had used for soldiers was answered by the fact that Admiral Sir Peter Parker's fleet, convoying a land force of some 2,000 troops from an Irish base commanded by Lord Cornwallis, had picked up Clinton by some prearrangement at Wilmington, North Carolina. Together they had proceeded from there to Charleston, arriving off the harbor bar about the same time that Lee rode in from the North to direct the defense of the city, which was until then in Moultrie's capable hands.

It is sufficient to say that the combined attack of a force led by Clinton and Cornwallis, backed up by Parker's marines, had failed to take Charleston. Moreover, the British fleet was so severely damaged by gunfire from the fort on the shore that it could only limp away, leaving the frigate *Actaeon* aground and burning. Casualties aboard the ships had been frightful, including a wound to the seat of the admiral's breeches, and were many times greater than the losses of the garrison on shore.

Satisfaction at New York over the Charleston victory was soon tempered by the arrival of more British ships in the Narrows. Instead of the expected Hessians, these were discovered to be carrying the battered remnants of the Charleston force commanded by Clinton and Cornwallis. Although it was an expedition which had suffered defeat off the coast of South Carolina, its arrival at New York to be added to Howe's already ominous potential created general astonishment and dismay at American headquarters.

One of the three *Cerberus* generals had returned to England from Boston or from Halifax—Burgoyne. While at home he had managed to get himself assigned to the Canadian forces under Sir Guy Carleton, based at Quebec. British strategy at Whitehall, conducted at long range and in deplorable ignorance of American local terrain, assumed that from Canada a British army could simply proceed down the Hudson and combine with Howe's forces at New York. From this governmental guesswork in London came the orders that would result in the battle Burgoyne was to fight and lose at Saratoga in October of the following year. Burgoyne's absence left Clinton—grouchy, jealous, and opinionated—to carry on his personal feud with Howe. And there had now arrived at the Staten Island camp that dangerous newcomer, General Lord Cornwallis, about to begin his long career on American soil, which would end at Yorktown five eventful years later.

Gates had been sent to join Schuyler's faltering Northern Command at Albany, a transfer which seemed at this time a misfortune to the defenders of New York, and Charles Lee was still at Charleston. Washington called on Congress for more field officers, an appeal which they answered by promoting those he already had, including Greene, to major generals and brigadiers. William Smallwood of Maryland came in with several companies composed of young men from the best Maryland families, wearing fringed hunting shirts as a uniform. Smallwood was a testy, red-faced man in a perpetual temper, a great trial to his associates but a reliable fighting man whose troops would stand fast. Also commanding Maryland men from Baltimore was Mordecai Gist, tall, handsome, and courteous, who after an interval of retirement was to see the war out at Greene's side in the Carolinas.

Still the British ships poured into the Narrows—ninety-six sail on the twelfth and thirteenth of August. Here were the Hessians at last, looking like toy soldiers in their cheap, gaudy uniforms and tall European-style headgear—human fighting machines whose officers treated them like dogs.

When it seemed that everything had happened that could happen, short of the first actual assault by the King's troops, another stunning blow fell on Washington. His right-hand man, who had reconnoitered and fortified Long Island and knew more about its defenses and its weak points than anyone else, was stricken with a raging fever which so robbed him of strength that he had to be carried away from his post at Brooklyn Heights to a bed in a house on Broadway, in the hope that careful nursing and rest would ensure his recovery. "I am sorry to inform your Excellency," wrote Greene's aide, Livingston, on August 17, "that General Greene has had a very bad night of it, and cannot be said to be any better this morning than he was yesterday."

Confronted by this terrible emergency, Washington threw into the vacuum the best officer he could lay hands on—John Sullivan. He had been camped alongside Greene at Cambridge until assigned to the disastrous Canadian expedition, from which he had just returned to rejoin Washington at New York. He was a stout, vigorous man, with graceful manners masking a violent temper and an oversensitive ego. Experienced campaigner though he might be, he had had no opportunity to familiarize himself with the Brooklyn terrain and fortifications, nor had he the advantage of Greene's many reconnoitering trips along the island's winding roads and shortcuts and the unexpected passes through the range of hills extending from Brooklyn Heights eastward to Jamaica.

On the night of August 21 the entire New York area was swept by a violent storm marked by blinding sheets of lightning and thunderbolts which killed several soldiers, even melting the tips of the swords belted to their blackened bodies, striking houses and barns and terrifying the population. The next morning was clear and fresh, with puddles of rainwater standing everywhere in the streets and roads.

At sunrise flatboats and other small craft began to ply across the Narrows between Staten Island and Gravesend, landing redcoats on Long Island. Howe was at last getting his attack under way. Cornwallis was there, commanding the reserves, and Grant and Rawdon and von Donop with his Hessian mercenaries. Clinton led the advance guard and found his landing unopposed. With Rawdon he set out on a scouting expedition which disclosed that the fourth and farthest pass through the rugged range of hills at Jamaica was too thinly guarded by the American line, which was extended along the crest from the redoubt on Brooklyn Heights.

When Washington learned of the British landing he threw more troops across the East River from Manhattan to reinforce Sullivan at the Heights and himself crossed over to observe. Returning to New York, he sent the veteran Putnam to supersede Sullivan, who continued as second in command and took the field opposite Clinton.

Though the Inglis house where Greene lay in misery was in a quiet suburban area of Manhattan, it was only three or four miles from the scene of the battle of Long Island when that finally began on August 24. He could hear the guns of both sides in the intervals of his prostration when he became aware of anything beyond his own painful struggle to survive.

Reports trickled in to his bedside, which set him groaning as much with impatience as with his crippling ailment. Clinton and Donop had advanced as far as Flatbush, where the enemy paused. Sullivan was out on the hills to the east of the Heights, Sullivan was where Greene had expected to be, and old Putnam, who knew nothing about Brooklyn, was in general command at the impromptu fort that had been begun by Lee on the Heights.

Washington was back and forth, perilously, across the arm of the sea which was the East River, maintaining touch with his rear, where Knox was at work on the defenses of Manhattan. Howe was attacking in earnest, with the Hessians, and the cannon fire rattled Greene's windows. Washington had seen the Maryland troops under Smallwood and Gist caught in the salt marshes of Gowanus Creek, with heavy losses, as they tried to hold off Grant's attack long enough for their comrades under Stirling to escape. Stirling, who they said had "fought like a wolf" against Cornwallis's Grenadiers, was reported missing, killed or captured. American casualties were running high from British bayonets, against which they had little defense but their clubbed muskets. Continental riflemen were giving a good account of themselves.

All day the sound of gunfire invaded the hot little room where Greene lay, burning with fever, too weak to stand on his feet—and still the dreary news piled up. But winds and weather were against the British. On the twenty-eighth a cold northeast gale brought torrents of rain, and Howe did not pursue his attack. By now, Sullivan was reported missing too. Clinton, who was accompanied by Cornwallis and guided by three local Tories, had turned Sullivan's flank at the Jamaica Pass and come upon him from the wrong direction. This news set Greene groaning again, for he well remembered that Jamaica road, about which Sullivan should have been warned. He learned later that Sullivan and his small force, already in retreat toward the Heights, had been confronted and overwhelmed by Clinton's dragoons and had recoiled in confusion upon the advancing Hessian bayonets. They fought desperately, hand to hand, while being driven backward and forward between the ranks of their assailants. Many broke through the gleaming fence of bayonets and sabers and escaped to the redoubt on the Heights, while their less fortunate comrades died in their tracks or were made prisoners, as were Sullivan and some of his officers. Sullivan had last been seen in a cornfield with a pistol in each hand, surrounded by the enemy.

It was still raining when the cannonade began on the morning of the twenty-ninth, and the British had begun to dig muddy earthworks in front of the redoubt on the Heights. Instead of a frontal assault, Howe had elected to begin a formal siege operation, which was felt even by some of his own officers to be a mistake.

Washington dared not strip Manhattan of troops to reinforce those on Long Island, lest with a change of wind the British ships could swing around and attack New York while his whole army was on Long Island. He had not enough men for both, Greene was well aware—but Howe could pour men in from the loaded transports. There were skirmishes all that day, and Greene surmised that by now the ammunition would be wet. The troops were soaked and hungry and had begun to disperse themselves without leave. Most of the American reinforcements had been hurried off from Manhattan without tents or blankets. The wounded were now a steadily increasing problem and had to be ferried back to New York across the East River in small craft.

The British were showing signs of moving toward Flushing near the north shore of Long Island, from where they could cross the East River to the mainland above Harlem and attack King's Bridge in Washington's rear. That would bottle him up, as they had been caught in Boston, between water and an enemy army. He had called a council, which Greene was still too ill to attend, and it was believed that they were discussing the evacuation of Long Island—which meant ferrying all those wet, weary troops and their equipment back to Manhattan in small boats across windswept water churned by a rapid current. It could never be done—but a fog was coming in now, and Glover's Marblehead regiment (composed chiefly of sailors and fishermen wearing round blue jackets and trousers) had been given the almost impossible task of collecting and manning boats to be brought to the ferry stairs at the foot of Fulton Street in Brooklyn.

By midnight a merciful shroud of fog covered the American companies parading silently at the ferry stairs to board the waiting boats, which with muffled oars plied back and forth to deposit their disheartened cargoes at the various wharves on Manhattan, only to slip away again into the fog for another load. Mifflin with two Pennsylvania battalions was in command of the rear guard, where there occurred some confusion in orders, until Washington arrived on the scene with his staff. All of them had been in the saddle all day and all night and were the last to be taken off from the ferry stairs, dismounting stiffly to step into the boat, while their weary horses were maneuvered into another just behind them. A British advance guard came pelting up from the lines around the Heights, just when the last boats had got beyond pistol shot.

The battle of Long Island was lost. Greene's presence in the field could hardly have altered the outcome, but at least he would not have been caught at Jamaica as Sullivan was.

New York might go next, and he bent all his will power to the necessity of getting on his feet again. "I have been very sick for near three weeks," he wrote when he was able to hold a pen. "For several days it was a hard struggle between nature and the disorder. I am now a little better, though scarcely able to sit up an hour at a time. I have no strength or appetite, and my disorder threatens me with a long confinement. I think the General proposes to retreat to King's Bridge, and there make the grand stand. If this is his determination, two to one that New York will be laid in ashes. . . ."

So the first pitched battle had been won by the professionals, and they held the ground. But Washington had performed a brilliant feat of improvisation, bringing off his battered troops with their baggage, field guns, equipment, even horses, from Long Island across water a mile wide, without the loss of a man in the crossing. He had himself been sleepless for forty-eight hours, most of that time astride a horse within sight of his men. But while he had saved the colonial cause from utter ruin, it was nevertheless a defeat and a retreat. Moreover, the escape was due at least partly to Howe's decision to lay siege at Brooklyn Heights instead of making a frontal attack on a weary, ill-organized army under confused and inexperienced officers.

Although Washington was criticized as an amateur bungler in strategy, even the British on the spot had to concede that his retreat from Long Island had been "a masterly military transaction, well timed and executed." To Washington the whole affair represented failure, both for himself as a commander and for his men as soldiers. No one knew better than Washington and his devoted officers that a successful evacuation did not win a campaign. After a day's inaction from exhaustion, he was in the saddle again, making ready for the next move of his powerful if leisurely enemy.

The surviving tents were drenched and almost useless, and the weather continued wet and miserable. The army quartered itself in the houses of the town, which caused the usual ill feeling, pilfering, and injustice. Washington divided his remaining troops into "three Grand Divisions" to be disposed for the defense of Manhattan. Putnam's was posted at the bottom of the island facing the East River. Spencer had temporary command of the division which would be Greene's as soon as he was sufficiently recovered, and this was stationed behind sketchy breastworks on a line from Putnam's north to Harlem, its center at Turtle Bay on the East River about where the streets of the East Forties run now. British small craft could be seen gathering opposite the cove just south of there known as Kip's Bay. The third division was under Heath at King's Bridge, watching the Westchester shore. Headquarters on Manhattan was well aware that the fighting had just begun, and there was no time to waste on making excuses or taking a breather. An epidemic of desertion set in as disillusioned militia succumbed to "cannon fever" and began to melt away homeward.

On September 5, when Greene was first able to report for duty again, he found headquarters opinion still divided on the immediate problem of New York itself. Could it be defended against both land and sea forces poised to attack? Or should it be abandoned, without another fight, to serve as comfortable winter headquarters for the enemy, who had only to walk in and occupy it? There was a third course, which Greene had at once recognized and which Washington was reluctantly contemplating. The city might be destroyed by deliberately setting fire to it, before it was abandoned to the British. Most of the property belonged to militant Tories anyway, as Greene pointed out, and once the British were allowed to settle in, they could not easily be dislodged again.

Washington wisely decided to leave so debatable a decision to Congress, which vetoed the destruction of New York, even if it could not be held, "having no doubt of being able to recover the same, though the enemy should, for a time, obtain possession of it." The enemy was to hold possession of it, as things turned out, till the autumn of 1783. But no doubt with a sigh the commander in chief accepted the verdict of Congress and turned to his maps.

Chapter 8

The town of New York occupied the lower two or three miles of an island thirteen miles long and more or less two miles wide. Beyond the town the land rose in rocky hills to Harlem Heights just south of the large unfinished earthwork called Fort Washington, which was designed to protect the approach to King's Bridge, where the Harlem River left the Hudson at Spuyten Duyvil to flow between the eastern shore of Manhattan and Westchester. From King's Bridge roads ran up into New England. Opposite Fort Washington on the Jersey cliffs Fort Constitution was situated to provide a crossfire above the obstructions which had been placed in the Hudson River to block ships coming upstream.

On September 7 another council was called at Washington's Manhattan headquarters and a heated argument took place. The

British were established on the south or Long Island shore of the East River, from where they could ascend the Harlem River to possess King's Bridge and bottle up Washington on Manhattan, forcing him to surrender either to the British or to starvation. Greene pleaded passionately for immediate evacuation northward into Westchester after rendering the city worthless to the British as winter quarters. Out of his textbook campaigning he reminded them of the King of France who laid waste whole provinces to starve and ruin the invading army of Charles V. He stated his conviction that there was no great reason to run any considerable risk for the defense of New York. He called their attention to the obvious fact that with the British in possession the city could never be recovered without a superior naval force, which the infant United States were not likely to have in the foreseeable future. Once occupied, the city would be at the mercy of the enemy, who might well destroy it themselves if ever they had no further need of it. He urged that the army be retreated to posts at King's Bridge and in Westchester, where barracks for the winter could be constructed. And he hoped that his good intentions would excuse his zeal.

He was overruled. The very thought of abandoning "the poor city," much less destroying it, gave some of his hearers "the horrors." It was decided by a large majority to try to hold New York with 5,000 men and post the rest along the retreat route of Harlem Heights, the Hudson River forts, and King's Bridge. Greene was the lowest-ranking major general in terms of seniority, and he held decided views on insubordination. But after consultation with some of the field officers who had not been present at the council, he presented to Washington a signed petition, with his own name at the top, for a review of the council's decision to defend New York. It seemed that Washington welcomed the opportunity to call a new council, where the decision of the first was reversed by all but three votes, and evacuation was ordered for the entire area south of King's Bridge and Fort Washington as soon as troops and supplies could be withdrawn.

When the reconsidered decision on New York was submitted to Congress, Washington received its assurance that he was not expected to remain in that city "a moment longer than he shall think it proper that the troops should be continued there." It was of course fully expected that he would fight defensively on the spot if attacked before he could withdraw in good order.

Fort Washington was to be garrisoned, for its defenders presumably could be removed to Westchester or New Jersey at need, while the rest of the army was to be brought together around the Harlem Heights defenses and organized as a single fighting unit. It was now to become a race between the wagons hauling army supplies and equipment out of New York and the boats which could bring the King's men to an advantageous landing place on Manhattan to cut off the retreat or attack the rear guard. Besides the removal of essential stores and ammunition, the American sick and wounded had first to be conveyed to a place of safety, and their transportation slowed the whole operation unavoidably.

Washington was at this point a little heartened by the arrival of Colonel George Weedon, an old friend from Fredericksburg, with a small reinforcement of Virginia Continentals, bringing to the weary commander in chief some familiar faces from home.

If Howe had at once followed up his advantage there would have been no time for debate at American headquarters. But the Howe brothers had been empowered by the Whig party in England to negotiate for a peaceful settlement of the colonists' grievances. They therefore delayed for a fruitless conference with a Congressional delegation from Philadelphia who arrived in response to an invitation from the British general delivered by the hand of General Sullivan, who was released on parole for that purpose. The British offer was of course unacceptable to Congress, and the Howes then prepared to resume their campaign, after a lull of two weeks which might have been put to better use by the Americans.

Washington established a new headquarters at a mansion on Harlem Heights belonging to the Tory Roger Morris, who had gone into self-imposed exile in London. He was accomplishing the belated withdrawal of troops and heavy equipment up the island of Manhattan when, on the hot sunny Sunday of September 15th, the British under Clinton suddenly crossed the East River and landed on Manhattan.

Under cover of a heavy bombardment by the guns of their frigates anchored in the East River, Clinton's landing barges, filled with scarlet coats and "looking like a large clover field in full bloom," crossed in four columns in front of the shallow breastworks that had been thrown up by the American defenders along the east shore of Manhattan. The unexpected deluge of British round shot and shell overwhelmed Spencer's nervous troops stationed there, and panic ensued. Almost without firing a shot in return, they began a mad stampede northward into the main road leading to Harlem and King's Bridge. The British and Hessians poured ashore at Kip's Bay without hindrance and set out in pursuit.

The first bombardment was heard at headquarters, where no warning intelligence had been received. Washington hastily left his desk for his saddle and, followed by his staff, rode toward the smoke and thunder at Kip's Bay. He met his disorganized troops streaming up the Post Road in a scene of disgraceful confusion and fright. Flinging themselves into the melee, Washington and his aides tried with shouted commands and the flat of their swords to turn the tide but were overrun by the fleeing troops and left behind with no defense but their own sidearms.

At the insistance of his aides, who feared that he would be captured by the enemy in his reckless fury, Washington at last allowed himself to be turned back to the Harlem defense lines. He had got his sick and wounded away from lower Manhattan in time, but the mounted cannon in the town and a considerable amount of army baggage such as tents and provisions and tools would now be lost behind the British occupation forces. Worse, several valuable men, including Putnam and Knox, had been left to organize the transport of army stores and artillery and were now marooned below Kip's Bay, where they would be taken prisoners if the British were able to hold on to the position they had so unexpectedly won at the waist of the island.

Howe with his vanguard reached Murray Hill early in the afternoon and paused at the mansion there to await the second wave of his troops who were still crossing the East River. During his halt he was served with the legendary cakes and wine by the Quaker mistress of the house, who was said to have encouraged him by her hospitality to linger on her cool veranda while Putnam slipped past the turning in the road where he might have been cut off from a safe retreat to Harlem.

The American officers, however desperately they tried to rally their men, were unable to control them, and some had been carried to the rear in the first rush. Greene had no command that day, owing to his recent incapacity and the fact that many of his men had been captured with Sullivan on Long Island. But he did get his first experience of an actual engagement while riding with Reed in Washington's wake.

Anxiety at Harlem headquarters for Knox and his subordinates, who had last been seen trying to save the mounted guns on lower Manhattan, was finally allayed by their appearance, without the guns and their baggage, from an obscure woods road leading up the west shore along the Hudson and bypassing the excitement which choked the roads northward from Turtle Bay. They had been guided to their escape route by one of Putnam's aides, a young man named Aaron Burr. Other scattered detachments either fought their way through or evaded the enemy by alternate lanes and bypaths. The Hessians, who had won a reputation for brutality on Long Island, had been warned by their officers of atrocities which might be expected from the American barbarians (such as scalping), and they butchered their prisoners without mercy, adding to the horrors of the headlong rout.

By the afternoon of that day New York was in Howe's hands, and British outposts had been set up opposite the American lines on Harlem Heights, which ran roughly east and west from the Harlem to the Hudson River. There had been no organized defense, no fighting in the streets to resist the invaders, no rearguard action. The city was lost.

When his shaken, exhausted troops had gathered themselves in the refuge provided by the Harlem fortifications, Washington reported on that dreadful day to Congress: "We are now encamped with the main body of the army on the Heights of Harlem, where I hope the enemy will meet defeat in case of an attack, if the generality of the troops would behave with tolerable resolution," he wrote.

Perhaps not altogether to his surprise, the same troops redeemed themselves in an unexpected encounter the following day when a reconnoitering party led by Colonel Knowlton and his Connecticut Rangers ran into a detachment of Hessians and Highlanders on Harlem Plain. Accompanied by his adjutant,

Colonel Reed, Washington again rushed out from headquarters toward the sound of gunfire, this time with reinforcements under Weedon.

Reed in a letter to his wife recounted the famous story that the enemy's bugles sounded the insulting *Tally-ho!* that is given on the hunting field at sight of the fox, "which seemed to crown our disgrace" of the Turtle Bay retreat, he added. But this time the fox did not go to earth nor give them a run. After a two-hour ding-dong fight in which Knowlton was killed in front of his men, Washington was obliged to call off his enthusiastic troops in order to avoid a full-scale, head-on engagement with British reinforcements led by Cornwallis, which he was not equipped to risk.

Although the field was held again by the British, the humiliated fugitives of the previous day had demonstrated that they could stand fire and even advance under it, and this limited success restored somewhat the morale of the American army. Behind their stout works at Harlem that night they were able to congratulate themselves, while the British enjoyed a riotous welcome from the Tories in New York.

Howe, as usual, was in no hurry, and the following day was uneventful. The British lines stretched from river to river across Manhattan around Bloomingdale, some two or three miles south of the American position on the Heights, with Harlem Plain between. From there Howe could have turned Washington's left by a landing in Westchester from the Sound and a sweep westward to threaten Fort Washington on the Hudson in Washington's rear. Or he could have made the frontal attack in force for which, since Bunker Hill, he had no stomach. He hesitated, allowing nearly a month to elapse, while with his headquarters established in the Beekman mansion at Turtle Bay he cut a figure in New York society and sent to London for more troops and more ships.

Washington strengthened Heath's position at King's Bridge and hastened work on the defenses at Fort Washington, which was commanded by Colonel Magaw, and wrote to his brother Jack that "if I were to wish the bitterest curse to an enemy on this side of the grave, I should put him in my stead with my feelings. I see the impossibility of serving with reputation, or doing any essential service to the cause by continuing in command, and yet I am told that if I quit the command inevitable ruin will follow from the distraction that will ensue." There was no one else, even he could see that. There was nothing to do but hold on where he was and wait for Howe's next move.

Greene was detached to a post of great responsibility in New Jersey, where a "flying camp"—the equivalent of the modern mobile reserve—had been established by General Hugh Mercer of Virginia, an old friend, neighbor, and comrade of Washington's since the French war twenty years before. Fort Constitution, on the east shore of New Jersey, was designated as Greene's headquarters, while he maintained touch with Mercer at Amboy. He had three brigades and two regiments, all below strength, and only a fraction of his men were from the original force which had accompanied him to Cambridge from Rhode Island. His task, like Mercer's, was constant vigilance in a Tory countryside, to protect the lines of communication between Washington at Harlem and the Congress at Philadelphia.

The assignment, though out of the firing line, was a well-earned reward for his past record of service, and no one grudged him its prestige and authority. "He is beyond doubt a first-rate military genius, and one in whose opinions the General places the utmost confidence," wrote Tench Tilghman of Maryland, who was serving as a volunteer aide under no obligation "but a tie of honor"—for, he said, "if we fail, nothing in this country is worth a thought." Slight of build, reddish-haired, gray-eyed and reserved, always willing and always present, Tilghman was to remain at Washington's side till the end of the war.

Although Howe had settled into inaction, which was to become a familiar pattern of behavior for him as time went on, Greene's watchfulness never relaxed, and he was busy recruiting, drilling, and foraging, until by the fifth of October he was prepared either for a confrontation on his side of the river or a summons from Washington to Harlem. He recognized a general loss of confidence in the wisdom of Congress, whose mistakes during the first year of the war had all been repeated, with embellishments, during the year about to end. The deep thoughtfulness, the sound basic knowledge, and the compassionate understanding of human nature which made Greene the invaluable man he would become were evident in his letters from New Jersey to the President of Congress.

In the lull of Howe's inactivity at New York, Washington regrouped his forces behind the Harlem works and welcomed back General Lee from his triumph at Charleston. Not everyone was pleased to have the bossy professional campaigner in their midst again. "General Lee is hourly expected, as if from heaven, with a legion of flaming swordsmen," remarked the caustic Tench Tilghman in his private correspondence. A council was called at Harlem on October 16 to receive the benefit of Lee's opinions on their present situation. Heath was still posted near King's Bridge, Greene was headquartered in Jersey, Sullivan and Stirling had been exchanged and were again on active duty. A new major general of Massachusetts militia, Benjamin Lincoln, had just arrived at camp. A benign, muscular man, deacon of the church in his home town of Hingham, he was never heard to utter a profanity and was capable of great courage and devotion to his friends. Washington placed Lee in command of all the troops around King's Bridge, where it was thought an attempt by Howe to turn his flank was likely to fall.

The difficulty of maintaining communications and of circumventing Tory activity everywhere from Staten Island to upper New York State was so great that the Council agreed that new positions must be adopted. To evacuate the works on Harlem Heights and fall back northward so that the army would no longer be divided by the Harlem River meant exposing Fort Washington to an alternate British attack, but Greene believed that it could be defended from the British ships which occasionally ran past the obstructions in the Hudson channel. Congress was demanding that the forts be garrisoned and the river held.

Even while Washington's council was sitting, Howe made the long-expected next move. Leaving Lord Percy to guard New York with a force of British and Hessians, Howe and Clinton, aided by Tory guides, made a landing at Throg's Neck above Turtle Bay and another still farther up the Sound at Pell's Point, where the road through Westchester to New Rochelle and White Plains lay open before them. Their force was now augmented by the second division of German hirelings led by General Knyphausen—an amiable veteran of the European wars, of whom legend says that he found the voyage to America so long that one night he interrupted the whist game in the captain's cabin to inquire earnestly, "Ain't we hab sailed *past* America?"

Washington fell back hastily to White Plains and took up a stand there before Howe and Clinton could come up with the whole British force. He had called in Stirling and Spencer and Heath to throw up shallow fortifications on rising ground called Chatterton's Hill. There was a battle at White Plains—hardly more than a sharp skirmish—but it was enough for Howe to recognize the same spirit which had finally faced him and stood firm at Harlem. After contemplating the situation at his leisure while the two armies lay almost face to face, Howe veered away westward toward Dobbs Ferry on the Hudson, in a maneuver which amounted to retreat. But at Dobbs Ferry he was a direct threat to Fort Washington and the New Jersey posts. Once again Washington's council faced the alternative of evacuating Manhattan altogether or being cut off.

As the end of the year again brought the end of enlistment terms, Washington's army was melting away homeward as it had done at Cambridge. Cold weather increased hardship and sickness, tents and blankets and warm clothing were all wanting, even cooking utensils were scarce, and it was said that in some regiments there was hardly a whole pair of breeches. To ask a man in those circumstances to reenlist was unreasonable, to say the least.

The council met again on November 6 and reached the same unhappy, inevitable conclusion it had faced before—more militia, called up in a hurry to serve only until spring—unwilling, untrained, unequipped militia, to maintain the appearance of what Washington himself called "a shadow of an army." Beyond Fort Washington, if that fell to Howe, lay the road to Philadelphia and the assembled Congress. A decision was taken to try to hold Fort Washington and the New York Highlands with detachments and retreat the main army across the Hudson into New Jersey to bar the road to Philadelphia.

Again Washington was forced to divide his dwindling army, leaving a garrison at Fort Washington and detaching more men under Heath at Peekskill and posting Lee above White Plains with another detachment to guard the Highlands. With the rest —about 2,000 men—he crossed the Hudson at Peekskill to join

Greene's New Jersey force at Fort Constitution (now renamed Fort Lee). He hoped to hold on there until by some miracle they could all be united again to confront the British at some future date. He anticipated that Howe would go into winter quarters soon, probably at New York, though it was possible that he might first make another attempt to gain a foothold in the South by a seaborne assault.

His most likely move was against Fort Washington, which stood alone on the rough plateau above the Hudson. It had been hastily constructed, had no palisade or ditch, and was still incomplete as to its redoubts. It was not stocked with fuel or supplies for a winter siege. It had not even a well. It was manned by two regiments of Pennsylvania troops and "a handful" of Virginians and Marylanders, all under Magaw's command. Greene thought it was adequate and that the river could be blocked with the aid of a crossfire from Fort Lee.

His natural optimism and desire to hearten his chief was valuable, but Washington received a distinct shock when he arrived at Greene's Fort Lee headquarters on November 13, 1776.

Chapter 9

He had left to Greene's discretion the question of evacuating Fort Washington or trying to retain possession of it. Greene had not only elected to reinforce its garrison but had passed more and more supplies and ammunition across the river to it. By the time Washington reached Greene's headquarters on the Jersey side, the British under Cornwallis and Percy and the Hessians under Rall and Knyphausen were closing in on Fort Washington along the Dobbs Ferry and New Rochelle roads.

At dawn on the sixteenth of November the commander in chief, accompanied by Greene, Putnam, and Mercer, crossed the river from Fort Lee in a small boat and interviewed Colonel Magaw, who agreed with Greene that Fort Washington could be held "till the end of December anyway." Their reasons for attempting to hold it were sound. Howe would not dare turn his back on it while its garrison could threaten his rear; another evacuation would further dishearten the dwindling colonial army; there would be time enough to get Magaw's men away across the river if the fort were actually threatened.

Their prospect of holding it against an all-out attack by the combined British and Hessian command seemed to Washington's superior experience very thin, but he was always willing to listen to other opinions. Moreover, his sheer physical exhaustion now inclined him to lean on someone else's decisions. His weary hesitation was apparent to his subordinates and at this crucial time caused some loss of confidence which with hindsight was later to grow into outright criticism of his capabilities as a commander.

While the four generals stood together in the redoubt at Fort Washington in anxious consultation with Magaw, gunfire on the outer defenses began, and they saw at once that the men posted there would not stand. Urged by a still confident Magaw, they made a hasty departure down the cliff to their waiting boat and were rowed back across the river to Fort Lee, followed by the sounds of increasing combat on the shore they had just left.

Within minutes of their departure the British were in possession of the very spot where they had stood. The whole garrison, except those slaughtered by the Hessians, went into captivity in occupied New York, and another sizable unit of Washington's army—some 2,000 men—was thus swept away. He lost his last foothold on Manhattan Island with their surrender, and Howe, with only 528 casualties, was now in a position to fall upon the New Jersey posts and drive on toward Philadelphia.

It developed later that an American deserter had turned over the plans of the fort to the British, for what reward is not related, though almost any Tory citizen could have done the same unhindered. This treachery without doubt expedited its fall, but its defenders were finally so crowded into the single redoubt that they could not long have subsisted there.

Washington at Fort Lee had been a helpless witness through his field glasses of the savage hand-to-hand fighting at Fort Washington as the Americans fell back within its walls. He saw the surrender flags passing in and out and watched the British standard run up to float above those walls. Greene was blamed for the loss of Fort Washington, for his unrealistic optimism, or for plain poor judgment. But the commander in chief was also present at Fort Washington and could have overruled a major general if he had himself been convinced that Greene was in error. The case for attempting to retain a Manhattan base was too good.

Again, there was no time for recriminations or apologies. Fort Lee was now vulnerable and useless, and there was no further hesitation about ordering its evacuation. The troops which had crossed the river with Washington on the twelfth of November had been encamped at Hackensack, and Washington went there, leaving Greene to empty Fort Lee as fast as he could get wagons for the transport of the flour, powder, and arms with which it had been stocked. The men of course had to walk, in steadily worsening weather.

Washington's little army was now utterly fragmented; his own feeble force, including men from Mercer's Fying Camp, lay on the far side of the Hackensack River; Stirling was roundabout Brunswick; Lee, Knox, and Sullivan were still above White Plains; Heath was at Peekskill anticipating an attempt by Burgoyne—unaccountably delayed—to lead a force from Canada in an attempt to unite with Howe at New York. Guards were posted along the Jersey heights of the Hudson River called Palisades to watch the enemy on the other side of the river, but they failed to give the alarm on the dark, rainy night of November 19 when an American patrol discovered too late that Cornwallis had crossed the Hudson at Dobbs Ferry and made a landing at Closter, above Fort Lee, dragging his cannon and equipment up the precipitous Palisades after nightfall.

Greene dispatched an express rider to warn Washington at Hackensack and put his remaining men under arms in an instant retreat toward the single bridge across the Hackensack River, where Washington met him. If the British had reached it first, they would again have been in a position to trap Washington's army between two rivers—the Hackensack and the Passaic.

Without enough wagons, forced in their desperate haste to abandon their mounted cannon, stacked tents and blankets, their tools, and nearly all the personal baggage of the officers, even leaving their cooking pots on the fires, Washington's army raced for the next bridge and the fords of the Passaic River, with Cornwallis close behind. Washington and Greene were still unaware that they were now measuring swords with a very different opponent from the leisurely Howe and Clinton.

Lord Cornwallis had arrived at Charleston the previous June with Clinton and Admiral Parker and had accompanied their defeated force to New York. He had been subordinate to Clinton until in this November Howe detached the latter to lead an expedition to Rhode Island. Howe was still in command, but by sending Clinton to occupy Newport he had rid himself of daily controversy with an always contentious subordinate. Cornwallis was the ablest and most active general the British had sent out from London to subdue the rebellious colonies. In this autumn of 1776, as second in command to Howe, he now took the initiative as Clinton had never done. He had had some army experience as a youthful aide to Lord Granby on the Continent during the Seven Years War, but on the death of his father he was recalled to take his seat in Parliament as the second earl. He represented the highest type of British aristocrat, enlightened and courageous, handsome in the portly fashion of the times, devoted to an invalid wife in England, and anxious to get this tiresome business in America over with and return home.

Washington's line of retreat in Jersey was still to be secured, and his army must be reunited. He pushed on across the Passaic River to temporary headquarters at Newark. From there he wrote letters calling in Lee from White Plains and Stirling from Brunswick. He sent the diplomatic Mifflin to Philadelphia to explain to Congress the almost hopeless weakness of the army and the immediate necessity for reinforcements and for funds to pay the men of the Flying Camp, who might then be persuaded to reenlist if allowed to visit their homes first. Adjutant Reed was dispatched to Governor Livingston of New Jersey, then at Burlington, with a similar plea for supplies and recruits.

Lee, whose rested and idle forces at White Plains were the only salvation Washington's desperate little army could hope for, was requested to bring his Continentals to New Jersey "by the easiest and best passage," but he delayed where he was, to write vainglorious letters to friends at Philadelphia—"I foresaw, predicted all that has happened. . . . I could say many things . . . let me talk vainly . . . had I the powers, might I but dictate one week . . ." It was a brazen attempt to discredit the commander in chief and by implication to show how much better qualified to lead an army Lee was himself than the Virginian everyone thought so highly of. Instead of moving his division southward as requested, Lee dispatched orders to Heath to send a small detachment from his own forces across the Hudson and down to Washington in Jersey.

Heath, holding to the letter of his instructions from Washington himself, refused to part with a single file and was promptly confirmed in this determination by a letter from headquarters. In the face of what seemed like deliberate insubordination on Lee's part, Washington could only assume charitably that Lee had misunderstood his first courteous orders, which were framed rather as a request, and sent Lee a second and very definite summons. Unless Lee's reinforcements were brought to Jersey, Washington would soon have no army at all, and the British were still on his heels. To turn about and confront Cornwallis in the present exhausted condition of the American troops was not to be contemplated.

On November 29, still with no word from Lee, Washington kept his temper and sent a third summons, quite unmistakably worded, and then fell back from Newark to Brunswick with the enemy so close behind him that they entered the opposite end of the town as Washington's rear guard left it. For some reason which was not apparent, the British did not attempt closer pursuit.

While he was at Brunswick, half stunned with fatigue and anxiety, Washington received a personal blow that was unexpected in the harmonious atmosphere which Lee's absence from headquarters always ensured. A letter from Lee arrived by express, directed to Colonel Reed, who was still absent at Burlington on his mission to Governor Livingston. Assuming that a communication addressed to the man who often acted as his secretary would contain some information about Lee's progress along the road to New Jersey, Washington opened and read the letter, which was a private one as between two friends. It was apparently written in reply to an unofficial letter from Reed to Lee and seemed to concur with some criticism of Washington already expressed by Reed, referring to "that fatal indecision of mind"—on Washington's part—"which in war is a much greater disqualification than stupidity or want of physical courage." The words were Lee's, but they read as coming from Reed.

Washington was hurt and incredulous. His trusted friend, the adjutant general—his respected counselor, the senior general—in secret disparagement and disloyalty at this time of his own personal calamity and self-doubt. Who, then, Washington must ask himself, who believed in him? In whom could he trust to uphold his weary hands during the coming weeks of suspense and almost hopeless endeavor? The aides, of whose devotion he had no possible doubt, were boys, looking to him for comfort and courage. But these other two—one of whom had for weeks shared his daily thoughts and witnessed his private despair— these two, so different from each other but both claiming his honest admiration as men of the world with more advantages than any country squire like himself could have—these thought nothing of him.

The wound to his pride and self-respect was deep. He wrote a brief, courteous letter to Reed, explaining the circumstances of having opened the letter himself, enclosed it, added his formal respects to Mrs. Reed, and turned grimly to the lonely business of war. There was still another river, the Delaware, to put between himself and Cornwallis, and expiring enlistments continued to nibble away the pitiful remnants of his army.

He gave orders for collecting boats on the Jersey shore around Trenton and for transporting baggage and equipment to the opposite bank, in Pennsylvania. From Brunswick they slogged on to Princeton, where Stirling was detached as a rear guard to discourage Cornwallis. There was still no report from Lee. From Princeton they marched for Trenton on the Delaware. Instead of overtaking Washington on the Princeton road as he might have done, Cornwallis had been detained at Brunswick by orders from Howe to await that general's arrival from New York. The campaign now seemed to Howe so nearly won that he desired to be in at the kill. He arrived at Cornwallis's camp in time to join what he called the fox hunt as Washington struggled on toward Trenton.

Washington accompanied his own rear guard on the road to Trenton and was observed by his men sitting impassive and patient on his big horse while the pioneer troops—as the engineers were called—tore up bridges and cut down trees behind them to impede the British progress. It was dusk when he arrived in the town, and he began at once to ferry everything that could be spared from daily necessities across the still unfrozen river. Orders went out that any form of water transport that could be found on the Jersey banks must be destroyed if it could not be taken across to Pennsylvania.

There was a rumor at Trenton that the British carried with them a supply of boats in which to convey their troops over the Delaware; and if they should accomplish such a feat there would be nothing between them and Philadelphia, where Congress sat defenseless. Or if the river froze solid, the enemy might find it possible to cross on the ice and occupy the capital city of the rebellion.

Although Reed returned to camp, after writing an affectionate and apologetic explanation of his correspondence with Lee, and although Washington made no further reference to the matter, it left an awkwardness between them which their former confidential association could not survive. In the spring of 1777 Reed would resign as adjutant general, to be succeeded in that post briefly by Weedon, St. Clair, and Pickering, one after the other, none of whom supplied the same mutual understanding which had once existed between Washington and Reed.

But even the strongest man needs friendship somewhere, and it is possible that Washington's growing dependence on the honest, warm-hearted, and loyal Quaker from Rhode Island stemmed from his disappointment over Reed's lack of integrity. He kept Greene so close to headquarters during the ensuing year as to cause some jealous comment, especially from Mifflin, who later became estranged also. Knox, like Greene, never wavered in his personal devotion to the commander in chief, and in a letter to Lucy he airily ascribed the humiliating retreat across Jersey to "a combination of unlucky circumstances."

Howe and Cornwallis lingered at Brunswick, reassembling and resting their weatherworn, complaining regulars. On the seventh of December they moved forward again, and on the same day Washington transported his few thousand men and horses across the open river at Trenton in a fleet of commandeered small craft which were then collected and moored on the Pennsylvania side. His army had been on the run for three weeks and had covered about eighty miles in their flight. The enemy had often been so close behind him that the "music"—the bands, drums, and bugles—of the pursuers and the pursued were heard by both armies. Yet no confrontation had occurred, thanks mainly to Washington's canny resolution to keep intact what force he had until some more favorable opportunity for an engagement could present itself. " 'Tis almost impossible to catch them," a disgruntled British officer had written. "They will neither fight nor totally run away. We seem to be playing at bo-peep."

As at Brunswick, it was again such a near thing at Trenton that Washington's last boatload pulled away from the shore as the British van reached the head of the two parallel streets which composed the town. The Americans left not a boat, skiff, or ferry on the Jersey side for miles up and down the bank. The British had brought none with them, as had been rumored, and were not sufficiently enterprising to commandeer lumber from the wooden buildings of the town and construct flatboats for their own use.

Washington set up a supply base near Newtown, in Pennsylvania, and his headquarters were at Keith's farm, nearer the river. Stirling, Mercer, Stephen, and Cadwallader were told off to patrol the entire Pennsylvania shore line, however thinly, lest the British find some means to cross in Washington's rear and take an undefended road to Philadelphia. General Putnam had been sent ahead to put the city under martial law and supervise the construction of its defenses. He promised the uneasy population that in no circumstances would Philadelphia be burned to deprive the British of its use. Mifflin was delegated to take charge of military stores there and try to raise militia.

On December 11 the British were in possession of Bordentown and Pennington, on either side of Trenton, which was occupied by the Hessians under Colonel Rall. The alarm in Philadelphia had reached such a pitch that on December 12 the Congress hastily loaded their papers and personal baggage into wagons and fled south to Baltimore, after voting emergency powers of dictatorship to Washington. The flight of Congress to a raw little town below the Susquehanna cannot be considered cowardice on their part, though at the time they were jeered at, even by those who were soon to follow their example. Apart from the probably fatal consequences to its members if they had been taken prisoners, the capture of the new nation's governing body would have been catastrophic. The British might have been cordially received in Philadelphia if they had managed to spend Christmas there, for its Tory population was crowing, and the Patriots were close to panic.

Calamity continued to pile up at American headquarters. On the thirteenth a hard freeze set in, which threatened to relieve the British necessity for boats to make the Delaware crossing. Bad news came from New England, where Clinton had taken part briefly in an expedition which had set a British garrison ashore at Newport on December 8. As at Manhattan, the defenders retreated to the north end of the island and escaped to the mainland, setting up camps at Tiverton and Bristol. At first sight of the British sails, the women and children had been sent inland from such centers as East Greenwich and Providence, and cattle and supplies were likewise removed from the shore area. The Rhode Island Assembly cried out for their favorite son, Nat Greene, to come and defend them, and Greene's anxiety was of course acute, for he had seen the Jersey countryside ravaged and the population abused by the professional foragers in Hessian uniforms.

The enemy in Rhode Island were apparently going into winter quarters there for shelter from the bitter New England cold, billeting the officers in all the best houses roundabout Newport. They had accomplished their objective, which was a safe anchorage for their ships, at the same time keeping the small American fleet of privateers bottled up at Providence. Clinton then left his second in command, Lord Percy, in charge at Newport, counseling inaction until spring, and sailed for England.

"The Eastern delegates made application to General Washington for me to come to Rhode Island," Greene wrote the governor from Trenton, "but the General would not consent. General Spencer and General Arnold are coming to take command at Rhode Island. Arnold is a fine, spirited fellow, and an active general. I hope they'll keep the enemy at bay."

Arnold had recently returned via Ticonderoga from the unsuccessful venture with Gates in the North, and he left Washington's Jersey camp for Rhode Island only a few days before the famous Christmas crossing of the Delaware which led to the battle at Trenton. Washington's decision to keep Greene at his side was an evidence of confidence and affection which did not sit at all well with some of the ambitious men who aspired to advancement at headquarters and glory in the field. This was true especially of Mifflin and Reed. The latter lived to regret his admiration of the showy European adventurer Lee and to give his allegiance to the Quaker general who so far had had scant opportunity to justify Washington's obvious preference for him as a right-hand man.

It was during that dreadful Christmastide of 1776 that Washington's iron composure gave way briefly in a letter to his brother, so that he wrote in a rare mood of despair: "If every nerve is not strained to recruit this new army with all possible expedition, I think the game is pretty near up." But even with his spirits at lowest ebb, he maintained his incredible resolution and a firmness of purpose which could hardly be called hope. A fantastic, dogged enterprise still simmered in the brain behind the impassive face he presented to the gaze of his anxious headquarters household and his wretched troops as he passed among them, his tall, cloaked figure still commanding their loyalty and endurance. If Lee ever came in with his reinforcements he was determined to make one last impossible gamble to confront the enemy on the Delaware and drive them back from in front of Philadelphia.

Then even that desperate resolution was seemingly wrecked by Lee, who had already caused enough distress by his reluctance to join his forces to Washington's on the retreat. Marching at last to overtake the main army in a leisurely way, he was for a time in a position to attack the British from the rear, pinning Howe and Cornwallis between his troops and Washington's. But neither Lee nor Washington had enough men separately to make such a maneuver feasible, and Washington's whole endeavor had been to avoid any direct encounter with the enemy. He sent Stirling to Morristown to meet Lee and hurry him forward past the British flank and to gather up another overdue contingent from Ticonderoga led by Gates. It was becoming a race with the weather too, till a sudden thaw set in and the ice in the river broke up into chunks driven by the current.

While Stirling was riding toward the junction with Lee at Morristown, Lee was taken prisoner at a tavern along the road, where he had turned aside to spend the night. There has always been some mystery about what Lee was doing at that wayside tavern three miles outside his own lines, with only a small body-guard, and how he came to be taken in his shirt and breeches by a British reconnoitering party who must have had information on his whereabouts. He was said to have offered no resistance, though his position with the British army was dubious, after having involved himself openly with the rebel command.

Rumors ranged from sordid allegations about the presence at the tavern with Lee of "a woman of easy virtue," to the suggestion of a deliberate design born of pique on his part to join the British without appearing to desert, so that the loss of his valuable services would be regretted by the rebels, who had not seen fit to give him the supreme command. Regret at his capture was certainly felt by the still deluded Congress and at headquarters —though by now it had begun to dawn unwillingly on Washington that his erratic second in command left much to be desired in loyalty and discipline. One of Washington's aides, young Sam Webb of Connecticut, put it in writing that "we shall find hard work to convince many officers and soldiers that Lee is not a traitor." Lee's Westchester army was still intact, and its command devolved on Sullivan, whose loyalty and courage were without question.

The Delaware had not accommodated the British by freezing solid, and the boats were all on Washington's side of the river. But Howe apparently had no intention of pursuing the miserable remnants of Washington's army across the river, frozen or not, being convinced that he could take Philadelphia whenever he chose. Professional armies like his habitually went into winter quarters and did not try to cope with weather which wet the powder and the flints and made the transport of heavy guns and wagons too slow and costly in wheels and horseflesh. He had already written off the Jersey campaign as won and retired from Brunswick to the comforts of New York, leaving New Jersey to the soldierly Cornwallis. In his turn, Cornwallis decided that it was safe to turn his back on Washington now, and he himself set out for New York, intending to sail for a winter leave of absence in England.

This left the main body of British troops at Brunswick in the experienced hands of General James Grant, the old campaigner from the Indian Wars who had such an arrogant contempt for all colonials. Colonel Rall's fancy-dress Hessians were garrisoned at Trenton. They had a nine-man band, which was required to stand playing in the snowy street under the windows of Rall's headquarters each morning while he shook off his hangover and donned his gold-laced uniform.

Most of the Hessians were housed in the comfortable stone barracks built nearly twenty years before for a British garrison, and Rall had lodged himself snugly in a Quaker household in King Street. He quite rightly felt some uneasiness at the proximity of Washington at Newtown just across the river and asked Grant at Brunswick for reinforcements. Grant, taking his tone from his superiors, replied to Rall's messenger: "Tell the colonel he is safe. I will guarantee to keep the peace in New Jersey with a corporal's guard."

There were small British outposts at Amboy, Princeton, and Mount Holly, and Donop had a brigade of the 42d Highlanders —the Black Watch—as well as his Hessians at Bordentown, where the Delaware makes a sharp elbow turning southward to flow past Burlington, Philadelphia, and Wilmington into the bay.

The German garrisons did not speak or understand English and were notorious for their drunken plundering of the population. Washington was somehow aware of the German custom of celebrating Christmas with riotous good cheer, including gambling, overeating, and swilling liquor. Their stock of the latter was now happily reinforced by a powerful local brew called applejack, which any German could pronounce.

Chapter 10

Washington lived in daily expectation that Sullivan would bring Lee's men into the camp at Newtown by a crossing well upstream and that Gates would also arrive shortly with a detachment from Ticonderoga. So long as he could cross the Delaware northward if he liked and the enemy could not cross it at all from Trenton—and so long as the river didn't freeze solid and his army didn't disintegrate entirely, which it would be at liberty to do when the year ended—he had a small advantage. He nursed a growing determination to make the most of this while there was still time and was maturing in his own mind a precarious plan of launching a surprise attack across the river on the Hessian garrison at Trenton.

With the belated arrival in a snowstorm of Sullivan, accompanied by Knox and followed by Gates, such a move became at least possible to contemplate seriously, though the reinforcements were fewer than he had counted on. Gates was gloomy and actually advocated retreating across the Susquehanna, which would uncover Philadelphia and leave Congress stranded in their temporary lodging at Baltimore. Gates did not remain long in Washington's camp but hurried on to Baltimore on the pretext of soliciting further aid and support from Congress. He was always to show a preference for fighting the war from the shelter of the Congressional wing.

With his usual courtesy to his subordinates, Washington called a council at Greene's headquarters near Newtown on the evening of December 24. It was plain to the grave-faced officers who crowded into the little room that his decision was already made, and no objections were raised when they heard it.

Some of the men who surrounded him in the yellow lantern light were old comrades of this new war—Greene, Knox, Sullivan, and Stirling. Others had only lately joined his army but had proved their worth, such as St. Clair of Pennsylvania, who had seen the Canadian campaign with Wolfe while Washington was fighting on the western frontier under Braddock's command in 1755. Since then St. Clair had retired to his farm in Pennsylvania but joined Washington in Jersey in November to help organize the local militia. Not present at the council but close at hand were other veterans of the Long Island defeat—Weedon and Mercer, both old friends from Virginia, Glover of Massachusetts, Smallwood and Gist of Maryland, and Starke of New Hampshire. There were also three junior officers at Newtown whose names would be heard again—Alexander Hamilton, James Monroe, and a young kinsman of the commander in chief, William Washington.

The Americans had by now lost five engagements, hardly to be called battles, with about 4,000 casualties, in the space of twelve weeks. Reinforced by militia from Pennsylvania and New Jersey, the army numbered about 5,000 men, raggedly clad and in some cases hardly shod at all, in remnants of shoe-leather held together with rags. But they were still in good enough health and spirits to follow wherever Washington led until their short enlistments were up. He now proposed to divide this pitiful force once again into three parts, keeping half of them under his own command—to transport them back across the Delaware River to

New Jersey under cover of darkness on Christmas night, march them cautiously along the shore to Trenton, and take the carousing Hessians by surprise before dawn.

Of the other two units, the Pennsylvania brigadier Cadwallader's militia, now at Bristol on the near side of the river, were to cross it there and occupy Donop's attention at Bordentown on Washington's right wing. James Ewing, commanding his own force of Pennsylvania militia, was to cross the river just below Trenton Falls and cut off Rall's retreat eastward over the Assunpink Creek bridge toward Bordentown.

Meanwhile Washington, with the main body, would cross the river at McConkey's Ferry nine miles above Trenton and proceed along a road which divided at Birmingham to enter Trenton at opposite ends of the town. With his own division he would take Greene, Knox, Stirling, Sullivan, Mercer, and a pot-valiant Virginia veteran full of reckless enterprise—Adam Stephen. If Ewing and Cadwallader could operate according to plan, all three forces would join at Trenton on the morning after Christmas Day for a combined attack on Princeton and Brunswick.

All afternoon of Christmas Day the boats were collected from the reeds and thickets along the shore where they had been hidden and were brought in to the landing place at McConkey's Ferry, which had been deactivated on the Jersey shore. Many of these were the "Durham boats"—long, light-draught, canoe-shaped craft, painted black, used to carry iron ore and freight between Philadelphia and the Jersey ports. They had steering sweeps which could be attached to either end and short masts and small sails, now useless, and long poles would be used to drive them against the current. They could carry thirty to forty men, needed five men at the oars, and capsized easily. The same "amphibian" Marblehead regiment under James Glover, who had manned the boats for the foggy Long Island retreat, were now called upon to maneuver these difficult craft through the floating, jostling ice chunks in the swollen Delaware, at night, in winter weather.

We must acknowledge here the famous painting of "Washington Crossing the Delaware" which has become the standard image of this crucial event in American history. The artist was a

German named Leutze whose parents had brought him as a child
to Philadelphia. He taught himself to draw. At the age of about
twenty-four he had returned to Europe to study art at Düssel-
dorf, where he married and made his home. For some fifteen
years he specialized in historical subjects, visiting their European settings for his backgrounds. In 1859 he returned to the
United States with his own family, and on the strength of his
accomplished work he was commissioned to do a mural for the
Capitol at Washington. The "Crossing" had apparently been
painted during his residence in Germany. He had never seen a
Durham boat, and his models were German. Common sense
should have told him that Washington would not have struck a
heroic pose standing up in a rocking boat on a rough, windswept
night. But the impressive canvas won him recognition at the
time and has passed into history along with the event.

Washington's Orders of the Day on that Christmas morning
in 1776 made grim hearing when read out to the cold, half-fed
men who had been on the run for weeks. The troops were to
carry three days' cooked rations and forty rounds of ammunition.
Each officer was to provide himself with a white paper stuck into
his hat for a field mark—in a snowstorm. The countersign, which
Washington wrote out in his own hand—*Victory or Death*—was
a strange one for so untheatrical a man. Once across the river,
the brigades were to form to march in subdivision on the right. A
profound silence was enjoined, and no man could quit the ranks
on pain of death. General Stephen was to cross in one of the first
boats and organize a chain of sentries at the landing place at
sufficient distance so that troops could form between it and the
shore and would detain any person who attempted to pass in or
out of the cordon. The sentries were ordered to rejoin their brigades as soon as the troops were all across.

Before twilight the rations were cooked and issued, along
with new flints and ammunition. When the regiments held their
evening parade there were snowflakes in the air, but instead of
returning to their quarters they were marched off toward the
ferry, into a northeast wind which stung their faces with the
snow. Those whose footwear consisted mainly of old rags tied
around their bare feet were already leaving the historic bloody
footprints in the snow.

The Delaware River at McConkey's Ferry was then about 1,000 feet wide. Washington and his staff, accompanied by Greene and Knox, arrived on the Pennsylvania riverbank as the winter daylight faded, hoping to complete the crossing between dusk and midnight. But it took nine hours to get the army over the river—the men first, clambering stoically into the rocking boats, guarding their muskets and powder as best they could from the wet, with bits of greasy rag wrapped around the firing-pans, then the horses and last the precious artillery.

Silence, of course, became a myth. The rising wind, the ice chunks in the river knocking the boats about, the horrified horses plunging and squealing, the profane and prayerful men who stumbled and fell and groped for ropes in the bitter dark between the bobbing lanterns made it almost impossible for even the necessary words of command to be heard. Washington, like everybody else, was laboring under a heavy cold and sore throat and wore a large woolen scarf tied around his neck over the bulky collar of his long blue cloak.

The men did their best to obey orders shouted by officers they could not even see, and once safely ashore themselves imag-ined that they heard cries for help from their friends still on the way—or was it only the wind?—imagined the crunch of boats stove in by the grinding ice, or boats carried away down-stream by the swift current and lost forever with their numbed and helpless cargoes. But not a boat capsized, not a man or a cannon was lost in that incredible nine hours of organized pandemonium.

Traditionally, Washington crossed in the same boat with Knox and after Greene. When his horse was brought to him on the far side, he mounted and rode among the men, with a husky word of praise or encouragement here and there. The troops straightened against the wind and dressed their lines in the dark to please him. Victory, Liberty, even Death, were only words. Washington was real; they could see him, touch him if they dared.

Then the artillery horses arrived on the Jersey shore, ice forming on their manes and tails. And then the guns came, lung-ing into the dragropes in the men's cold, stiff hands, or else dead weight against them, till the horses could be put to again, to take the strain. An anonymous staff officer, sheltering now and then in the ferry house, somehow found presence of mind to scratch a few notes in his pocket diary, aware that he was a witness to history. At 3:00 A.M. he wrote: "The troops are all over, and the boats have gone back for the artillery. We are three hours behind the set time. Glover's men have had a hard time to force the boats through the floating ice, with the snow drifting in their faces. I have never seen Washington so determined as he is now. He stands on the bank of the river, wrapped in his cloak, superintending the landing. The storm is changing to sleet, and cuts like a knife. The last cannon is being landed, and we are ready to mount our horses."

The sentries were called in, the ragged lines were formed, and they moved off, shepherded by their officers—dim, comforting shapes on horseback, with the snow lying white in the folds of their cloaks. The ring of horses' shoes on rock and frozen rut, the rumble of the gun carriages, the hard breathing of many men, the low, reassuring commands were all swallowed up in the roar of the storm. There could be no turning back now, no falling out, no lagging behind. They lurched forward into a murky dawn that would soon reveal their presence to the countryside. They had to go on, but they knew they were a forlorn hope, and they knew the usual fate of forlorn hopes, which was to be cut to pieces in brief, inconspicuous glory. The question lay heavy on all their minds: When they came back to the boats, how many of them would cross the river again to the Pennsylvania side?

At Birmingham, beyond the Bear Tavern, the troops were allowed a brief halt for breakfast from the cooked rations they carried in their knapsacks. There was of course no hot food or drink. Most of the officers ate without dismounting. Some of the men fell asleep in their tracks and had to be shaken and kicked awake by their comrades when the order came to fall in. Again Washington was among them on the tall bay horse, calm and collected, wrapped in thought as in his long blue cloak. "Press on, boys," he urged them gently. "Stick close to your officers, boys—press on—press on." And they stumbled after him again.

The wind was everywhere—in their faces, holding them back —behind them, whipping their frozen rags forward. And wherever they trod, the new snow was stained with their bloody footprints.

The road divided at Birmingham, both branches running south and east to enter Trenton at opposite ends of King and Queen streets. Sullivan had been assigned to the lower one, which followed the river. As he filed off to the right he reported that the storm was wetting the muskets and rendering them unfit for service. "Tell General Sullivan to use the bayonet" was Washington's grim reply. But the men had little confidence in what was to them a new and awkward weapon which the British regulars handled with appalling efficiency. Sullivan was soon lost to sight, and with him went about half the troops and cannon.

Greene, with the rest, led off to the left on the parallel track, and Washington rode with Greene. It was about five miles to go on either road, and the design was to arrive simultaneously at opposite ends of the town before the Hessians could form a battle line—though a converging movement at night with a chancy time element was a thing even an experienced general would always hesitate to employ, and Sullivan was already famous for courageous blundering.

The same sleet storm that battered at the marching men had also kept the festive mercenaries from manning their usual picket posts. There was probably not another night during the Hessian occupation that their patrols did not cover the very ground over which Washington had to pass on his way to attack the town.

Slipping, sliding, and stumbling on the treacherous frozen road, the men who followed Washington and Greene reached a point a mile from Trenton where the Hessian sentries were sheltering in a cooper's shop by the road. There was a belated challenge in German from the doorway as they passed, and some muskets were fired after them before the startled men on duty there gathered themselves into an attempt to give the alarm. Almost simultaneously there was firing on the right, indicating that Sullivan was keeping pace with them and had roused a picket on his road.

Washington and Greene rode in silence, for their plans were all made and their throats were closed with their colds. Greene's men followed them at the ragged "long trot" which kept up with the officers' horses. Together Washington and Greene reached the high ground at the upper end of King Street, where the Princeton road cut in from the north to join theirs, and they left a detachment there to block it as an escape route from the town.

The Hessians were just as drunk and demoralized by their holiday celebrations as Washington had anticipated. Colonel Rall, who thought so little of what he called "these country clowns" that he had not seen to his defenses, was with difficulty got on his feet from the gaming table in a very unbuttoned state, after the firing had reached the very streets of the town, amid shrill astonished shouts of *"Was ist?"* and *"Der Feind!"* and *"Heraus!"* A hastily scrawled message warning of unexpected activity on the Birmingham road was found crumpled up in Rall's pocket, apparently unread, after it was too late.

Knox planted his big guns at the top of King and Queen streets, and young Captain Hamilton swept both with a cannonade. Sullivan, getting it right for once, had arrived on time and was driving in the pickets on the lower road at the other end of the town where a bridge across the Assunpink Creek led to the Bordentown road. The Hessians, pouring out of their barracks into the street in half-awake confusion, found themselves between two firing lines as the village was raked by American grapeshot and musket balls, and gunsmoke as well as sleet obscured the air. When the Hessians tried to wheel their parked cannon into position to reply, Greene's men shot the artillery horses, while Captain William Washington and Lieutenant Monroe rushed the disabled guns. Monroe took a slight wound in the shoulder during the scrimmage around the guns, and the younger Washington was wounded in both hands.

This is the first notable appearance of the commander in chief's kinsman, who was to distinguish himself under Greene's command later in the war, and of James Monroe, who at eighteen had left the college at Williamsburg to join the army and who would be elected fifth President of the United States exactly forty years later. Captain Alexander Hamilton's artillery commanded the scene from the top of King Street. He was not yet twenty-one and had been seen at New York to pat his cherished brass cannon as though they were horses.

American riflemen ran through the fields at the waist of the town and fired into the street from behind barns and fences, driving the bewildered Hessians into Sullivan, who controlled the only escape route, across the Assunpink bridge. Rall stumbled to his horse and tried to rally his panicked Hessians, riding boldly up the street shouting and swearing in German, until he was struck by two musket balls and reeled from his saddle into the arms of his aides. Instead of rallying to avenge him, his men fled into an orchard behind the Quaker meetinghouse and raised their tall hats on the points of their swords in a token of surrender.

When the storm finally got to the powder and firelocks of Washington's men, the fight went to bayonets, gun-butts, and swords taken from the enemy. Little groups of dazed, surrendered Hessians were rounded up by the American officers, who collected their sidearms and colors and prepared to march them off as prisoners.

Once the American troops saw through the haze of sleet and powder smoke the captured swords and colors in the hands of their own generals Sullivan and Greene and the crowds of hung-over Hessians in their ridiculous pigtails and huge mustaches begging for mercy in fluent German, they began to cheer themselves loudly. Then they cheered their officers, and, having started, they got a kind of hysteria and couldn't stop cheering and throwing their hats into the air, which was soon full of battered wind-blown headgear. They had won. After that long licking, from the Hudson to the Delaware, they had taken their first prisoners and captured enemy colors. They cheered till they set Washington laughing, and he sent to say it was enough. The entire battle had not lasted two hours, and the enemy had not succeeded in killing a single American soldier. They breakfasted better than they had eaten for months, on the Hessians' Christmas leftovers, and some of them found more than a drop of something in which to drink to their victory.

Things had gone almost too well. But Washington and Greene now became aware that both Ewing and Cadwallader had failed to navigate the icy river and were not now where they were supposed to be, having doubtless assumed that Washington at McConkey's Ferry had also been forced to turn back. Without the three-point maneuver that had been planned, it was still possible for the enemy to reorganize on Washington's flanks and push him back against the river with no time to reembark his men and equipment. Also, there were prisoners to transport, before they could be retaken by their own side.

After a hurried conference in the street, which still rang with victory, the American generals decided to retrace their steps at once to the ferry landing so as not to lose their miraculous gain by grasping for more. Their total casualties were two privates who had frozen to death and the minor wounds of William Washington and James Monroe. The Hessians had lost at least six officers and about thirty men killed, besides the wounded and the prisoners who were still being hunted down in the barns and alleys.

Rall's wounds were mortal, and he was carried back to his quarters on a pew taken from the Methodist church. Greene and Washington heard of his condition and visited him where he lay in the care of his servant and his Quaker landlady. It was plain that he could not live through the night, and he asked the favor that his men might be kindly treated as prisoners. Washington with his quick compassion promised that his prisoners would be as well lodged and fed as his own men—which was not as well as they were accustomed to—and returned with Greene to the street.

The withdrawal from Trenton, although it took place by daylight, was even slower and more difficult than the advance had been, for they were encumbered now with prisoners and booty, the men were completely exhausted, and not a few of them had contrived to get gloriously drunk. "We did not get to our tents," one of the young officers wrote, "till next morning—two nights and a day in as violent a storm as any I ever felt."

A captain from Connecticut recorded that on reaching his quarters in Pennsylvania after the battle and the second crossing he sat down to a hot meal at last and fell from his chair to the floor with weariness, awaking some hours later with the spoon still in his hand. Some of Washington's men had marched about forty miles since Christmas afternoon when they assembled at the ferry, and all had gone sleepless for twenty-four hours on cold rations. Without his indomitable leadership and the incredible fortitude and endurance of his troops, the war might have ended in Jersey in the year 1776 as a British victory.

Tench Tilghman drafted Washington's report to Congress from the Pennsylvania headquarters on the twenty-seventh. With his characteristic understatement Washington "had the pleasure" to congratulate them on the "success of an enterprise I had formed against a detachment of the enemy lying at Trenton, and which was executed yesterday morning."

Philadelphia was in an uproar that night. Church and fire bells rang all over the city, and many Patriots ran to General Putnam's camp for confirmation of the intoxicating rumor that Washington had finally won a battle. The Tories remained truculent and unbelieving, so that some private wars were fought in the streets before they were convinced. All doubts were ended when on January 1 the Hessian prisoners, who had been sent across the river under guard the night after the battle, were paraded with their nine-man band through the streets of the capital, their outlandish appearance and toy-soldier uniforms creating great astonishment.

"Rall's defeat is a most unfortunate business," wrote General Grant at Brunswick to Colonel Donop at Bordentown, with notable restraint. The Hessians claimed that the sleet had made their muskets useless, and they couldn't get at the Americans with the bayonet because of all that lead flying through the air. Actually, their weapons had been under cover until their drums beat to arms when the Americans were already in the streets. But Washington's men had kept their firearms wrapped and dry all the way through the blizzard so that they were able to fire a few rounds before the touchholes clogged up and the flints refused to spark—after which they went to the bayonet without waiting for orders.

The mortification of the British command in New York can be imagined. Howe sent a frantic recall to Cornwallis, who had gone aboard a ship with his luggage and was on the point of sailing for his proposed leave in England. Cornwallis rushed back to Brunswick to give General Grant a wigging and himself lead a march on Trenton—a little late. Both Howe and Cornwal-

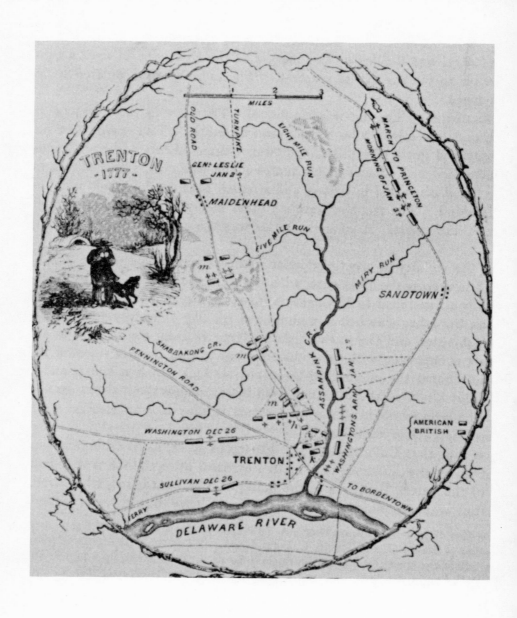

lis were doubtless furious with the provincial general who should have recognized that it was not the thing to campaign in winter time.

Chapter 11

Because of Ewing's failure to get across the Delaware into Jersey on Christmas night, several hundred of Rall's Hessians escaped to Donop at Bordentown before his hasty removal from there to Amboy. Trenton was deserted by the enemy, but there were still British garrisons at Princeton under General Leslie and at Brunswick under Grant.

The taste of triumph at Trenton, plus renewed exhortation by their officers in the Pennsylvania camp, was encouraging even the faint-hearted among Washington's troops to reenlist, while a slow recruitment was actually beginning again. Some of the regiments had been reduced to scarcely a hundred men by sickness and the departure of those who insisted on going home. Congress had sent specie through the banker Robert Morris at Philadelphia for back pay owing the troops, and Washington himself had appealed to the New England regiments for continued service from these veterans who had already experienced enemy fire. On his own responsibility and by pledging his personal funds, he also offered a $10 bounty to each man who would commit himself to another six weeks after his term of service expired.

Washington allowed the elated, though still cold and hungry, troops in the Pennsylvania camp four days to recover from their exertions at Trenton. Then, on the night of December 30, preceded by Greene's brigade, he took them across the Delaware again in cruel cold—the fourth crossing in a week—and reoccupied Trenton. He found no sign there of the enemy and could get no information beyond a rumor that Cornwallis, with fresh troops from New York, had joined Grant at Brunswick and that Leslie at Princeton was fortifying and stocking that town as a supply base. British stores and the pay-chest were known to be at Brunswick, and it was suspected that Charles Lee was held a willing captive there.

Cadwallader was at Trenton waiting for Washington, having got across the river belatedly on the twenty-seventh, and Mifflin had brought over some Pennsylvania militia. The road to Philadelphia ran from Brunswick through Princeton and Trenton, and the recovery of Trenton raised Washington's hopes of making the attack on the British stores at Princeton and Brunswick which his exhausted men had been unable to undertake after the Trenton victory.

In acute need of an intelligence system, he sent Cadwallader to occupy Bordentown—where he found only Donop's sick and wounded—and detached a troop of Philadelphia Light Horse under Colonel Reed to reconnoiter toward Princeton. They reported that Cornwallis had left his luggage at Brunswick and was moving southward on the Trenton road, leaving a garrison lodged in Nassau Hall at Princeton as a rear guard, while Leslie was posted similarly at Maidenhead midway.

Washington promptly withdrew his men from Trenton to high ground on the far side of Assunpink Creek, where he could command the single bridge leading out of Trenton to the east. He had no intention of confronting Cornwallis in a contest for the battered little town, and he dispatched Greene on the run with a detachment to harass and slow the British advance.

At Boston the winter before he had at least possessed an entrenched position and a fairly adequate commissary. Now winter quarters must soon be found for his army, and he thought enviously of the snug Princeton buildings and the British supplies housed in them.

Greene's men encountered the British van north of Trenton and fell back slowly according to plan, skirmishing as they came, to rejoin the main army, which had dug in on the east bank of the Assunpink, while Knox posted artillery to cover the bridge. Cornwallis drove Greene back through the town and made three attempts to storm the bridge, only to be thrown back each time by determined musket fire and Knox's well-served cannon, till the ground on the Trenton side of the creek was red with disabled British. As darkness fell, Cornwallis gave the order to encamp for the night around the town and promised confidently that he would "bag the fox in the morning." His men were tired from marching since dawn, and Washington's boats were now all beached above Trenton and at the enemy's disposal. Cornwallis was on the Delaware, but Washington hoped to get between him and his main base at Brunswick, cutting his communications.

At a council at St. Clair's headquarters behind the Assunpink Washington came to his perilous decision. He had a bad choice of giving battle on the spot or of retreating down the Delaware to make a stand outside Philadelphia, or, as a second alternative, he could withdraw quietly that night from his present position and under cover of darkness march by a new unfinished road that led around Cornwallis's flank to Princeton through a swamp spanned by small bridges. Such a detour might enable him to take the enemy rear guard by surprise at dawn, beat up the quarters, and possibly go on from there to seize the baggage and stores at Brunswick. This move, if it were successful, would force the British to evacuate Trenton, relieving the threat to Philadelphia. It would be the second consecutive night march for his army, and one must wonder again at the endurance of his troops in winter weather.

His generals agreed to the third undertaking, and soon a muffled bustle began in the American lines. Scouts were sent out to make sure the British had not found the back road. The mud was freezing in an opportune change in the weather, and cannon could be moved on hard ground. Reinforcements for Cornwallis would follow the Post Road to Trenton, through Maidenhead, already traveled by the British force now at the Assunpink bridge. Local Patriots were brought in to serve as guides to Washington, and they confirmed that the flanking movement around the British left could with any luck be accomplished.

The campfires burning on the American side of the bridge were replenished with cedar fence-rails from the nearby countryside, and fatigue parties were assigned to create a noise as of digging new earthworks and setting up an overnight camp for a battle in the morning. The British fires were scarcely a hundred yards away across the icy creek, and the pickets of the two armies could hear each other's voices as they took up their posts. The American guards on the east end of the bridge kept up their rounds noisily, making sure they were heard all night by the enemy.

Behind the screen of this staged activity, the sleepless preparations went on. For the sake of quiet and because of the bad road, the army must march to Princeton without its baggage. Horses were hitched to baggage wagons which were quickly loaded and sent off into the darkness with General Stephen in command—bound for Burlington, where Putnam would ride out from Philadelphia along the Pennsylvania bank to receive them. The wheels of the gun carriages were wrapped with rags and even with strips of cloth torn from precious blankets so that their bare metal rims would not ring on the rocks and frozen ground of the new road.

With orders given in lowered tones and passed on in the same way, creating a dramatic hush instead of the usual hullabaloo of breaking camp, small detachments moved back from the blazing fires that faced the British and, screened by their light, fell in and were marched off to the unfinished track through the woods where stumps and cut boughs were a peril to horses and transport wagons. The whole operation was accomplished so smoothly and silently that even the American sentries could hardly hear the departure of their comrades.

By one o'clock on the morning of January 3, the main army was under way for Princeton. Mercer's brigade led the column, followed by St. Clair's, which was accompanied by Washington and his staff, with Greene and two six-pound guns in Knox's care. Lastly, the fatigue parties built up the fires again, showed themselves in the light, and then slipped away to rejoin their marching regiments ahead. At dawn the campfires at the bridge were still burning, but the troops had disappeared, along with their baggage.

The new road led through deep woods where the intense darkness hid treacherous pitfalls from the weary men, so that there were heavy falls and muttered cursing and frequent halts to right an overturned cannon or a floundering horse which blocked the way. During these pauses in the march the men often fell asleep standing up, leaning against each other in the ranks, or supported by their muskets, only to stagger forward again in a walking nightmare of exhaustion, which was described by an American sergeant who was there: "At this time our troops were in a destitute and deplorable condition. The horses attached to our cannon were without shoes, and when passing over ice they would slide in every direction and could advance only by the assistance of the soldiers. Our men too were without shoes or other comfortable clothing; and as traces of our march towards Princeton the ground was literally marked with the blood of the soldiers' feet."

When they emerged from the woods into the barrens below Stony Brook it was easier going, and when daylight finally came they had reached a little bridge two miles from Princeton. Mercer's men were leading, in files, without flankers, Sullivan on his right and St. Clair just behind, when they discovered and simultaneously were discovered by two British regiments under Colonel Mawhood, marching along the Post Road under orders to join Leslie at Maidenhead and continue from there to Cornwallis at Trenton.

Taken by surprise and supposing Mercer's to be only fugitives from the skirmishing at Trenton, Mawhood wheeled toward them and both detachments raced for the high ground which lay between them. Mercer got there first and formed his battle line in a field below an orchard, throwing a volley into the British charge at a range of forty yards.

Unaware that the whole American army was behind Mercer, Mawhood ordered his regulars forward to take their losses and go in with the bayonet. After a savage fifteen minutes of hand-to-hand fighting the Americans broke, and Mercer's big gray horse went down under him with a leg wound, leaving him on foot trying desperately to rally his men. In the melee he was struck on the head by a musket. As he fell, he was somehow mistaken for Washington, and a cry went up for the "rebel general" to surrender. Mercer refused to give up his sword and identified himself. Beaten down and bayoneted, he feigned death and was overrun where he lay.

Washington, approaching with Greene and St. Clair, heard Mercer's guns and spurred into the fight with reinforcements at the double, followed by some battle-wise riflemen. Placing himself at their head, he led them into a hail of British lead. At a distance of about thirty yards from Mawhood's lines he reined in his well-disciplined horse and sat immovable among his men while at his order they paused to pour a volley into the British, and smoke enveloped the scene. There is a story that at this moment, when he exposed himself so recklessly to the fire of both sides, one of his aides, young Colonel Fitzgerald of Virginia, so feared to see his chief killed outright that he covered his eyes with his hat. He looked up again at the shout which greeted Washington's appearance among Mercer's retreating men and beheld him still unscathed, sitting his horse amid the smoke and roar of the battle. Fitzgerald, who was still new to the war, burst into tears of relief and spurred to Washington's side, crying, "Thank God your Excellency is safe!" He was calmly bidden by Washington to bring up more troops, as the battle was nearly won.

Mawhood could see Washington, Greene, and Cadwallader among their troops bringing rapid order out of chaos, and he suddenly found himself outnumbered as St. Clair's regiment poured in at the double. His regulars had had enough, and he knew they would not stand to load and fire again. He could only abandon his guns and wounded, while his men fell back headlong toward the college on the way to Brunswick, or down the Post Road toward Trenton.

It was said that as they retreated Washington gave chase briefly, with the rest of his army, waving his hat and hallooing like everybody else. When he recollected himself and rode back to his outdistanced infantry, he paused here and there to praise them or to take his sweating officers by the hand. He paused also to speak to the British wounded on the ground and placed a guard to protect the helpless men from being robbed or murdered by the ghouls who always gathered on a battlefield after the action.

The college buildings at Princeton had been used as barracks by the British, and some survivors of the battle had taken refuge in Nassau Hall. These promptly surrendered when young Alexander Hamilton—recently from the college to be known as Columbia—set his artillery to lobbing shells at the building. Sullivan, bringing up his troops at a run from his post in a lane west of the main action, took the prisoners as Hamilton flushed them out.

Washington and some of his officers enjoyed a hot breakfast at the deserted British headquarters in President Witherspoon's house before they learned that Mercer lay critically wounded in a house near the bridge on the Post Road. Washington had been told that his old friend was dead, and now he had no choice but to leave him where he was and mount up again, because word was brought that Cornwallis was pounding up the road from Trenton with his army, in an incredulous rage at having been outgeneraled again by the rebel commander. Washington rose from the table as the Long Roll was being beaten in the streets. His tired but triumphant men fell in again, and the column got under way northward, clearing the town just as Cornwallis crossed the bridge at the other end of it.

At Kingston beyond Princeton the road forked right toward Brunswick and left over another bridge to Somerset Courthouse and Morristown, where various invalids and stores were already established in the care of General Maxwell. At the fork there was a brief council of mounted officers while the army, led by Greene, filed off to the left. Once more, as at Trenton in December, Washington was forced to be content with what he had gained and, with Cornwallis in his rear, dared not order his weary men onward another seventeen miles to make an attempt on Brunswick. Again, his troops had been some forty hours under arms without rest and with no fresh rations since they struck camp at the Assunpink, and many of them were falling asleep on the ground at every halt. He gave orders for the Kingston bridge to be destroyed when the army had passed over it,

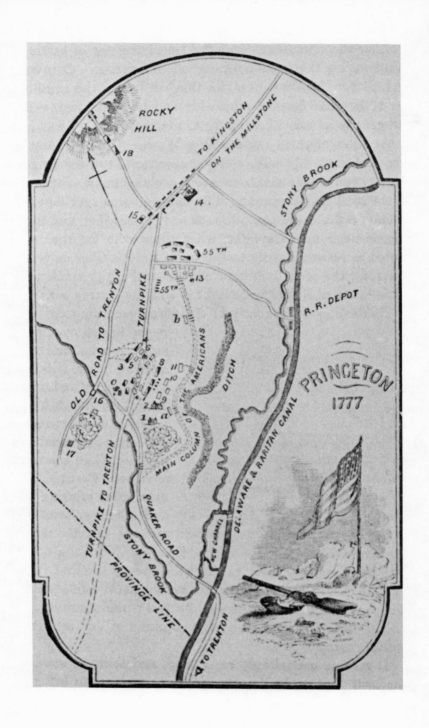

ROCKY HILL

18

TO KINGSTON ON THE MILLSTONE

STONY BROOK

14

15

55 TH

13

55 TH

b

R. R. DEPOT

TURNPIKE

OLD ROAD TO TRENTON

6

3 5

8

11

10

2 9

1 a

OF THE AMERICANS

DITCH

PRINCETON 1777

16

17

MAIN COLUMN

QUAKER ROAD

STONY BROOK

TURNPIKE TO TRENTON

NEW CHANNEL

DELAWARE & RARITAN CANAL

PROVINCE LINE

TO TRENTON

and he himself delayed to see it done before turning left in Greene's wake to Somerset, which must be reached before they could safely halt for the night.

It was soon apparent that Cornwallis's concern for Brunswick, too lightly held for his peace of mind, would cause him to renounce pursuit of Washington and hurry down the right-hand road to protect his precious pay-chest and baggage.

Mercer, with seven terrible bayonet wounds, lingered in agony for several days, nursed by the Quaker household at Princeton that had received him from the battlefield. Learning that he was still alive, Washington sent a white flag to Cornwallis, asking the favor of being allowed to send his nephew aide, George Lewis, to attend a fellow Virginian. In what was for the most part a gentleman's war, his request was granted, and Lewis was accompanied by Dr. Rush, one of the best physicians to be found in Philadelphia. But Mercer died in Lewis's arms on January 12.

The British losses at Princeton amounted to nearly four hundred killed, wounded, and prisoners, about ten times that of the Americans, who lost several valuable officers besides Mercer. They had gained two fine brass cannon, the horses to draw them having been killed during the battle, a large store of ammunition, bales of new blankets, and other military supplies, which were already loaded into wagons destined for Trenton.

Washington was to declare in his report to Congress that if he had had a thousand fresh troops at that fork in the road he could have made a forced march on Brunswick, ahead of Cornwallis, captured its precious booty, and possibly even have ended the war. And if Cornwallis had mended the bridge and overtaken the exhausted victors he might have ended the war in another way. But his own men's level of endurance was lower than that of Washington's dogged troops, and his professional leadership, however capable, lacked the inspiration of the tall Virginian who set an example of fortitude and determination his troops felt bound to equal.

At Somerset that night the American army slept on the frozen ground, many of the men without a blanket. Early on the fourth they marched to Pluckemin, where they were allowed to rest two days while nearly 1,000 stragglers caught up with them. Moving on again, they arrived at Morristown in the Jersey hills, where they were to pass the second winter of the war.

Chapter 12

At Morristown a chain of rugged rocky hills and the winding Passaic River lay between them and the baffled British on the seaboard. Due to the astounding ability of the American amateur soldier to absorb hardship beyond the limit of human endurance as understood by the British professional and the German mercenary, an incredible reversal of the situation on Christmas Day had taken place. Howe's forces had been within sixteen miles of Philadelphia and were now driven from all of New Jersey, except for small posts at Brunswick and Amboy which were without communication with the New York headquarters except by sea. Cornwallis and the Hessians had been made to look foolish, and it was up to Howe at New York to leave his diversions and take the field himself against an enemy which Cornwallis should have been able to whip with one hand tied behind him.

It is impossible to exaggerate the effect on both armies, in Congress, and on the people of Washington's two resounding victories after the autumn depths of 1776. Fulsome praise of the commander in chief replaced the grumbling and doubts expressed during his long retreat to the Delaware. Moreover, there was a recognition—in some quarters a reluctant one—of the embarrassing fact that he had done it in Charles Lee's absence and without the benefit of the arrogant British adventurer's advice.

Five American generals had emerged in this time of crisis to support and justify Washington's own resolution and courage— Greene, Knox, Sullivan, St. Clair, and Stirling. It might be alleged that Greene had lost Fort Lee and that Sullivan had lost Long Island. But Greene had become a solid personal bulwark of loyalty and faith, with a limitless capacity to learn and grow in the job. Sullivan was able and brave, and even with his difficult ego, at his worst he was better than most. Knox was an indispensable standby, stouthearted, indestructible, and a wizard with his guns. St. Clair and Stirling were useful veterans, loyal, intelligent, and inspiring confidence in their men.

Between Washington and Greene the habit developed of harmonious private discussion and mutual decisions taken after exhaustive consideration of the various dilemmas confronting them. It was at Morristown in the spring of 1777 that young Alexander Hamilton was transferred from the line, where his artillery company had served gallantly from New York to Princeton, to the headquarters staff. Possibly the change had been made at Greene's instigation, for he had noticed the nineteen-year-old captain of artillery at Manhattan before the battle of Long Island.

Now that the immediate peril was past and Philadelphia was a safe place for Congress to return to (in March, 1777), there were those among its members who resented the exceptional powers granted to the commander in chief at the time of their flight to Baltimore. It became increasingly plain that he had critics who would like to see him replaced by someone who could be kept more under their thumb—such as Charles Lee, or such as Gates, both of them openly jealous of Washington's prestige and prone to bask idly themselves in Congressional esteem. Congress was also increasingly divided between a conservative element, represented by the delegates from the South, and the radicals led by John Adams, who at this time wrote disparagingly of "the superstitious veneration that is sometimes paid to General Washington."

Washington was aware of an undercurrent of hostility at Philadelphia, even while he knew himself to be hamstrung by the difficulties encountered in reenlistment and recruiting, the scarcity of food and clothing for his winter-bound army, and the horrors of an inadequate hospital system. "I do not think that any officer since the Creation ever had such a variety of difficulties and perplexities to encounter as I have," he confided wearily in one of his frank family letters at this time.

If he could have been in two places at once and journeyed to Philadelphia to appear in person before that always contentious assembly and explain to them his perpetual problems of man-power and commissary, the very force and integrity of his personal character might have made a sufficient impression to put at least a temporary check on the criticism there. But among his many cares was a threatened epidemic of smallpox in the Morristown camp and the immediate necessity to see the entire army subjected to inoculation against the disease. Having nearly died of smallpox as a boy, he was himself immune, but his undernourished, badly housed troops were defenseless against infection, and he dreaded that a panic desertion might set in before drastic measures for their protection could be accomplished.

Finding it impossible to leave the army at so critical a time, he sent the man he considered to be most fitted to be his deputy —Nathanael Greene. It was Greene's first visit to Philadelphia and his first encounter with Congress, though he was already accustomed to addressing the Assembly in Rhode Island. In his long, harassing days of question and answer and diplomatic argument, he made no record of his sensations when with some ceremony he was ushered into the State House to face the cautious, only half-friendly curiosity of the men on whose often wayward decisions now rested the fate of the whole army and its absent leader.

Congress saw a sturdy, forthright, self-possessed man in a coat of Continental blue with buff facings and underdress, such as Washington wore—but the uniform, with its handsome epaulets and bright buttons, had been sent to him before the long retreat through Jersey began and had become weather-stained and rubbed almost threadbare in places. The halt in his step was attributed by some to a recent injury, and they tactfully ignored it. The first session lasted two hours and was followed by evening meetings with a committee of five, where the discussion was full and free.

Released from the immediate anxieties of the past year, Philadelphia had relaxed into a round of social gaieties. Greene now had little patience with the dinner parties, dancing assemblies, concerts, and full-dress entertainments, though he could not have overlooked a new element in the glittering society he would once have enjoyed—the Europeans, the professional adventurers, who were arriving in the provincial capital like flies around a honeypot, clicking heels, kissing hands, and demonstrating the latest dance steps from abroad. There were spectacular Frenchmen, heavy-handed Germans, and showy Poles, all peacocking in fancy uniforms usually of their own design. All of them clanked with swords and spurs and decorations and spoke in a variety of more or less intelligible accents.

Some of these pretentious strangers came with credentials from the American agents who had been sent abroad to wangle aid from European politicians sympathetic to the new American doctrine of independence and freedom from ancient tyrannies. Dr. Franklin was in Paris with Silas Deane and Arthur Lee, commissioned to negotiate for both money and weapons, which had begun to arrive secretly as a result of his presence there. Deane was recklessly recruiting a corps of European fire-eaters who flocked to commit themselves to the American army in hopes of free pickings among the amateurs across the Atlantic. Among these were a few sincere believers in the American cause, but inevitably American jealousy of what could only be considered corrupt opportunists was foreshadowing serious questions of rank and seniority that were to plague Washington and his senior field officers for years to come.

His mission accomplished to the best of his considerable ability, Greene set out for Morristown as soon as Congress would let him go. Crossing the Delaware northward again and passing the Princeton battlefield, he reached the sheltering mountains behind the Passaic River. Doubtless as he rode he revolved in his mind the conflicting personalities and policies he had encountered during his brief stay at the seat of government. Naturally, too, his thoughts would stray to faraway Rhode Island, still in the grip of British occupation, where Kitty was awaiting the birth of their second child in the household of his brother Jacob at Potowomut. His "superstitious" anxiety about her condition was relieved soon after he reached Morristown by a letter announcing the safe arrival of a daughter. Lucy Knox also was prevented from coming to winter headquarters that year by the birth of a son, who would die in infancy. Many other wives came to Morristown, Mrs. Washington and Lady Stirling among them.

During the early weeks of 1777 the mounted foraging parties of both armies engaged in constant skirmishes. On the American side the daring raids were largely composed of young Virginia horsemen riding their own thoroughbred mounts. Henry Lee in particular soon distinguished himself at this risky hit-and-run game. His opposite number in the British dragoons based at Brunswick was an equally young and much more ruthless officer whose name became a bogey word to frighten children with— Banastre Tarleton. It was largely due to the spectacular leadership of Tarleton and Lee—the famous Green Dragoon and Lighthorse Harry—that cavalry became a factor to be reckoned with on both sides as the war went on.

General Lincoln was posted at Bound Brook, watching the British at Brunswick, for there was doubt as to whether Howe's next move would be toward cooperation with Burgoyne's Canadian force or an independent attack on Philadelphia launched from the remaining British foothold in Jersey. Meanwhile, Howe remained in his gay social circle of Tories in New York, and the campaign lay dormant well into the spring of 1777.

Kitty had been very ill after the birth of the child, and Greene was oppressed by his anxiety over her health and his desire to see her again. His cordial neighbors near the Morristown camp were urging him to send for her and offered their hospitality for her comfort if she would make the attempt to join him. "If you think your health and strength will endure the journey, my heart will leap for joy to meet you," he wrote in May, 1777. "Mr. Lott's family have engaged you to spend the summer there. It is about nine miles from this place, and they are one of the finest families you ever saw. Mr. Lott's son-in-law, Mr. Livingston, was one of my aides-de-camp last year, which introduced me to the family. You may learn music and French there, too. Adieu, my second self."

The new daughter was named Martha for Mrs. Washington. It was to be Greene's destiny to live in Washington's headquarters family for another three years, his daily presence a source of support to his harassed general. The drabness of existence at Morristown was relieved by the simple amusements they contrived, such as games, amateur concerts, sewing circles, and frugal dinner parties attended by the first families of the Jersey countryside as well as by the feminine relatives of the officers, courageous women who braved the hardships, deprivations, and alarms of camp life to be with their men. And there was still the happy absence of Charles Lee, still a prisoner of the British, now received in the highest Tory circles in New York and somehow escaping censure for his former connection with the rebel cause. Gates, too, was away in Philadelphia, creating an impression of important affairs which required his presence there.

The European arrivals at Philadelphia soon caused active resentment among the American officers who had been steadfast through uncounted disasters in the field. A man named Conway, with introductions from Silas Deane in Paris, so impressed Congress with his swagger and credentials that the commission they granted him was considered an insult to the rank and seniority already won by American officers who had served from the beginning at Boston. He was followed by a man named du Coudray, who claimed that Deane at Paris had promised him the supreme command of the artillery of the American army. This would have given him rank over Knox, who promptly offered to resign. Knox was supported by similar threats from Sullivan and Greene.

The situation caused poor Washington mountains of paper work and considerable diplomatic effort, until it was even suggested that a separate European corps should be created to accommodate these aggressive adventurers from abroad who considered themselves appointed by a higher—if not a divine—authority to show the Americans how to run a war. Du Coudray eventually rode his horse onto a ferryboat crossing the Schuylkill River, against more experienced advice, and in midstream the nervous animal dumped him over the side into the water to drown. Conway remained a thorn in Washington's side for months to come.

The summer of 1777 arrived with many alarums and excursions, and there was marching and countermarching, which wore out the soldiers' shoes and accomplished very little else. By the first anniversary of the Declaration of Independence the British had withdrawn entirely from New Jersey to their Staten Island base. Howe's pet project of marching on Philadelphia seemed to have been abandoned in favor of a thrust up the Hudson to meet Burgoyne, who was at last leading an army from Canada toward Fort Ticonderoga, where St. Clair was posted to face him.

Soon after Kitty had been happily installed in the Lott household, the whole camp was startled by the news that St. Clair had evacuated Fort Ticonderoga before Burgoyne's advance, leaving Burgoyne with a clear road ahead to Albany, where Schuyler had only an inadequate force. At Albany Burgoyne would be in a position eventually to join hands with Howe on the Hudson and descend in force via New York on Washington's main army guarding Philadelphia. Benedict Arnold had just arrived in the capital from New England and was complaining to Congress about promotions which bypassed him and elevated his juniors to a higher rank than his. He was soon placated by orders directing him to the Northern Army headquartered at Albany.

Reports that Howe had suddenly loaded his army into transports and left Sandy Hook for an unknown destination reminded Washington that Philadelphia might be taken from a landing on the shore of either the Chesapeake or the Delaware Bay, as well as by an overland march across Jersey. Such a move now would mean that Howe had abandoned the possible junction with Burgoyne which would have united the British forces for a combined assault on a vastly outnumbered American army.

Weighing these latest developments, Washington remained incredulous that a general of Howe's experience would undertake to move on Philadelphia without waiting for Burgoyne's cooperation, which had seemed on the brink of accomplishment. No one, including his own generals, had counted on Howe's obsession with the capture of the rebel capital, which was not even a strategic city like New York. But Washington's army left the Morristown hills and encamped around Middlebrook on the Raritan River, collecting itself and its equipment to meet a sudden marching order either northward or toward the Chesapeake. And Howe seemed to have disappeared into the Atlantic.

Someone had to be sent to the North against Burgoyne, who,

if they had only known it, was still as ignorant of Howe's intentions as Washington was. Again the commander in chief showed reluctance to part with Greene at headquarters, and Greene was naturally unwilling to leave the vicinity of Middlebrook while Kitty was so recently lodged nearby with the Lotts. It was General Lincoln, who had demonstrated his courage and ability ever since the action at Harlem, who was sent to Albany instead. Gates was soon to succeed Schuyler in the Northern Command, outranking both Lincoln and Arnold, who would be under his command. And Greene remained at Washington's side, while they awaited the reappearance of Howe at any one of several possible landings.

The summer of 1777 was passing, and still the campaign hung fire. Burgoyne moved cautiously toward Albany, with a watchful eye on his retreat route to Fort Ticonderoga, in daily expectation of orders from Howe.

It was during those hot, inactive days in the camp outside Philadelphia that the young French volunteer, Lafayette, was commissioned major general and took his place in Washington's family at headquarters. He at once dispelled all previous prejudice against the European interlopers by his youthful enthusiasm, his modest observance of military etiquette, his open idolatry of the commander in chief, and a still undefined and inexplicable charm which won him an almost filial place in Washington's regard. He spoke a fluent if somewhat baroque English, and so far from making demands on the American treasury, he supplied his own horses and equipment, asked for no salary, and vowed that he had "come to learn and not to teach." This attitude alone was enough to make the tall, slender youngster—he was not yet twenty—the outstanding exception to the conceited fortune hunters from abroad who had preceded him.

The health of the army while encamped near the Delaware suffered from inaction and a lack of sanitation in the summer heat. Washington reported to Congress that "our soldiers have scarcely tasted any kind of vegetables, had but little salt, and did not receive sufficient vinegar, drink, or soap."

Toward the end of August, after weeks of uncertainty respecting Howe's whereabouts, a breathless express rider brought the news that the British ships had entered the Chesapeake.

Howe was coming at Philadelphia by the back door, bypassing Delaware Bay, which led directly into the water defenses below the city. But from the Chesapeake he must disembark so far from his goal that Washington might be able to interpose his army between the landing place and the city.

The wives scattered home again as Washington called in his regiments and himself set out for Philadelphia. Just at this time of flurry and stress, unexpected good news arrived from the North. A strong detachment of British and Hessians foraging ahead of Burgoyne's advance toward the Hudson had been defeated on the sixteenth of August near the village of Bennington in what was then called the New Hampshire Grants. A body of militia led by General Starke had fought a decisive battle and inflicted heavy losses which Burgoyne could never replace. Although the full effects of this victory were not at once realized, it would lead eventually—combined with Howe's desertion of the Hudson campaign in favor of his own willful determination to take Philadelphia—to Burgoyne's surrender at Saratoga in October.

Any report of any success at this point was valuable to the morale of the army which must at last confront Howe in a defensive stand on the road to Philadelphia. It was decided at headquarters that a parade of the army through the threatened city would both straighten the men's backs and impress the uneasy population, which was strongly laced with Tories. Since they still lacked anything resembling a general issue of standard uniforms, the regiments were ordered to wash their nondescript garments and burnish their miscellaneous arms. Each man's hat was to be dressed with a fresh green sprig, symbolizing "an emblem of hope." If he had no hat he was to wear a wreath of greenery.

It was a Sunday morning, and the streets and windows along the line of march were crowded with spectators. Washington, on his best mount, wearing his blue and buff uniform with gold epaulets and a cocked hat, rode near the head of the column, with Lafayette, sporting his major general's scarf, at his side. They were surrounded by the uniformed aides, all spit and polish, on spirited horses of their own.

The field officers were all there that day, following their chief

—Greene, Sullivan, Stirling, Weedon, Stephen, Knox—and Wayne of Pennsylvania, whose service so far had been mainly in the North, where his long personal feud with St. Clair had begun. Called in to join Washington at Morristown in the spring of 1777, he brought with him a reputation—"Where Wayne goes, there is always a fight." Also, where Wayne went, the ladies were always captivated —though he had a wife and family at the farm called Waynes-borough not far from Philadelphia. Polly Wayne, as the saying went, "enjoyed poor health," was violently jealous, and eventually became mentally unstable. Wayne attracted nicknames too—"Mad Anthony," though he was merely reckless and unacquainted with fear; "Dandy Wayne," though his finery wore out and he became famous for a cloak made from an old rose-colored blanket.

Each brigade was assigned its place in the line of march, which led down Front Street and along Chestnut to the Common, and thence by the floating bridge across the Schuylkill River to Darby on the west bank. On August 25, 1777, the British army came ashore at the mouth of the Elk River, which formed the northernmost tip of Chesapeake Bay. Men and horses alike had suffered from seven weeks on board the overcrowded transports, where they ran short of fresh water. The horse vessels had been obliged to throw many of their animals overboard, so that it had become necessary to collect new mounts from the countryside. The enemy therefore delayed to engage in ruthless raids and pillage, skirmishing with American scouting parties sent out to hinder their progress.

The heat was oppressive to everyone, and Greene recorded that a dusty bed at a roadside lodging had touched off an attack of his chronic asthma. But Washington had time to dispose his forces on ground of his own choosing, along Brandywine Creek, which flowed into the Delaware roughly parallel to the Schuylkill and about twenty miles below it. The creek was deep enough to require the use of fords, and there were several of these, both above and below Chadd's on the main road, which was considered the most likely crossing for an army marching northward toward Philadelphia.

Here Washington stationed himself, with Greene and Wayne at the center of his line; Sullivan, Stephen, and Stirling were above him on the right, with Sullivan commanding; Armstrong's

Pennsylvania militia took up their position on the left, below Chadd's. It was the hot, foggy morning of September 11 before Howe was ready to attack, and the battle of the Brandywine began in sweltering late-summer heat.

Chapter 13

Howe had left Clinton in New York and brought with him Cornwallis and his veteran Grenadiers and Highlanders, Knyphausen and his Hessians. He had enough men to divide into two columns, and one of these he sent with Knyphausen to create a diversion at Chadd's Ford in front of Washington. There a heavy cannonade, to which Greene responded, occupied several hours and, so far as Washington knew, could have developed into the major engagement for which he was prepared.

Simultaneously, Howe accompanied Cornwallis and the second column on a long cross-country detour, by which they passed behind Knyphausen, crossed the creek at Jeffries' Ford above Chadd's, and, shrouded by the fog, bore down on Washington's right and rear, threatening to engulf Sullivan in a wide flanking movement very like the maneuver that had succeeded at Long Island. There was unlucky Sullivan again, outflanked and surprised, lacking reliable intelligence in a hostile Tory and Quaker countryside. His outnumbered and ill-trained force was unable to execute the quick wheeling movement which was re-

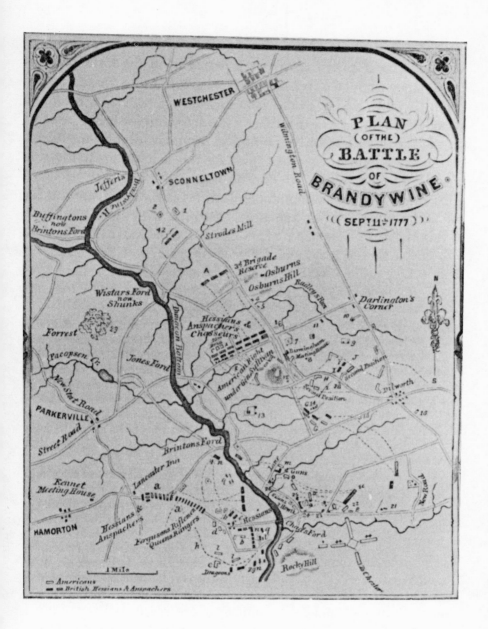

PLAN (OF THE) BATTLE OF BRANDYWINE. (((SEPT 11th 1777)))

WESTCHESTER

SCONNELTOWN

Jefferis

Buffingtons now Brintons Ford

Strodes Mill

Wistars Ford now Shunks

Forrest

Pacopsen Cr.

Jones Ford

New Stet Road

PARKERVILLE

Street Road

Kennet Meeting House

HAMORTON

Hessians & Anspachers

Lancaster Inn

Brintons Ford

Fergusons Riflemen Queens Rangers

Dragoons

Rocky Hill

Chads Ford

Hessians

3d Brigade Reserve — Osburns
Osburns Hill

Hessians Anspacher's Chasseurs

American Fight under Gen. Sullivan

Birmingham Meeting House

Darlington's Corner

Second Position

Dilworth

Guns

N
S

1 Mile
Americans
British Hessians & Anspachers

quired to change front and re-form at right angles in time to
meet the British advance, which was made in columns from Os-
borne's Hill, where the two mounted generals impassively
watched the smoky panorama that developed below them.

A British battle line had a terrible beauty, with a band playing a quick march and the sun striking the polished arms and
clustered buttons of the scarlet uniforms cross-belted with white,
the gold lace and epaulets and powdered hair of the mounted
officers, and the arrogant discipline of the red ranks marching
into gunfire as though on dress parade. In the face of it, Sullivan
saw his half-formed wings collapse into hopeless confusion, while
his center, where Stirling was, received the full weight of the
British attack. Two of his aides were killed outright, while Stirling
strove profanely to re-form and hold his lines against a spreading
panic. But this time Greene was in health and in the field, and
Washington dispatched him to Sullivan's support.

With two brigades of Weedon's Virginia Continentals Greene
made a famous four-mile march over broken country from
Chadd's Ford, with such speed as to get him into position in time
to allow Sullivan's exhausted men to fall back through his ranks,
which then closed again in front of Cornwallis. Washington arrived on the spot as daylight was fading, riding cross-country
toward the hottest fire, as was his habit, and with his aides and
Lafayette at his side attempted to rally the fugitives. Greene's
men stood fast until the sheer weight of British numbers forced
them back, step by step, into the general withdrawal toward
Chester.

Wayne's position at Chadd's Ford had been fatally weakened
when even Washington rushed to support Sullivan. As a result,
Knyphausen was able to pin down an entire brigade by attacking
across the ford. Darkness fell on stubborn fighting on both sides,
and gradually the noise and confusion of battle ceased in the hot
twilight. The action had been costly to both sides, and the field
was strewn with dead and dying men and disabled horses.

The desperate stand of Greene's brigade had prevented a
total rout and made possible a more or less planned retreat by
Washington to Chester. He was not pursued by the punished
and equally exhausted enemy and was even able to bring off
some of his baggage and artillery. But it was midnight before the

tangled regiments were collected and sorted out at the camp around the meetinghouse that served as a hospital where the surgeons were at work.

Lafayette had got a bullet through his leg while he was on foot trying with his drawn sword to encourage Sullivan's men. He attempted to conceal the wound, until someone pointed out that his boot was full of blood. After reaching Chester later that night, he fainted. Washington ordered him conveyed by water to Philadelphia, where his wound could be properly dressed. He was then taken in a carriage to a tedious convalescence at Bethlehem, which was already crowded with refugees from Philadelphia, where the rumble of the guns at Brandywine had been clearly heard.

It was November before Lafayette was able to wear a boot again, and he missed the action at Germantown, where his place was more or less filled by a new member of Washington's family —young John Laurens of South Carolina, whose father was a delegate to Congress. Lafayette was able to rejoin Washington at the Whitemarsh camp in time to accompany the army to Valley Forge.

Washington and Greene were miraculously unscathed after exposing themselves recklessly to enemy fire in a battle where casualties ran high on both sides. Howe's men were still feeling the effects of their long confinement in the transports in hot weather and were in no condition to pursue Washington's army, which fell back from Chester across the Schuylkill to camp at Pennypacker's Mill, twenty miles above Philadelphia. On the night of September 21 Wayne's rear guard was badly cut up in a surprise attack at Paoli.

Two days before what came to be known as "the Paoli massacre," an urgent message from Washington in Hamilton's handwriting arrived at the State House: "If the Congress has not left Philadelphia they ought to do it immediately without fail; for the enemy have the means of throwing a party this night into the city." Once again Congress fled the capital, along with other Patriots and their families, this time westward to York in Pennsylvania. They had had time to remove precious stores and records to Reading and were able to function in the courthouse at York, where they remained until the following summer.

When Howe and Cornwallis marched into Philadelphia at the end of September, they left between themselves and their seaborne communications from New York two small American fortified posts on the Delaware River called Forts Mercer and Mifflin. But it was time for winter quarters soon, and Howe intended to enjoy himself in Philadelphia as he had done in New York. The main part of his army were ordered into camp on Washington's old ground at Germantown, while many officers were billeted luxuriously in the city, and detachments were scattered along the Delaware banks to watch the Americans who manned the little forts. It was soon plain that the capture of Philadelphia was of less consequence than had been supposed by both sides, and except for the triumphant Tories the population at first preserved an uncordial neutrality.

Washington's troops at Pennypacker's Mill were singularly undepressed by the loss of Brandywine field and assured each other in colorful language that they would do better next time. Washington soon decided on an attempt to dislodge the enemy from the Germantown area before their winter quarters could be completed and occupied. A movement against the camp there, designed to push Howe's army back against the Schuykill River, required a maneuver similar to that which had succeeded at Trenton. Instead of the two-pronged drive that caught the Hessians in King Street between Sullivan and Greene, the new plan depended on the junction of four coordinated columns on four converging roads into the village.

The too elaborate scheme failed, though the mystery of what went wrong to turn the early appearance of an American success into just another defeat has never been explained, and no two accounts of the battle agree. There was a fog, bad intelligence work, shortage of ammunition, and an unpredictable delay in the arrival of Greene's division, caused by his guide's mistaking the road, which was four miles longer than the one assigned to Sullivan and had confusing cross-lanes.

Washington rode this time with Sullivan and Wayne, on the most direct middle road, with Greene and Stephen on the one leading in from the left, Smallwood on their left, and Armstrong on the right. Washington intended a surprise attack at dawn on October 4, but their approach was discovered too soon by a

CHEW'S HOUSE.

British patrol which sounded the alarm. A sharp skirmish developed around the large stone mansion owned by Chief Justice Chew, which stood isolated in spacious grounds adorned by statuary, a little short of the fork in the road where Greene and Stephen should have joined Sullivan, Wayne, and Washington for a combined attack.

The Chew house was occupied by a British outpost under Colonel Musgrave of the 40th, who had barricaded themselves inside and with musket fire from the windows were able to obstruct the American advance. The stout walls of the mansion withstood Knox's fieldpieces, even though some of the balls passed clean through them into the handsome rooms; the fine

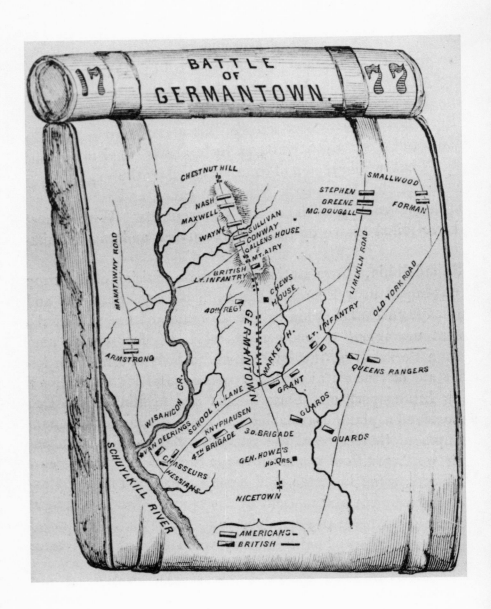

oak doors were riddled with bullets, and the statuary in the garden was decapitated. The house also refused to catch fire, though one of Sullivan's aides was killed while attempting to plant a firebrand against the foundations. The British outside the house were in actual flight, but it was against the rules, said Knox the scholar, to leave a fortified post in one's rear even in order to pursue a retreating enemy.

The delay caused by the stubborn defense of the Chew house and the unwise assignment of American reserves to overcome it upset the timing all around, while what Weedon called the worst fog he had ever seen in his life rolled in, making it impossible to distinguish friend from foe, and Greene did not come up with Stephen as expected. On their belated arrival some of Stephen's men collided with Wayne's rear guard and they fired into each other in the fog and fled in opposite directions. Because he was in danger of being outflanked and surrounded, Greene retreated from the village, firing as he went and saving his guns. The enemy pursued him "at a civil distance" for about five miles. Sullivan's men, having run out of ammunition, had to fall back. Washington finally marched his exhausted army all the way back to Pennypacker's Mill before he allowed them to halt for a night's rest, and from there he withdrew to Whitemarsh, six miles above Germantown.

The British were certainly left in confusion, and although some members of Congress tried to blame Greene for being late on the field, or wanted to court-martial old Adam Stephen for being drunk, Washington blamed the poor visibility which allowed the British to come in with the bayonet and the delay caused by the defense of Chew's house.

Except for Forts Mifflin and Mercer on the Delaware, Howe was now free to settle down to a comfortable winter in Philadelphia. But Cornwallis was an active man, not content to share Howe's social life in the captive city, and soon made ready to attack the Delaware forts in conjunction with Howe's brother, the admiral. Greene was sent down to Mount Holly to join Varnum in their defense but was slow to go into action there for fear of the demoralizing effect of another defeat. "The cause is too important to be trifled with to show our courage," he wrote Washington, adding that if the commander in chief desired him to advance, he would do so. But while the British held Philadelphia, Mount Holly was always a precarious base, and Greene was soon recalled to camp. In the end, both forts fell to the British after heroic resistance.

At Whitemarsh Washington was as always pressed for bare necessities, but he refused to be drawn into another battle for Philadelphia which would almost certainly end in another failure. The well-read Knox was quoting the King of Prussia on the necessity for "tranquil" winter quarters to enable an army to rest its horses, repair its guns and wagons, and recruit reinforcements. He was therefore urging Washington to retire still farther from the city, to some defensible place where they would not be subject to constant little raids and alarms by the enemy.

Washington's army was melting away again, as it had done the previous winter at Morristown, and the need of shoes, blankets, and clothing became more acute every day. But the tough American soldiers were learning, as Washington constantly reminded them, "that the enemy are not proof against a vigorous attack, and may be put to flight when boldly pushed." In spite of privation and the physical miseries resulting from a sudden early winter, the morale of the American forces was in general surprisingly high.

At the same time the commander in chief was becoming increasingly aware of growing criticism of his so-called "Fabian" policy of evading head-on conflict when he knew he could not win and his apparent lack of military *élan*. The disappointment of the failure at Germantown was formidable, both among members of Congress and in the country at large. Dr. Franklin at Paris was negotiating an alliance with France, and Congress believed that a single fortunate stroke, such as a victory at Germantown might have provided, would be enough to bring Louis XVI openly to their assistance. No one was yet aware how deeply impressed the French already were by Washington's indomitable spirit which had led him to attack at Germantown so soon after the disastrous day at Brandywine.

Washington's prestige was still further damaged in the eyes of Congress late in October by news from the North, where Burgoyne had run his head into a noose and surrendered his whole army at Saratoga to an American force led by Gates, Arnold, and

Lincoln—a spectacular victory which only emphasized Washington's recent defeats. It meant, for one thing, that the Hudson was no longer a separate liability dividing the American army by the need of constant vigilance for its protection. Putnam could now send in seasoned troops from his post in the Highlands, and Virginia militia could be brought into service nearer home. It began to seem possible that American forces might ultimately wear down and outlast the British professionals.

Burgoyne had been sacrificed to Howe's obsession with Philadelphia, but while Burgoyne himself gave the credit for his defeat to Arnold, Gates was quick to snatch all the glory. Arnold had behaved with conspicuous courage at Saratoga and received a wound in the leg which would disable him till the following spring. Gates was later said never to have come under fire at all during the two days of hard fighting that resulted in Burgoyne's surrender. But Gates, having superseded Schuyler by the favoritism of Congress, was now acclaimed the victor of Saratoga, and this success compared to Washington's loss of Philadelphia and the Delaware forts could be turned to his disadvantage by his enemies.

Furthermore, the whole personnel of Congress had now changed, by death and replacement, until less than half a dozen now remained of those who attended the session in 1775 which had unanimously named the Virginian commander in chief. Many Congressmen now voting had never laid eyes on the tall, modest man they were measuring against the pompous, vain, and ambitious Gates.

No one at headquarters begrudged the Saratoga victory, which acted as Germantown might have done to further the essential alliance with France. But it was at the same time an added discouragement to the loyal officers around Washington, who must quickly decide on a safe site for a winter cantonment for soldiers already suffering from exposure and hunger.

Chapter 14

They chose a triangular valley enclosed by bleak hills and two creeks which ran into the Schuylkill and with the river itself formed a natural defense line some nineteen miles west and north of Philadelphia. The march of the army from the Whitemarsh camp was begun on December 11, when winter had set in suddenly with snowfall and severe cold. Again, the fresh snow on the frozen roads was stained with blood from the rag-wrapped feet of the soldiers who had no shoes.

When they arrived on the campground at Valley Forge there was no shelter from the wind and snow except the few tattered tents they still possessed, until with their own axes and saws they were able to build little log huts. These were chinked with mud, had a door at one end and a clay fireplace at the other, with rough double-deck bunks along each side. The regimental officers stood over them, laying out parallel rows of huts facing each other in little streets, easily patrolled and picketed.

Washington pitched his double marquee field-tent, sharing the wind and the cold till all the men were hutted before he moved into the small fieldstone house at the upper end of the valley, owned by a Quaker named Isaac Potts. Here, with the whole camp between it and the only entrance road, his Life-guards in a cluster of log huts behind it, he established his head-

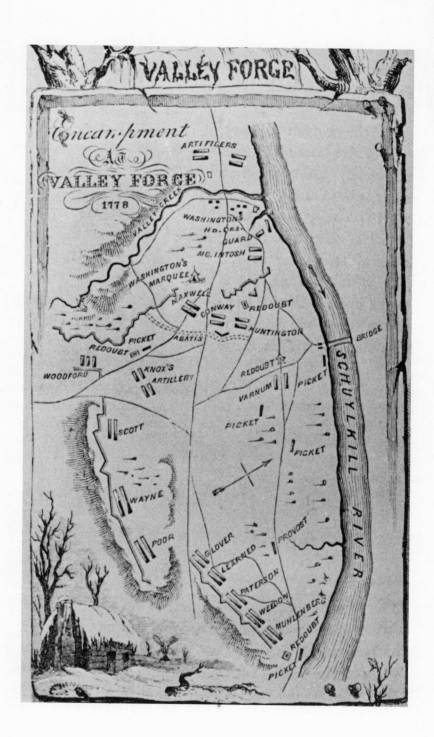

quarters. A log addition was built onto one end of the house to serve as a dining room for the staff.

Greene, Knox, Stirling, and Lafayette were among the officers who found crowded accommodations in the few spartan farmhouses scattered around the edges of the camp. Others made do with log huts only a little more commodious than those constructed by the soldiers for themselves. On January 3, 1778, Greene wrote to his brother Jacob that the men were greatly distressed for want of clothing and shoes:

"The Quartermaster-general's department has been in a most wretched condition. Colonel Mifflin, who ought to have been at the head of the business, has never been seen with the army since it came into Pennsylvania.

"General Conway is a man of much intrigue and little judgment. He is a great incendiary, of a restless spirit, and always contrives to puff himself off to the public as an officer of great consequence. General Gates is a child of fortune; General Arnold and General Lincoln are in high esteem; and it is said that General Burgoyne gives Arnold the credit for the successes obtained over him [at Bennington and Saratoga]. I am happy that the work is done, I do not care who does it."

Greene's estimate of Conway was a just one. The Irish adventurer remained to cause trouble for months to come, first as the originator, with Gates, of what came to be known as the Conway Cabal—designed to force Washington to resign out of pique or frustration if he could not be dismissed. But being Washington, he placed the task in hand before everything else and maintained a dignified composure under what soon amounted to persecution. The conspiracy against him, which came to a head during this crucial Valley Forge winter, only served to try him almost beyond human endurance, coming as it did on top of the other burdens laid upon him at the same time.

Mrs. Washington arrived at camp promptly, as she always did when the autumn guns fell silent, and shared with him the cramped quarters of the Potts house. She brought with her, as she always did, the gracious hospitality and the illusion of family life she was able to create for her husband and the young, bored, homesick aides and officers who surrounded their chief.

Kitty Greene stowed her two babies with their uncles in

Rhode Island and arrived at Valley Forge late in February. She had a small stock of schoolgirl French, and, limited as it was, it brought the tongue-tied European volunteers in the camp to her door, beaming with their hope of being able to communicate with somebody somehow.

The rooms of the stone house near Valley Creek which had been assigned to Knox were larger than those of the Potts dwelling, which was considered to be a safer location and therefore more suitable for the Washingtons. The sewing parties and singsongs gathered there to bask in Lucy's indestructible good humor and enjoy her ingenious concoctions out of nothing which she called collations. But the grim knowledge of the army's hunger and sickness could never be banished for long, and the dreary chant of "No meat—no meat" which echoed from the little regimental streets of huts haunted the ears day and night.

The elegant Thomas Mifflin of Philadelphia, who had begun so well at Cambridge, served as quartermaster until his resignation on the grounds of ill health. He then remained at home in Philadelphia, like Reed, and was drawn into the Gates–Conway circle there, a defection which he was later to deny. The quartermaster department being left without a head, things went from bad to worse. Hospital huts had been among the first shelters to be built at Valley Forge, but they were soon overcrowded with wretched men who died as soon as they were brought in, to make room for more to do the same; or they lingered on in misery, complaining that there were not enough medicines even to cure them of the itch. The shortage of forage was such that Knox had to see his gaunt artillery horses literally starve to death, after they had chewed the bare wood of their shelters to splinters in their agony of hunger.

The whispering campaign known as the Conway Cabal, designed to undermine the commander in chief by destroying confidence in him, so that he could be arbitrarily replaced by a more successful man—such as the self-styled victor of Saratoga—finally involved even a faction of the Congress at York. A correspondence had developed between Gates and Conway approximately like that between Lee and Reed during the Jersey retreat, and some of Conway's sarcastic *bon mots* about "weak generals" and "bad counsellors" had leaked out into the taprooms and

streets. Washington was of course one of the last to receive concrete evidence of Conway's perfidy, but inevitably it was reported
at headquarters by an authentic source.

The aides were dancing with rage and yearned for Conway's
blood—and Mifflin's, to say nothing of Gates's. Washington's only
comment at first was a rueful smile. When Congress was induced
to appoint Conway inspector general of the army and he visited
Valley Forge to strut his new rank, he was received by Washington with such icy courtesy that the chill penetrated even his thick
hide, and he took mortal offense. After his return to York he wrote
bitterly to Washington, protesting his reception and threatening
to resign and return at once to France. Unlike the situation with
Reed the previous year, no personal friendship had ever existed
between Washington and either party to this new canard, and he
resolved to lay the thing before Congress, expressing his private
opinion of their protégé—"General Conway's merit as an officer
and his importance in this army exists more in his own imagination than in reality," he had already written to Richard Henry
Lee, who was himself strangely inimical to his fellow Virginian.

When Gates learned from Mifflin that a copy of his correspondence with Conway had reached Washington's hands he was
apparently seized by panic rather than contrition and wrote incoherently to the commander in chief alleging that someone had
tampered with his letters. He demanded to know who the in-
former was, professed that the offensive phrases quoted had been
forged, and insisted that he was not a party to the backstairs
calumny. Washington was neither deceived nor placated by
Gates's wordy hedging. On the very day that Mrs. Washington
arrived at Valley Forge he had been closeted with Hamilton, who
as secretary assisted him in constructing the crushing letter to
Gates which with scrupulous courtesy and almost legal clarity
would point out that Gates was lying. He felt that the thing was
finished then—that there was nothing more to say.

Later, with Gates serving as president of the new Board of
War and Mifflin as a member of it, Washington's enemies soon
hatched another scheme, intended to seduce the young Marquis
of Lafayette from Washington's side by offering him a gilded
command in a proposed expedition against the British in Canada.
Official papers were forwarded to him at Valley Forge, informing

him of his appointment to a northern command and enclosing instructions to proceed at once to Albany, where he was to await further orders.

Realization that the appointment had been made without consulting Washington put the Marquis on his guard, but Washington made no effort to detain him. When he arrived at Albany, he found Conway already there, behaving, said Lafayette, "like a man sent from heaven for the liberty and happiness of America," and he refused point-blank to accept the flashy Irishman as his second in command. In their eagerness to annex the Marquis and with him the whole European element in Washington's army, the conspirators hastily agreed to the substitution of Lafayette's friend and traveling companion on his voyage to America, the honest and amiable Baron de Kalb.

But the Canadian venture was suddenly abandoned by Congress, and it was not long before Lafayette returned, simmering, to the camp at Valley Forge. He had learned without surprise that several other generals besides Gates had been concerned in the victory at Saratoga.

By the third week in February, 1778, it seemed impossible that the situation at Valley Forge could longer endure. "For some days past there has been little less than a famine in camp," Washington wrote Congress on the sixteenth. "A part of the army has been a week without any kind of flesh, and the rest for three or four days. Naked and starving as they are, we cannot enough admire the incomparable patience and fidelity of the soldiery, that they have not been ere this excited by their sufferings to general mutiny and dispersion. Strong symptoms, however, of discontent have appeared in particular instances; and nothing but the most active efforts everywhere can avert so shocking a catastrophe. . . ."

But the commander in chief underestimated the fidelity of his soldiers. They even contrived a surprise for his birthday, which was celebrated according to the New Style calendar on February 22. The cook at headquarters concocted a dinner of boiled fowls and parsnips, and there was rum and water in which to drink the general's health. During dinner Knox's artillery band paraded to headquarters and played "The Old Continental March," standing in the snow and the biting wind in front of the Potts house—after which they were all invited inside and given a present of hard money and a gill each of something warmer and made their bashful bows to a smiling Mrs. Washington.

Chapter 15

Because the Tory population of Pennsylvania persisted in its selfish preference for the profitable British market in Philadelphia for its produce, Washington was forced to use his ultimate power of seizing food, forage, and blankets wherever they could be found. Greene was put in command of this painful duty, and he accepted it with a natural reluctance. But from the beginning of the conflict he had maintained that war itself was a state of violence, subject to harsh laws of its own, and that those who were not for their country were against it. Once having undertaken the distasteful job, he acted vigorously in its accomplishment. "I sent in yesterday nearly fifty head of cattle," he wrote Washington from the field in February, "but the country is much drained; the inhabitants cry out and beset me from all quarters, but like Pharaoh I harden my heart."

His expeditions provided the camp with temporary relief, but a visiting committee from Congress was convinced on the spot that something must be done about the neglected post of quartermaster general, and they nominated Greene for the thankless duty. He protested that he had not the qualifications and abhorred the paper work involved. Only his love for the weary commander in chief induced him to quit his place in the line for the semi-civilian kind of drudgery entailed in providing the army with clothing and provisions. "No one ever heard of a quartermaster in history!" he complained in a letter to his brother. But he agreed to accept the post for one year on condition that he might appoint his own subordinates—Cox of Philadelphia and Pettit of New Jersey, both recommended by Reed—retain his major general's rank and pay, and not have to do the accounts.

Congress was desperate enough to accept these rather odd stipulations, and voted the customary percentage of all funds issued to the department to be divided among Greene, Cox, and Pettit. The newly organized Board of War undertook to procure clothing and shoes by donation from the several states—belated reforms which somewhat relieved the soldiers' immediate necessities. But Greene always considered himself a field officer and chafed at the desk work and political duties imposed upon him by the quartermaster's office.

Within a remarkably short time he had established a chain of depots from Head of Elk through Delaware, Pennsylvania, and Jersey to the Hudson, so that cloth, canvas, cattle, grain, and forage began to trickle in from regions not as yet swept bare by both armies. The incompetent Mifflin, who had been eliminated entirely by Greene's appointment, tried to play up an already existing jealousy of the friendship between Greene and Washington and was heard to imply that General Greene was glad to be out of the way of bullets. The remark of course came back to Greene, who used Washington's tactics and sent Mifflin a written request for an explanation. Mifflin at once denied that he had ever said any such thing, and the matter was allowed to drop.

Except for Lafayette, who had returned to camp after the collapse of the Canadian project, and Louis Duportail, the capable, unsociable French engineer who had laid out the encampment at Valley Forge, they had long since had enough of foreigners at headquarters. But when Baron Friedrich Wilhelm Augustin von Steuben, Knight of the Order of Fidelity and former aide-de-camp to Frederick the Great, arrived at camp with recommendations from the American commissioners at Paris and from Congress at York, he came, like Lafayette, with an adequate amount of rank and resources behind him. Unlike Conway and the rest, he possessed a lovable warmth and modesty behind his rather formal Prussian-style exterior. But he had come to teach and had been given the appointment as inspector general which Conway had coveted for himself.

They laughed at Steuben at first in the camp. But his earnestness, his dedication to the profession of war, and his genuine, constitutional kindliness under the rough exterior gradually won everybody's respectful attention. In the beginning he had not a word of English with which to make himself understood by his amused or exasperated pupils, though he spoke a sort of very bad French fluently. Traveling with him was his articulate and good-natured aide, Pierre-Etienne Duponceau, who could interpret the Baron into understandable French. They were at once fortunate in acquiring as linguist a young New Yorker, Benjamin Walker, who stepped out of the ranks during the first day's drill and offered to translate Duponceau's French into English for the benefit of the bewildered companies and the spluttering drillmaster. Somewhat to everybody's surprise, they all began to love Steuben.

No one was more aware of the army's need for a competent drillmaster and a book of rules than the commander in chief. So far, each state had used its own drill system, based to some degree on the British manual of arms. Steuben drew up a whole new training program adapted from the Prussian and written out in single daily lessons in French, which had to be put into English by Hamilton and Laurens. There was no way to print the result, so each brigade commander was required to copy the lessons one by one in English and pass them down to the regimental officers, who made their own copies.

Instead of leaving the drill duty to the American officers, themselves deficient in the procedure, Steuben elected to set the pattern himself, conducting the drill with the musket on his shoulder like a sergeant, while the American ranks learned to load, reload, and fire in unison at command. They were taught the musket manual with a smart slap and thump in handling the weapon. Above all, they learned from Steuben not to fear the bayonet but to use it for something more than an implement on which to roast a hunk of meat over a campfire. He tramped tirelessly up and down, leading his squads in the routine of facing right and left, wheeling, marching in columns of fours, deploying from column to line and line to column, halting smartly at the word—until the parade ground became a daily show as the Baron, wearing the impressive jeweled star of his European order —"the size of a dinner plate," someone said—set the pace for his harried companies.

The return of Lafayette to Valley Forge enlivened the evening gatherings with his colorful stories of his recent adventures at Albany, which his hearers found as good as a play. A less welcome return to the headquarters family was that of Charles Lee, whose exchange Washington had labored to accomplish and himself appeared to regard with satisfaction. Lee's undisciplined, short-tempered dogs came with him and were fed from his own plate at meals, as was his habit. Captivity with the British had not improved either his manners or his appearance. He was still impudent, still lacking in respect for his betters, and still not clean.

While Lee's arrival may have caused some private misgivings, headquarters could at least congratulate themselves that they had seen the last of Conway. After fretting at Albany for a while after Lafayette's departure, he had sent in his resignation to Congress in a rage because they had refused to give him a division to play with. He confidently expected to bring them to heel again by threatening to remove his valuable presence from their councils. To his furious surprise, the astute Henry Laurens, who was now President of the Congress, saw to it that the resignation was snapped up without delay, and Conway found himself out of a job. He rushed down to York to explain that he didn't speak English very well, having lived so long in France, and that he must have expressed himself badly and been misunderstood. But nobody was interested in him any longer. The unmoved, immovable man at Valley Forge had sat it out.

Conway did not carry out his threat of returning at once to France, and the following summer his forked tongue was still busy with slander and innuendo against Washington's reputation, till he ran afoul of gallant Cadwallader, who had seen the commander in chief in action at Trenton and Princeton. In a burst of fury he challenged Conway to a duel. Shots were exchanged according to protocol, and while Conway's shot went wild, Cadwallader's bullet struck Conway in the jaw in what was at first thought to be a fatal wound. He survived, however, to write Washington an abject apology and to live out an undistinguished career in France and India.

The daily life of the camp dragged on into spring. Steuben's eternal drilling began soon after breakfast, in a rasp of commands and a dogged shuffle and tramp of marching feet, interrupted by a motionless silence beneath a flood of trilingual invective at which no one in the ranks dared to grin. Because the drums were relied on to give notice of a sudden alarm, an order prevailed against random beating by idle drummer boys. But two authorized and required practice beats from 5:00 to 6:00 A.M. and from 4:00 to 5:00 P.M. were added to the regular camp beats which began with the reveille at daybreak and ended with the tattoo at 9:00 P.M.

As warmer weather arrived, a general housecleaning of the whole encampment was ordered by the commander in chief. Bedding was aired, clothing was laundered, the streets between the log huts were tidied, dirty straw and refuse were burned, with a fine smoky stench which drifted from one end of the valley to the other. Fresh boughs and hurdles were placed to screen the necessaries, and at least two windows were required to be let into every hut. Bathing parties, supervised by a sergeant with watch in hand, swarmed into the icy streams. Soap, vinegar, new shirts, and even shoes were coming in under Greene's competent quartermastering. A run of shining shad up the Schuylkill was chased into nets by sending the cavalry into the water to drive the fish, which provided days of wholesome feasting and plenty more to be salted down. Fresh vegetables began to appear in the rations, and small garden plots were optimistically laid out by the country-bred lads.

The universal sprucing up came just in time for the mammoth picnic which celebrated the completion of the French alliance on the sixth of May. Most of the Pennsylvania countryside population came in to see the troops parade and hear the cannon salutes and the running fire of musketry from right to left and left to right in the *feu de joie*, as Steuben had taught them, and to join in the cheers for the King of France and the American states.

It was Steuben's hour. With his jeweled star flashing in the sunshine, his hair powdered and dressed Prussian style, he led the inspection of the ranks assembled under arms and pronounced them ready. Mounted to review his army, Washington and his staff moved into their appointed places on the slope, and the ladies clustered under a marquee of tent cloth, surrounded by a throng of excited civilians. The signal gun boomed, the fifes and drums struck up, and the whole American army, Stirling commanding on the right, Lafayette (wearing a dramatic white scarf) on the left, swept forward to perform the drill they had so laboriously learned under Steuben's exasperated but fatherly guidance. These were the ragged, groaning, cursing human skeletons who not long ago had huddled in their murky huts coughing up their hearts—these washed and mended and self-respecting soldiers, stepping out with their heads up and their accouterment rustless and polished, performing their drill with confidence and precision. This was an army to be proud of—and it could be seen by Washington's rigid face and statuelike stillness in the saddle that he was gripped by an emotion almost too deep to bear.

It was a great day to remember, as they were all to do, ruefully, many times over, while they awaited the slow fulfillment of its promise. France had undertaken to come to America's aid, it was true, and the French navy would be of immediate value against the strangling British fleet. But it would take time for French supplies and reinforcements to arrive. The ragged Continentals had still a long way to go alone and with all the same vexations. At a council on the eighth of May it was decided to remain at the Valley Forge encampment and await the next British move. There were still too many sick and too many shortages to risk any decisive action.

Once again the wives watched the ominous staff conferences and busy dispatch riders which always preceded a new campaign. The secretary-aides were swamped with table work, so that the scratch of their pens and the drone of dictation went on till the small hours in the little office behind the parlor at the Potts house, and there was always the sound of hoofs and the clink of spurs as the riding-aides came and went on their endless errands.

Among the wives the familiar reluctant preparations began also, for it was time for them to go home again before the guns began. Kitty Greene was among the first to depart, for she had been too long away from her two small children for even such a lighthearted—some said lightheaded—creature as had married Quaker Nat. After a visit to the Lotts, where she had spent the previous summer, she was accompanied as far as the Hudson by her husband, who was bound there on quartermaster business. They said their farewells along the road, and she proceeded to Rhode Island and he returned to camp to find an exhilarating rumor going round.

The British were said to be preparing to evacuate Philadelphia. Without a fight? Greene asked incredulously. Washington thought that unlikely. But General Howe had been recalled to London to defend his inactivity, and Clinton was appointed to succeed him in the command at Philadelphia. And Clinton was perhaps uneasy at the prospect of French ships arriving in the Delaware below the city. If he intended to withdraw his forces in order to consolidate at New York, it might be possible for Washington to catch him on the wrong foot somewhere along the way.

Philadelphia and the British lay between Mrs. Washington and Mount Vernon, and her husband wanted to be sure that she was safely home before any trouble began. She said goodbye to Valley Forge on the eighth of June, a little comforted by the French alliance, a little homesick for the Potomac, but rent asunder by her comprehension of the lonely anxieties the commander in chief must still endure in the rooms they had shared.

Left to himself in the comfortable quarters at Moore Hall on the Pottstown road which apparently went with the quartermastership as some compensation for its pains, Greene sent a letter after Kitty within a few days of his return to camp: "I have only time to tell you now that I am here in the usual style, writing, scolding, eating, and drinking. But there is no Mrs. Greene to spend an agreeable hour with. I hope you got safe home. Pray write me a full history of family matters; there is nothing will be so agreeable. Kiss the sweet little children for their absent papa. You must make yourself as happy as possible; write me if you are in want of anything to render you so."

There would be another child, he knew, in the summer.

Chapter 16

Clinton had arrived in Philadelphia from New York on May 8, 1778, to encounter all the gaieties designed to speed the popular Howe on his way home—Howe having found plenty of friends among the Tories there, while his handsome aides in their scarlet regimentals had dazzled the younger set. Cornwallis returned from leave in England early in June to become second in command to a man with whom he could never agree about anything.

The British began to move out of Philadelphia during the second week in June, and the Americans repossessed it on the eighteenth. Benedict Arnold, still crippled by a leg wound received at Saratoga, had reported for duty at Valley Forge just in time to be appointed by Washington military governor of the city—an unwise assignment, as it turned out, for Arnold had little tact and less discretion and was soon living like a lord in the best mansion in town, driving the best carriage, and entertaining lavishly both Tory and Patriot society, with a noticeable preference for the former.

Accompanied by Cornwallis and encumbered by an enormous baggage train and hordes of Tory refugees and unruly camp followers laden with loot, Clinton moved slowly out of the city and crossed the Delaware at Gloucester Point, which brought him to Haddonfield and the road through Mount Holly to Brunswick. Washington followed cautiously, crossing his army above Tren-

ton in a pouring rain on June 21 and pausing at Hopewell for a
council. Clinton moved so slowly that he was suspected of an
intention to swerve suddenly to advantageous ground and confront them in battle array.

Greene's multiple duties as quartermaster on the march kept
him in the saddle most of the time. His efficiency, combined with
Steuben's discipline, caused Washington to note that they were
able, "with great facility, to make a sudden move with the whole
army and baggage from Valley Forge in pursuit of the enemy."

When Clinton reached Allentown he discovered that Washington had gained a position almost on his front, at Kingston
above Princeton. Rather than risk an engagement encumbered as
he was, Clinton changed course eastward for Monmouth and
Sandy Hook, where he hoped to embark for New York. Washington then felt safe to close in and harass the rear guard and so
marched for Englishtown. The sandy roads he and Clinton traveled ran almost parallel and were so narrow that in some places it
was impossible for two columns to pass each other, and there
were few east and west intersections. The weather turned in-
tensely hot and thundery, which exhausted the marching men on
both sides.

At a council on June 24 Charles Lee loudly opposed any
attempt to overtake and attack the clumsy British column, while
Greene, Steuben, Wayne, and others disagreed with him. The
old guessing game had begun again for Washington, dependent
as he was on inadequate intelligence reports—spies—and a knowledge obtained from unreliable local informants of the terrain
separating the two armies. His generals wrangled—some in favor
of striking Clinton while he was in motion and at a disadvantage,
others convinced that it would be folly to throw the weakened
survivors of Valley Forge against the British regulars who had
wintered more comfortably around Philadelphia.

Hamilton, now an influential staff officer and much in Washington's confidence, Lafayette, and Greene all protested the
council's decision to avoid a general engagement with Clinton
until French cooperation was assured, and it was probably due to
their representations that the orders were issued which led to the
battle of Monmouth on June 28. Lee, as senior officer, had command of the advance force, for Washington persisted in accepting

him at his own high evaluation, even though Lee had expressed violent opposition to bringing on a battle at that time.

On the morning of the twenty-eighth Washington received word that Clinton was about to leave his camp at Monmouth Courthouse. He at once dispatched orders to Lee that he was to advance and force a fight there, while Washington moved his main column forward in support. John Laurens and another aide were sent to reconnoiter as the army was put in motion, with Stirling leading the left wing and Greene again in command of his own division on the right.

It was a blazing hot Sunday—96 degrees in the shade—and there was very little shade. The British wore scarlet wool uniforms, heavy with buttons and braid and colored facings, and they carried sixty-pound packs on their backs. The officers, although they were mounted, were no better dressed for the heat, and they drove the men in the ranks relentlessly. About noon Washington could hear cannon fire up ahead from the direction of the Courthouse, and both Hamilton and Knox rode in from there to report confusion among Lee's troops. Then the firing slacked off, and a breathless fifer-boy informed them that Lee was falling back, which would leave Lafayette, Wayne, and Varnum unsupported.

Washington was still incredulous even of Knox's report and himself pushed on toward what should have been the front. Soon he encountered the first stragglers in retreat from where he supposed the firing line to be. Knox was not surprised to see them, since he had been all over the field placing his artillery and had witnessed the "confusion" around General Lee. More aides were sent galloping ahead to learn what Lee was doing, and more troops came straggling back, not in panic but definitely without leadership and in retreat. Then Washington saw Lee, with members of his staff, riding toward the rear and away from the Courthouse. He spurred out to meet Lee and sharply demanded an explanation.

Lee stammered defensively that "contradictory intelligence" had caused "confusion," that his orders had not been properly carried out, and that anyway he had never approved of the decision to attack. Washington replied hotly that he expected his orders to be obeyed regardless of Lee's own opinions. A blustering attempt by Lee to justify his behavior brought on an explosion of Washington's famous but seldom visible anger, so that, as a bystander reported later, the commander in chief "swore like an angel from heaven" and "cursed till the leaves trembled on the trees" before riding forward himself to rally the fainthearted men who were retreating through the withering heat without having fired a shot at the enemy.

Arriving at what should have been the front line and was now chaos, Washington was stunned to learn from Wayne that Clinton was only fifteen minutes' march away and advancing. Colonel Tilghman produced a local man who knew the district, and with his reluctant guidance Washington was able to intercept and rally some of the fugitives. Steuben joined him, and they posted some of the disorganized companies behind a useful hedgerow, took advantage of a protective swamp in front of them and a wooded lane to the rear, and formed a line that would stand to face the enemy, while Knox's artillery kept up a brisk cannonade.

"I never saw the General to so much advantage," Hamilton wrote later. "His coolness and firmness were admirable. He instantly took measures for checking the enemy's advance, and giving time for the main army to form and make a proper disposition. General Greene and Lord Stirling rendered very essential service and did themselves great honor."

Wayne came up in the nick of time with an unshaken brigade, and Greene and Stirling proved capable without orders of establishing themselves on the wings. In the paralyzing heat of the day, Washington was everywhere on a sweating white horse which finally collapsed beneath him—recklessly exposing himself to enemy fire while Stirling's well-served guns began to tell against the Highland Foot.

Clinton made a determined effort to break through Greene on the right and sent in Cornwallis with his Grenadiers and Guards. Knox, by now the most brilliant artillerist on either side, supported Greene with an enfilading fire that mowed down the close-ranked British line like dominoes, and Greene's infantry stood rock-steady to pour their volleys into a British bayonet charge. Cornwallis saw his men crumble and break and had to retreat some of Britain's finest. Steuben's work at Valley Forge was paying off. For the first time American artillery had fired a defensive barrage over the heads of its own men, who had proved their ability to obey the words of command and to wheel and form again without stepping on each other.

A lull in the fighting occurred in the late afternoon, for sunstroke and thirst became another weapon. As the brassy sun began to sink in the west, the firing on both sides finally died away, while the two spent armies were left facing each other across the swamp. The battle was practically a draw, but the Americans had rallied under fire, had withstood a cavalry charge and a pounding by the Royal Artillery, and they remained on the field.

When Washington's hard-ridden horse died under him, he had mounted another, to ride unscathed through the hail of British lead. At the end of the day he lay down on a cloak spread on the ground, with Layfayette beside him and Greene stretched out under a tree not far away, and they all slept the sleep of exhaustion, there among the dead and wounded.

Another hot dawn roused them to the astonished discovery that the entire British army had crept away during the night, leaving their dead unburied and their wounded to the mercy of the American surgeons, who were already working their way across the bloody field. By sheer discipline and desperation Clinton had got beyond pursuit along the road to Sandy Hook, where Admiral Howe's transports awaited him. Washington had to let him go, in view of the overpowering heat, a lack of drinking-water for his troops, and the distance already gained by Clinton's dogged night march, which had saved his army and most of his baggage train. Nevertheless, both British generals were unhappily convinced that they were up against a very different army now from the rabble that had fled before them at Kip's Bay and Brandywine.

Washington could recognize that, disappointing as the day had been, Monmouth was still the closest thing to victory they had yet achieved in a pitched battle against a British force of any size, and for the first time they had held the field against a British army. Clinton's losses were heavier than his, and Clinton was in retreat.

Washington himself was able to withdraw the next day at his leisure, on a hot, thirsty march to Brunswick, where he arrived on

July 2. Greene had to find replacements for the horses lost on the battlefield and during the march, when many animals had died of heat and thirst.

While the army rested at Brunswick, Washington was confronted by Lee's haughty demand for a court of inquiry on what he termed insulting language from the commander in chief and undeserved censure on his conduct. The proceedings, which amounted to a court-martial on three counts of disobedience, misbehavior in the face of an enemy, and disrespect toward his commanding officer, were opened formally on July 4, with Stirling acting as president of the court and the younger staff officers like Laurens, Hamilton, and Lafayette expressing vehement criticism of Lee.

The hearing dragged on for weeks—"a certain preconceived and preposterous opinion of his [Lee's] being a very great man will operate in his favor," wrote Hamilton on July 5. And "No attack, it seems, can be made on General Washington but it must recoil on the assailant," Lee discovered incredulously on the twenty-second. After a somewhat inconclusive hearing, during which Lee impudently conducted his own defense, he was suspended from command for a term of twelve months and went off to Philadelphia to spread his own version of the day at Monmouth and to belittle Washington in every possible way. The commander in chief was soon too much occupied with a new venture to comment on the verdict.

The army was moving to familiar ground around Paramus in New Jersey. During the march the general and his staff paused at the picturesque Passaic Falls to picnic rustically on cold ham, biscuits, and grog. There a rumor reached them, soon to be confirmed, that the French Admiral D'Estaing had arrived with a fleet off the coast near Sandy Hook. Since Clinton was again ensconced in New York, this might result in a French blockade of the harbor with a British admiral immobilized inside.

Chapter 17

D'Estaing's ships had been eighty-seven days at sea because of contrary winds, and he was anxious to put his sick ashore. The Jersey pilots refused to take the "long-legged" French ships across the bar at Sandy Hook because of their deep draught, and to the admiral's puzzlement no one came out at once from the shore to meet him. He detached the *Chimère* to Philadelphia, bearing Conrad Gérard, who had made the voyage in company with the returning American commissioner Silas Deane and who bore credentials as the first French Minister to the United States.

The difficulty of a joint operation with the French allies would soon become apparent, though the language barrier could be surmounted to some degree with the aid of Hamilton and John Laurens, both of whom spoke fluent French, besides the helpful and dauntless Lafayette. Young Laurens was finally chosen to make the risky trip through thrashing seas in a small boat to come aboard the French flagship *Languedoc*, off Long Branch on July 16. He found the French very short of fresh water and nursing a growing number of men afflicted with scurvy, while the pilots were still unable to find a channel deep enough to allow D'Estaing to attack the British fleet "lying snug within the Hook."

Washington at Paramus then received a proposal from Congress, following their first conference with Gérard, that D'Estaing might be directed northward to attack the British garrison at

Newport in Rhode Island, and he put matters in motion to further that effort. Hamilton was sent after Laurens to explain to the French admiral that the American army would at once cross the Hudson to its old camping ground near White Plains and would there be in a position to cooperate with an attack by the French on either Rhode Island or New York. The aides returned shortly to report that such a move had already occurred to D'Estaing and was approved by the French council aboard the *Languedoc*. Having sent his water boats ashore for a fresh supply, D'Estaing put to sea on July 29 for Rhode Island.

The British had been in possession of Newport Island ever since the grim autumn of 1776, when Washington was making his long retreat across New Jersey above the Delaware. At that time General Howe, always with a jealous eye to the prestige of capturing Philadelphia, had disposed of his captious second-in-command by sending Clinton with a detachment in Admiral Parker's ships to seize the undefended harbor of Newport as a winter anchorage for British ships. The Rhode Island forces which gathered hastily to dispute the landing had fallen back just as hastily to positions on the mainland north of Newport, and an uneasy occupation had ensued, marked by great severity on the part of the British.

Clinton had soon left Lord Percy to occupy for him so insignificant a post as Newport, and in January, 1777, he sailed for England to express to Parliament his dissatisfaction with the way things were being done in America. He returned to New York in July but was not present with Howe at Brandywine the following year, remaining inactive (except for an abortive attempt to relieve Burgoyne) until he was named to succeed Howe at Philadelphia in May, 1778. Lord Percy had followed him to England, leaving General Richard Prescott to hold Newport.

Prescott was to figure in one of the half-forgotten episodes of the war when in July, 1777, a raiding party from Tiverton under William Barton captured him in his bed and carried him off to Providence as a prisoner. General Sir Robert Pigott was then sent up from New York to take over the Rhode Island command, and he still held that post at the time of D'Estaing's arrival off the coast. Prescott was considered valuable enough to be exchanged for Charles Lee, and he eventually returned to Rhode Island in the autumn of 1778.

General Spencer had succeeded Arnold at Providence early in the year, and the city became an armed camp during the British occupation of Newport. The Rhode Island Assembly moved there from East Greenwich, just as Congress had fled from Philadelphia to York. The British erected defenses north of the town of Newport and made themselves as comfortable as possible by billeting among the snug farmhouses on the island.

Early in March of 1778 Washington had ordered General Sullivan up from Valley Forge to Providence, replacing Spencer, who had resigned after being criticized for incompetence. The Rhode Island Assembly's council of war voted Sullivan the supreme command when he arrived there, at the time the first news of the French alliance was raising new hopes in the American camps. Rhode Island enlistments were being mustered under Colonel Varnum, who had asked to be transferred there from his duties with Washington's army after the winter at Valley Forge.

Sullivan was notified of the approach of the French ally and was requested to promote the recruitment of Rhode Island militia. With Clinton back in New York and Washington at White Plains, the two armies appeared to have returned to their stalemate positions of two years before. But now it was plain even to the cautious Washington that with D'Estaing's arrival the balance of power could shift in his favor.

Greene at White Plains had certainly felt a sharp disappointment when Sullivan was chosen instead of himself to play a leading part in the forthcoming Rhode Island campaign, but he was resigned to the prior claims of his quartermastership, which detained him at Washington's headquarters. It was unfortunate that his feelings had recently been ruffled by a misunderstanding with Washington, who appeared to complain unjustly of Greene's temporary absence—on his quartermaster duties—during the recent crossing of the Hudson on the way to White Plains. Greene was at the same time obliged to see Lafayette and Glover depart to Rhode Island to reinforce Sullivan and cooperate with Lafayette's newly arrived countrymen, while Laurens and Hamilton—none of them Rhode Islanders—were also assigned to what promised to be the next field of action.

The unusual strain on the friendship between Greene and the commander in chief—arising apparently from Washington's desire to have Greene in two places at the same time—was already relieved and forgotten when Washington finally recognized the value of Greene's local prestige and personal knowledge of the Rhode Island countryside and ordered him to follow Lafayette. He carried letters from Washington directing that Sullivan's forces be arranged in two divisions, with Lafayette in command of one and Greene of the other, both subordinate to Sullivan.

It can be imagined that the young Marquis was enchanted at the prospect of joining D'Estaing with an army of his own, and he wrote Sullivan a hasty note to say that the admiral was a friend and relation of his and that with the French and his own brigades joined to what Sullivan could muster at Providence they would have "a pretty good reinforcement," adding with disarming enthusiasm, "For God's sake, in the name of your own love of glory, do not begin before we arrive! I avow that if I were to arrive too late I should wish to hang myself!" The ardent young Frenchman nevertheless welcomed generously the news that his first independent command was to be divided with his friend Greene. His unfailing grace and deference to the commander in chief made him one of the few comforts Washington could enjoy at this time.

Greene wrote to Sullivan from Coventry on July 31 that he had ridden there from the White Plains camp in three days and was "a little fatigued" but would see him at Providence the next day, unless his earlier arrival there was imperative. And then, for the first time in three long years, he sat down at his own table under his own roof and with his wife and two babies around him. Until now he had not made the acquaintance of the little daughter born in March, 1777, and named for Mrs. Washington while the army was at Morristown. The baby called Martha had been left at home with her uncles when Kitty came to New Jersey belatedly for the brief stay with the Lott family, before the army moved out toward Brandywine, and neither child had been brought to Valley Forge.

Friends and neighbors at Coventry now poured into the roomy white house on the hill to hear the latest about their friends still in camp with Washington, and the other Greene brothers rode in from Potowomut for a general reunion.

The British occupied the oblong Newport Island, separated from the mainland by wide water ways, called passages, on the east and west, and by narrow straits on the north where ferries ran to Tiverton and Bristol. The town of Newport was at the south end of its island. Providence, the principal American base, was on the mainland some distance north and west, at the head of Narragansett Bay.

On the first of August some Rhode Island farm boys, who had been compelled by recent British reinforcements to labor for the enemy with their fathers' teams, were hauling stores for the garrison on Newport Island when they noticed a certain agitation among the British officers who were directing their labors. The next time they reached a slight elevation on the road with their loads and looked south and west toward Point Judith, they saw to their delight twelve tall ships of the line with attendant frigates, standing in for Newport harbor. The French allies had arrived. "Darsn't laugh—not then," one of those who witnessed that exciting day related many years later when he was an old man. But all Rhode Island was laughing in its sleeve as the British withdrew hastily from their outer fortifications into their entrenched camp at Newport town. They then blew up a couple of their smaller vessels in hopes of blocking the east passage and prepared to stand a siege as the French ships ran in under a British cannonade and established a blockade.

D'Estaing ran two ships up to Conanicut Island, which lay between Newport and the mainland on the west, and prepared to land troops where the British had deserted their works only the day before. The British blew up, grounded, or burned some of their own vessels to prevent their capture, and Rhode Island recruits poured into Sullivan's camp at Tiverton, across Howland's Ferry from the north end of Newport Island. Spirits were high with the determination to demonstrate that Rhode Islanders were anxious to do their part in the expected conflict on their own ground.

Greene was doing double duty as quartermaster general and commander of a field division, which required an additional aide, Lewis Morris, who was to remain with him until almost the end of the war. On the sixth of August he marched his division from Providence to the camp at Tiverton, followed by Lafayette. A conference with D'Estaing aboard the *Languedoc* ran into some bilingual argument over precedence and procedure but produced a plan for simultaneous action on August 10 by 10,000 French fighting men and the American forces under Sullivan. Then on the ninth the always impetuous Sullivan jumped the gun and landed a detachment from Tiverton on the island to occupy the abandoned British works at Butt's Hill north of Newport town. This unexpected move offended D'Estaing, who had been promised due notice for a joint assault on the following day, and he began hastily to set his troops ashore on Conanicut Island, following the lines of the strategy which was to hem in Pigott at Newport and force him to surrender.

But even while the French transports lay at anchor off Conanicut unloading troops, thirteen of Admiral Howe's British ships of the line and as many smaller vessels appeared out of a fog off Point Judith, about fourteen miles across the Sound from Newport, heading into the anchorage D'Estaing had just left. Clinton had decided to save Pigott before moving against Washington at White Plains and was preparing an expeditionary force at New York to follow Admiral Howe to Rhode Island. To avoid being bottled up, D'Estaing promptly reembarked his soldiers from Conanicut. Convinced that his chief object was after all to destroy the British fleet wherever he found it, he collected his scattered vessels and put out to sea to engage Howe.

He notified Sullivan that he would return "in any event, dead or alive," to assist in the conquest of Newport—ignoring the awkward fact that he was leaving Sullivan stranded a long way from his base, committed to hold the deserted British works and to storm the inner fortifications of Newport without any support from allied forces on the west shore.

In the torrent of recriminations and protest which ensued, Sullivan always maintained that if D'Etsaing had been content simply to defend the mouth of the passage between Conanicut and Newport against the entrance of British ships all would have gone well. Instead, D'Estaing allowed himself to be drawn farther and farther down the coast in pursuit of Howe while they both maneuvered for the weather gauge. During a hot engagement at

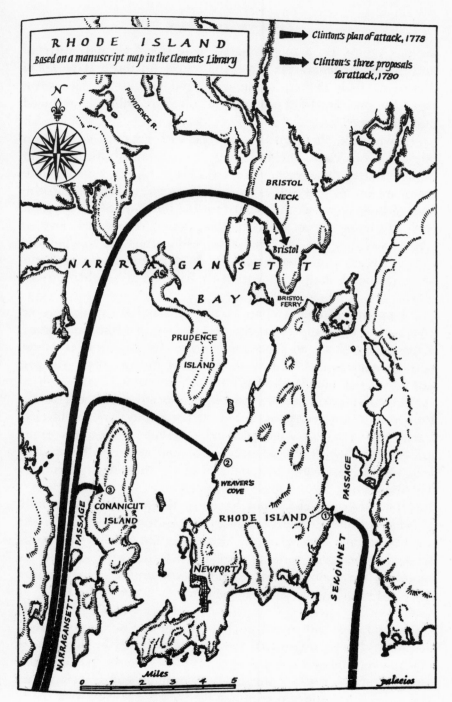

Rhode Island campaigns, 1778 and 1780

sea on August 12, a sudden severe gale swept in and scattered both fleets, drenching the American forces on shore as well and destroying their shelter, ammunition, and provisions. The storm raged for two days, and even animals on shore collapsed and died under its fury.

Howe made off toward New York with his crippled ships, as might be expected, but D'Estaing had promised to return to Newport after the engagement at sea. Hasty repairs were made to the army camps and Sullivan moved forward toward the British lines outside Newport in preparation for the planned joint action with D'Estaing's support when the admiral reappeared. Greene wrote to Kitty from his farmhouse headquarters on Newport Island, replying characteristically to the anxieties and complaints of a nervous young wife with two babies and another on the way.

"I am sorry to hear you are getting unwell. I am afraid it is the effect of fearful apprehensions. Remember that the same good Providence protects all places, and secures from harm in the most perilous situation. Would to God it was in my power to give peace to your bosom, which I fear is like the troubled ocean.

"I thank you kindly for your concern for my health and safety; the former is not very perfect, and the latter is in the book of fate. I wish to live but for your sake, and those little pledges of conjugal affection which Providence has blessed us with. Those dear little rogues have begun to command a large share of my affection and attention.

"The French fleet has not returned. We are within two miles of Newport, and are to begin our approaches tonight."

There were times when the Quaker in him still showed, in his somewhat pedantic tone toward his volatile wife and in his speech, when the habitual *thee* and *thou* recurred, even while he delivered some of the strongest military language to be heard in camp.

Several days had passed since the storm and nothing was seen or heard of D'Estaing. From the roof of Greene's headquarters a lookout kept constant watch over an empty ocean, while below him the routine work of digging and manning gun emplacements and parallels went on in preparation for the siege of Newport.

Then a solitary frigate appeared, bringing a letter from the

Nathanael Greene. From a portrait by Charles Willson Peale. (*Indepen-dence National Historical Park Collection, Philadelphia*)

Henry Knox. From a portrait by
Gilbert Stuart. (*Courtesy, Muse-
um of Fine Arts, Boston*)

George Washington. From a
miniature by Charles Willson
Peale, probably painted at Valley Forge, showing an unusually
youthful aspect of the general,
who was forty-five in 1777.
(*The Mount Vernon Ladies'
Association*)

Daniel Morgan. From a portrait by Charles Willson Peale. (*Independence National Historical Park Collection, Philadelphia*)

Thomas Sumter. Engraved after a portrait by Charles Willson Peale. (*Library of Congress*)

Anthony Wayne. After a portrait by Peter Rothermel, based on John Trumbull's study. (*The Historical Society of Pennsylvania*)

Baron von Steuben. From a portrait by Charles Willson Peale. (*Independence National Historical Park Collection, Philadelphia*)

Washington's retreat at Long Island, August 29, 1776 (*Emmet Collection, Manuscript Division, New York Public Library*)

Landing of the British on the Jersey palisades, November, 1776. From an
original drawing attributed to Lord Rawdon, who served at the time as

engineer officer on Cornwallis's staff. (*Emmet Collection, Manuscript Division, New York Public Library*)

Capture of the Hessians at Trenton, December 26, 1776. From a painting by John Trumbull. (*Yale University Art Gallery*)

View of the upper Harlem, scene of the September action, 1776 (*Spencer Collection, New York Public Library*)

Washington at Valley Forge

"Massacre" of Colonel Buford's regiment in the Waxhaws by Tarleton's dragoons, May 29, 1780. "Tarleton's quarter." (*Emmet Collection, Manuscript Division, New York Public Library*)

Encounter between William Washington and Banastre Tarleton at the Cowpens, January 17, 1781. Engraved after a painting by Alonzo Chappel. (*Frick Art Reference Library*)

Francis Marion crossing the PeeDee (*Emmett Collection, Manuscript Division, New York Public Library*)

The Cypress Swamp, scene of the South Carolina campaigns of 1781. From a photograph taken by the author.

admiral. He wrote that his shattered ships must go into port to refit and that his officers were convinced that their safety depended on making their way at once to Boston for repairs—of course with the intention of returning eventually to Rhode Island to cooperate against Newport.

Sullivan's famous temper erupted at what he considered base desertion by an ally. He sent Greene and Lafayette out to the flagship to entreat the admiral to bring his ships back to Narragansett Bay, where he could refit as well as at Boston, and at the same time detach troops for Sullivan's support.

They found the tall French flagship disfigured by British broadsides, and D'Estaing's bland good manners were shadowed by his careworn aspect. Greene had to speak through Lafayette at the council of war which courtesy compelled D'Estaing to assemble in order to hear Sullivan's plea. His officers at once confirmed their earlier decision in favor of a retreat to Boston, overruling both the incredulous protests of their guests and D'Estaing's halfhearted attempt to live up to his commitment to Sullivan.

When Greene and Lafayette returned to camp to report their failure, a formal written protest was composed by the American officers—promising fresh water, trees for masts, tar, paint, workmen, everything Boston could provide, if only D'Estaing would bring back the troops without which Sullivan's preparations to attack Newport were hopeless. It was signed by all but Lafayette, whose French loyalties were torn between his kinships and his adopted cause.

Laurens was therefore chosen to be dispatched in a fast sloop, which overhauled the *Languedoc* as it was about to enter Boston harbor. Referred to by the easily offended D'Estaing as "Sullivan's colonel-bailiff," Laurens was received coolly aboard the flagship when he presented Sullivan's petition, doubtless reinforced by some urgent youthful remarks of his own. The admiral read the document with studied calm—ordered refreshments sent aboard Laurens's boat—and proceeded into Boston port.

When Laurens arrived back at the Rhode Island camp to confess his lack of success, Sullivan's angry reaction was audible everywhere, even in his General Orders which were read out to the troops next day. This led to widespread and undiplomatic criticism of the French allies, which required enormous effort on the part of wiser men to suppress. Lafayette found himself in a very unenviable position; his feelings were genuinely hurt, his pride was suffering, and his friendships were threatened, after his own loyal energies had been freely spent on America's behalf. A violent quarrel took place between him and Sullivan, who had been his friend since Monmouth and was now dangerously close to provoking a challenge. Washington intervened promptly from White Plains in his calm, unhurried handwriting, which at once cooled off the Marquis. Sullivan retracted some of his rudest allegations, and Lafayette consented to ride to Boston himself, seek out D'Estaing there, and make another attempt to secure his future cooperation.

All this was not an auspicious beginning to the new alliance. If the more temperate Greene had been in Sullivan's place, things might have gone differently, though he had written to Pettit that "the devil had got into the French fleet; they are about to desert us, and go round to Boston. I am afraid our expedition is now at an end; to evacuate the island is death; to stay may be ruin."

But they stayed.

Wrought upon by his young kinsman's distress and eloquence, the chivalrous D'Estaing offered gaily to imagine himself an American colonel and serve under General Sullivan in command of a small French detachment. This *beau geste* was instantly voted down by his council of officers, and Lafayette could only dash back to Rhode Island—seventy miles in seven hours—to find that in his brief absence the bloody battle of Rhode Island had been fought on the twenty-ninth of August—the only head-on conflict of that whole campaign.

Having already approached to within two miles of the Newport town fortifications, Sullivan had been compelled by D'Estaing's absence to abandon the attack. When he attempted to withdraw his little force, diminished by desertions, northward toward the ferry that would evacuate it to Tiverton, the British under Pigott came out after him, and a furious engagement was fought. The British were supported by armed vessels offshore which cannonaded the right flank, where Greene and Varnum were stationed, and the carnage on both sides was considerable. Every cannon fired that day was distinctly heard at Coventry, and the smoke of the battle could be seen from the doorstep of

Greene's home. At nightfall both armies reoccupied their respective camps, and Greene wrote to Kitty from the vicinity of Bristol: "We retreated back here last night, with an intention to hold this part of the Island. The enemy advanced upon us early this morning, and a severe action ensued with nearly the whole right wing. I write upon my horse, and have not slept for two nights, therefore you'll excuse my not writing very legible, as I write upon the field. Colonel Livingston is slightly wounded. My aides all behaved with great gallantry."

Livingston had been with him, at his right hand, since Long Island. The Quaker general was now inured to wounds.

The young Marquis was disappointed at having missed all the fun and was chagrined by his failure to persuade his countrymen to return at once to Rhode Island waters. But his ruffled feathers were now smooth again, and his devotion to the American cause was undamaged, especially since the receipt of a fatherly letter from Washington, which reminded him that "the censures which have been levelled at the officers of the French fleet would, more than probable, have fallen in a much higher degree upon a fleet of our own (if we had one) in the same situation."

For a few days after the battle Greene was stationed on the west shore of Narragansett Bay, with headquarters at his own home, while his quartermaster duties again occupied his attention. Forage and food were scarce and prices were high, and in Providence the people literally could not find enough to eat. In the middle of September he rode to Boston, where D'Estaing and his officers were still enjoying the hospitality of John Hancock. From there he wrote a full account of the Newport battle to Washington, who was still stranded at White Plains in acute anxiety not only for the outcome of the Rhode Island campaign itself but for the strained relations which now existed with the touchy new ally as represented by D'Estaing and Lafayette.

Sullivan's first violent resentment against the French admiral was expressed in his letters to the governor of Rhode Island. These were just about to be read aloud to the Legislature assembled at East Greenwich when they were hastily suppressed by Greene's whispered advice to the Speaker. This opportune precaution against the spread of adverse comment on French behavior was due to Greene's characteristic tact and sense of justice and temperance in all things. Further to assuage outraged French sensibilities and bury the accusation that D'Estaing had failed the new nation at the first test of the alliance, the diplomatic Steuben was sent to Rhode Island as general adviser to the camp there. D'Estaing's own discretion and restraint contributed to a slow cooling off at Boston, before he sailed for the West Indies in November—without vouchsafing to Washington the slightest hint of his destination or intentions. He and Washington had never met during the admiral's sojourn in American waters.

On October 5 Greene wrote again from Coventry to Washington, largely on the subject of his quartermastering difficulties in the vital matters of forage and clothing, the depreciation of currency, and the prevailing uncertainty as to what anyone, including themselves, was going to do next: "I was told yesterday that General Sullivan had wrote to your Excellency to have me stationed here this winter," he added. "However agreeable it is to be near my family and among my friends, I cannot wish it to take place, as it would be very unfriendly to the business of my department. I wrote yesterday to General Sullivan for leave to join the grand army [at White Plains] and expect his answer today. I have the honor to be, with the greatest respect and regard, Your Excellency's most obedient and humble servant, NATH. GREENE."

On Greene's departure, Sullivan was left with a handful of discouraged troops at his old position on the mainland. He was still in danger from possible British reinforcements by Howe's refitted fleet at New York, as was evidenced by the arrival at Newport of nearly seventy vessels sent to relieve Pigott—Clinton being unaware that the "siege" of Newport had already been raised by the retirement of Sullivan's dwindling force, now so reduced in numbers it was not considered worth chasing farther. Sullivan recognized with dismay that he had less than 2,000 men to defend the extended Rhode Island coastline from possible assault by the British from their Newport base.

But Pigott soon returned to England, leaving the post in Prescott's hands again, and Sullivan was succeeded in the Rhode Island command by Gates, who was received with great enthusiasm. Gates soon contrived a transfer to the more prestigious command at Boston, at which time Heath took over at Providence.

Chapter 18

The autumn of 1778 saw another of the periodic crises that boiled up into an apparently hopeless outlook, this one being agitated by the rivalries and ambitions of the European officers, by the growing necessity to recruit cavalry when there was not enough forage to keep the horses from starving, and by the persistent intrigues and burrowings of the Gates faction in Congress and the army, the conspirators having convinced themselves that Boston would be the next point of attack and therefore was in urgent need of defensive measures.

Henry Laurens, as President of Congress, was inclined to a conviction shared by Washington that the British would soon make another attempt to subjugate the Southern ports, Charleston in particular. But the current "scare" of a New England invasion from Rhode Island caused Congress to designate their favorite, Gates, for the Boston command.

Under the still debatable new British threat to the South, President Laurens at Philadelphia was sponsoring the appointment of General Lincoln to the Southern command, to succeed the relatively unknown North Carolinian, Robert Howe, who had fought under Moultrie and Charles Lee during the first British attempt on Charleston in 1776. This American Howe had recently retreated to Savannah from a disastrous campaign against the British posts in Florida. Lincoln was the Massachusetts general

who had been disabled by a leg wound at Saratoga—the day
Gates claimed the victory and other men got the wounds—and he
had been recovering painfully at his Hingham home during all
the months of Valley Forge and the Monmouth campaign. He
now considered himself fit for duty, though he would go lame all
his life and was further handicapped by his enormous weight.

He had joined Washington at White Plains in time to receive
the appointment which was the first link in the chain of events
which in 1780 would lead Nathanael Greene southward into the
great adventure of his life. Traveling overland, Lincoln set out for
Charleston in early October, 1778, unaware that a British seaborne expedition under Sir Archibald Campbell would overtake
and pass him, bound for an attack on Savannah.

When Clinton returned to New York after Monmouth in June
of that year, he had found himself no better off than Sir William
Howe had ever been, and he was not content to endure any
longer the exhausting deadlock with Washington. Therefore, in
November of 1778 he dispatched Campbell from New York to the
coast of Georgia, in command of a force which was carried by
Commodore Sir Hyde Parker's fleet. In 1776 they had failed to
take Charleston from the sea. Now Clinton decided to come at
the city overland, and the mouth of the Savannah River afforded
a more vulnerable landing place than Charleston harbor.

In that worrisome autumn of 1778 it seemed unlikely that the
British would undertake another winter campaign in the North,
in which case the White Plains position became ineffective.
Washington could do no better than arrange his army in a vast
arc from Connecticut through West Point and Fishkill to New
Jersey. He set up his main headquarters near Middlebrook, where
the army began to arrive in detachments early in December, to
find boards, bricks, and other building supplies collected by the
quartermaster and awaiting them. A new house at Somerville
under construction by a man named Wallace was taken over to be
finished for Washington's occupancy, and the men's huts were
laid out roundabout.

After inspecting the position around Middlebrook, Greene
and Washington left Stirling in charge of the camp and together
rode to Philadelphia, to confer with Congress on the complica-
tions of the French alliance and the ever-pressing daily necessities

of food and clothing for the army. They found Mrs. Washington already there, as a guest in the home of Henry Laurens, resting from her annual journey from Mount Vernon to winter headquarters.

The Washingtons enjoyed the hospitality of the President of Congress during the Christmas season. The city had become even more riotously gay under the American commandant Benedict Arnold than during the British occupation under Howe. Arnold was popular with all the wrong people, was criticized for his extravagant style of living, his apparent Tory bias, and his conquests among the ladies, notably the pretty Peggy Shippen, who had been such a belle with the British officers. But Washington knew Arnold for a fine fighting man when his blood was up, and he had given him the Philadelphia appointment because his honorable Saratoga wound kept him still a cripple, unable to stand without the supporting arm of his orderly, and therefore still useless in the field.

It was a further discouragement to Washington while at Philadelphia during that winter of 1778 to realize that Congress had become a commonplace body of selfish politicians, where graft and high living were canceling out the effort of a few noble exceptions like Henry Laurens and the two Morrises, Robert and Gouverneur. Charles Lee was also in Philadelphia, still snarling about the verdict of the Monmouth court-martial. Like Conway before him, Lee could not stop trying to vindicate himself at Washington's expense and had publicly implied that, thanks to his own wisdom and valor at Monmouth, there had been little left for the commander in chief to do but strip the dead. There are always little people ready to snigger at jibes directed at the man in popular favor, just as there are always loyal people longing to silence the detractor forever. Steuben had already challenged Lee to a duel in defense of Washington, and Lee had sidestepped it with adroit explanations of having been misunderstood.

Not so easily to be fobbed off with palaver, young John Laurens sent a challenge to Lee, which was received with a slurring remark about Washington's need of a champion—which so infuriated the aides that the duel somehow took place in a wood outside Philadelphia before Washington got wind of it. Hamilton acted as Laurens's second. Lee's shot missed, and, like Conway, he learned at the cost of a bloody though not fatal wound that it did not pay to slander the commander in chief. Washington was angry at what he considered a frivolous episode, but Laurens *père* was amused and perhaps gratified, and the opposition was squelched again.

With a new campaign ahead of him for 1779, perpetually haunted by depreciated currency and divided councils, Washington could feel only uneasiness amid the festivities devised by Philadelphia society in honor of himself and his wife. Although Mrs. Washington enjoyed the opportunity to visit her friends again before the usual winter austerities at headquarters closed in, they were both glad to escape early in February, 1779, to a crowded, noisy, informal life in the Wallace house near Middlebrook. The carpenters were still at work there and were required to fashion for the commander in chief's wife extra cupboards and conveniences and a little sitting room of her own, with blue and white tiles let into the mantelpiece—a cozy separate retreat from the reception room across the hall where official visitors were sent to wait.

There was also a bedroom upstairs set aside for Lafayette, although he was off to France in January on a mission to speed up the promised aid to America which had begun to arrive in driblets—warm uniforms, flimsy shoes, and blankets too small to cover a brawny American soldier. Practice had improved the ability of the officers and men to erect their villages of huts chinked with mud, but there was always the daily problem of food, because money wouldn't buy enough of anything any more, even when money was to be had. Still, Congress continued to delude itself that French aid would soon relieve them, even fractionally, of their own obligation to provide.

Kitty Greene finally arrived at Middlebrook, bringing with her not only little Washington, now nearly four years old, but the two girl babies, "Patty" and last summer's little newcomer born during the Rhode Island campaign and named Cornelia for a friend in the Lott family. The Greenes were housed in a brick farmhouse on the bank of the Raritan River not far from headquarters. The Knoxes were nearby at Pluckemin, the site of the artillery park, surrounding a building which consisted of a single long room with plastered walls and a dais. Here Knox held what he called "the Academy," or riding and artillery school, where lectures on gunnery, tactics, logistics, and similar subjects were demonstrated on the spot. Lucy Knox had produced her annual addition, another girl, named Julia.

Wayne, Sullivan, and Steuben, all philosophically bachelor as usual, lodged roundabout the neighborhood, Stirling was living *en famille* at his Baskingridge home with his wife and daughter, while some of the younger officers found accommodations at the Van Horne homestead under the same ample roof with five accomplished Van Horne daughters. After Valley Forge, Middlebrook was a paradise.

The weather continued mild that year, and Morristown and Baskingridge were near enough so that the Lott family, the Stirling and Livingston ladies, and other old friends could visit the Middlebrook headquarters. Besides the usual sewing parties and tea drinking in Mrs. Washington's little parlor, there were subscription dances and amateur concerts, charades and readings at which the gentlemen entertained and were entertained. The first anniversary of the French alliance was celebrated with fireworks and a ball held at Knox's "Academy" which the whole countryside attended. Washington wrote his brother that seventy ladies and over three hundred gentlemen were present, and they danced all night. The commander in chief, always an accomplished dancer, opened the ball with Lucy Knox, who, in spite of her girth, was graceful and light on her feet. Greene's lighthearted Kitty was not to be outdone and soon sent out invitations to an evening party at the brick house on the Raritan. When the drawing room was cleared of furniture there was room for six couples to take the floor in a minuet and more for the country dances.

Kitty had recovered her health and figure after the birth of Cornelia and declared recklessly that she could dance forever without sitting down. Washington overheard her and remarked that forever was a long time. Kitty replied saucily that she could dance as long as he could, anyway. Smiling, he rose and bowed and led her out on the floor. When he signaled to the fiddlers the other guests fell in behind them, and the contest was on.

Greene, who was conscious of his stiff knee and his asthma, sat down beside Mrs. Washington, who didn't dance at all, and took out his watch. "We had a little dance at my quarters a few evenings past," he wrote later to a friend in Rhode Island. "His Excellency and Mrs. Greene danced upwards of three hours without once sitting down. Upon the whole, we had a pretty little frisk. Miss Cornelia Lott and Miss Betsy Livingston are here with Mrs. Greene. This moment they have sent for me to drink tea. I must go."

Uneventful as the winter of 1778 and the following spring at Middlebrook might seem in retrospect, it brought Greene a great deal of hard, exasperating and thankless labor. Some of his subordinates and agents were untrustworthy. Some were merely imprudent or ignorant, but the blame always came home to him. The depreciated money caused many mistakes and misunderstandings, for values fluctuated overnight, and the quartermaster department was wantonly accused of overexpenditure.

Congress wasted precious time in endless, profitless discussions without arriving at decisions. Short enlistment terms continued to plague the regimental officers, who could never count on their brigades being at full strength. The countryside around Middlebrook suffered from the inevitable levies made by their own army on stores, cattle, and transport, often where the British had already plundered. When it took sixteen hundred dollars to buy a suit of clothes, there was a halfhearted endeavor to fix a scale of prices, and an attempt was made to pass laws to protect private citizens who owned horses and forage and the always precious wagons. But committees on finance were useless against the daily necessities of the army.

During the deceptive lull while the army lay at Middlebrook there came disturbing news from the South, where at the end of December, 1778, the Carolinian Robert Howe surrendered Savannah to the British seaborne force under Campbell. Lincoln was already at Charleston on the way to Howe's relief, and more detachments, including Pulaski's cavalry, were hurried off from Jersey to Lincoln's support. A new problem then confronted Washington at Middlebrook—how to prevent the British from overrunning the Carolinas while he himself was pinned down on the Hudson-Delaware line of defense which had been drawn to keep them out of Jersey and Philadelphia.

It was an open winter, and spring came early to Middlebrook.

In May, 1779, a military review was staged in honor of a visit from the French Minister Gérard, who had arrived in America the previous summer with D'Estaing and had remained after the sudden departure of his countrymen. A stage with seats for the ladies was erected, and Steuben's pupils outdid themselves beyond the Valley Forge review. Major Harry Lee's Virginia Light Horse, clothed at his expense in smart, short-coated green uniforms with buff underdress, made a sensational display in formal maneuvers for cavalry.

At the beginning of June, 1779, there was ominous activity among the British on the Hudson. The American army was preparing to defend that vital spot at West Point above New York, and the wives were ordered to pack. Kitty Greene set out for Rhode Island after confiding to Mrs. Washington that another baby was due in time to spoil her return to headquarters next winter—unless, she added defiantly, she brought it along and had it there. Mrs. Washington warned her, from hard experience, that they might not be so comfortably situated next winter. Before Lucy Knox started for Boston, the baby Julia had succumbed to a summer teething complaint and was buried in the Dutch churchyard near their Pluckemin headquarters.

The army under Washington had spent that summer of 1779 fortifying West Point and enduring the dull, scant rations, along with an anxious inactivity on the *qui vive*, and the perpetual, humiliating recurrence of general nakedness for lack of an adequate issue of army clothing—while awaiting the French reinforcements and supplies that could be expected to increase after Lafayette's return to America.

John Laurens, having rushed down to South Carolina on leave from headquarters to join the fight for the South, rode all the way back to Jersey to plead for reinforcements for Lincoln at Charleston and to urge Washington to come down himself and turn the British out. It wasn't feasible, he was told. Washington sent his cousin William with some cavalry instead and detached two Virginia regiments, which were all he could spare.

As the autumn of that strange year came in sight, it was evident that the British had wasted the campaigning weather around New York. Nobody had won the war, and Washington was still in the field, unbeaten. He had refused to take the bait of little nuisance raids in Connecticut and New Jersey, and thus lay himself open to an unequal show of force. Clinton, on the other hand, had not been strengthened for any decisive move.

The loss of Savannah had caused repercussions in Congress that led to the renewal of contact with D'Estaing in the West Indies. In late August invigorating news of his imminent return to American waters caused a flurry of correspondence in an attempt to learn his intentions. Acting blindly on the assumption that the French fleet would appear off the Jersey coast as before, Washington again shifted troops toward the Hudson in preparation for joint action with D'Estaing against Clinton at New York if and when the opportunity arose.

Then they could only wait. On September 3 D'Estaing suddenly arrived off the Georgia coast in a position to attack the British garrison at Savannah, which had been in possession there since Robert Howe's surrender to Campbell the previous December.

The humane, efficient Campbell had been recalled to England, and he was succeeded by Augustine Prevost, who had come up from the British posts in Florida to join Campbell at Savannah. Prevost was a tough, seasoned campaigner and had already carried on months of costly sparring with the South Carolina partisan, or guerrilla, forces defending Charleston. As soon as D'Estaing's fleet was sighted off the mouth of the Savannah River, Prevost called in his detachments from Sunbury and Beaufort and prepared to stand a siege at Savannah.

Lincoln scraped together a meager force at Charleston and marched to meet D'Estaing. On September 16, when he reached Miller's plantation three miles from Savannah, he learned that D'Estaing, who was always in a hurry, had already landed troops and summoned the British garrison to surrender "to the arms of France," without reference to America. Prevost was stalling for time until his reinforcements could arrive from the coast.

After a two-week siege under drenching rains, a combined French and American attack on Prevost failed, with disastrous losses. D'Estaing was twice wounded, and the gallant Pulaski was killed. On October 20 D'Estaing suddenly put to sea again, and just as at Rhode Island the year before, he left everything worse than it was when he came. Lincoln retired with his angry and disheartened survivors to Charleston.

The news of the defeat at Savannah reached Washington's Morristown headquarters at the beginning of what was to be the worst winter of the war, surpassing even Valley Forge for pitiless cold, desperate privation, and blasted hopes. For this second Morristown winter Washington occupied with his staff the big white house belonging to the widowed Mrs. Ford, who was allowed to retain one room for the use of herself and her family. His Lifeguards built their huts in the meadow south of the house, and the regiments as they converged on Morristown in December were again set to felling trees and piling logs for the winter cantonment, while the wind tore holes in their sleazy canvas shelters and snow blanketed the ill-clothed men sleeping on straw in tents.

Working "half-leg deep in snow," the soldiers by the first of the year 1780 had constructed a log-house city on the site chosen by Greene, on the hillsides of a place called Jockey Hollow. A system of signal lights and gunfire was arranged to sound the alarm in case of an incursion by the British, who were near enough, it was feared, to attempt a raid to capture the commander in chief. Hunger was a constant companion. In their extremity men gnawed birchbark sticks and even tried to roast and eat the sodden leather of their shoes. Plundering, under the name of foraging, was inevitable though the punishment was severe, and the soldiers, said Washington, "had to eat every kind of horse food but hay."

Though Clinton had been unable to win in the North, he believed that a new opportunity for the British now existed at Charleston. He therefore evacuated Rhode Island and appointed the Hessian general Knyphausen to command the New York garrison, to free himself for the venture. On December 26, 1779, a year after Campbell had set out on a similar enterprise, Clinton embarked with his main army in a fleet commanded by Admiral Arbuthnot. Cornwallis, recently returned from a visit to England during which his beloved wife had died, sailed with Clinton, as did the ruthless green-clad cavalry of young Banastre Tarleton.

It was a nightmare winter voyage. Clinton's ships were buffeted and scattered by gales and mountainous seas and paralyzed by severe cold. The men in the crowded transports suffered acutely, and most of the horses died at sea. Clinton and Cornwallis had learned not to try to take Charleston from its harbor and followed the pattern set for Campbell the year before.

In late January, 1780, Arbuthnot landed them in very bad shape at Tybee, at the mouth of the Savannah River. Collecting all available reinforcements and equipment from the Savannah garrison and sending out a call for Tory militia, Clinton reembarked and on February 14 moved cautiously up the coast to a landing on Simmons (now Seabrook) Island southwest of Charleston at the mouth of the Edisto River. After four years of war and several false alarms, South Carolina was now about to become the cockpit Jersey had been.

The situation somewhat resembled that at New York in the summer of 1776. Lincoln occupied Charleston with a motley force of Continentals and local militia and amateur cavalry and was under pressure to hold the city at all costs, just as Washington had been bound by Congress at Manhattan. He was therefore immobilized in a posture of defense within hastily constructed fortifications. Charleston lay at the end of a marshy peninsula between the Ashley and Cooper rivers. Like Washington at Manhattan, Lincoln had a single escape route—up Charleston Neck and along the Cooper River to the north. If the British could march around the landward defenses and gain a foothold on the neck above the city, while their navy controlled the harbor, Lincoln would be trapped as Washington might have been on Manhattan had he lost the Harlem engagement four years before.

To maintain his line of retreat, Lincoln had posted the South Carolina general Isaac Huger with about five hundred mounted troops at Monck's Corner, near the head of the Cooper River. With Huger were William Washington and John Laurens, each commanding a small cavalry force. Against them Clinton threw out the savage Green Dragoon, Banastre Tarleton, who defeated Huger's whole force at Biggin's Bridge and drove the Americans into the swamps, capturing their horses and stores.

Huger's defeat closed the door on the escape hatch and left Lincoln caught inside Charleston. Webster, Rawdon, and Tarleton were now across the neck, and Charleston was cut off from evacuation as well as from reinforcements.

Clinton held the cards. Knyphausen at New York would give

warning if Washington started to move his army—already weakened by sending detachments to Charleston. A French attack on Arbuthnot's ships in the harbor was unlikely. And instead of coming out to fight where there was room to maneuver, Lincoln was adding every available man to his garrison inside the crowded town.

In a series of well-executed moves Clinton marched up the shore south of Charleston until seven weeks after the landing at Tybee he had erected batteries on the southwest bank of the Ashley River opposite the neck. At the same time Arbuthnot got ships over "the infernal Bar" in the harbor and was anchored off Sullivan's Island where the old 1776 Fort Moultrie still stood. Clinton was able to put his troops across the Ashley River unopposed, and on April 1 he broke ground on the neck for siege works. He sent detachments inland under Tarleton and Cornwallis to find more horses, and these skirmished with scattered detachments coming from the North to Lincoln's aid. On the tenth he summoned Lincoln to surrender.

William Moultrie, modest hero of the 1776 attempt on Charleston, was Lincoln's second-in-command, and he kept a journal of the siege which was later included in his memoirs. Provisions were running short in the city. But "without consulting anyone," Lincoln replied that his duty led him to hold out "to the last extremity." At the same time he undertook to preserve a civil government for South Carolina by persuading Governor John Rutledge to slip through the lines and escape from what even Lincoln recognized as inevitable surrender.

The brothers Rutledge—John, Edward, and Hugh—were among the first citizens of Charleston, and two of them had served as delegates to the Congress at Philadelphia. By the time Lincoln arrived at Charleston John had been unanimously named governor of South Carolina, while Edward and Hugh were with the army. John established headquarters at Orangeburgh, about two hundred miles north of Charleston, and began to recruit militia, though he never wore a uniform and had no military rank.

When Clinton returned for his second attempt on Charleston the Assembly voted Governor Rutledge dictator powers in his absence and he came back to Charleston to discuss the defense of the city. He listened in enigmatic, noncommittal silence to the heroic oratory of the Council, which demanded that Charleston be defended to the last man, and people whispered that Dictator John had lost his nerve. When he consented to leave Charleston secretly they were sure of it, and there were angry sneers and some insulting remarks from the fire-eaters, which he ignored and rode out unchallenged on his big white horse, Caesar. He went to Charlotte, which was then a "hornet's nest" of Patriot volunteers, and from then on, the seat of the South Carolina government was said to be in the governor's saddle.

On the thirteenth of April Clinton opened fire on Charleston with his cannon and mortar batteries. For days the city was subjected to pitiless shellfire, causing numerous casualties among the population, destruction of property and homes, and civilian terror. By the end of the month Lincoln's situation was desperate, and Moultrie recorded in his journal that the fatigue of the garrison was "so great that for want of sleep many faces were so swollen they could hardly see out of their eyes." He added that during one of his visits to an advance redoubt to give the necessary orders "we were constantly skipping about to get out of the way of the shells thrown by their howitzers; they were not more than 100 yards from our works, and throwing the shells in bushels on our front and flanks."

A second summons came from Clinton on May 8, confirming that Fort Moultrie was in his hands and alleging that the remains of the American cavalry had been cut to pieces. Meat and rice had run out in the garrison, sugar and coffee were nearly gone. Lincoln consented to a truce to consider the terms of capitulation, which were harsh. His counter-proposals on the ninth were termed "inadmissible" by Clinton, who added curtly, "Hostilities will in consequence commence afresh at 8 o'clock."

The Americans fired the first gun, and there followed a tremendous cannonade in which, Moultrie wrote, "the fire was incessant the whole night; cannon balls whizzing and shells hissing continually amongst us; ammunition chests and temporary magazines blowing up; great guns bursting and wounded men groaning along the lines. It was a dreadful night! It was our last great effort, but it availed us nothing; on the 11th of May we capitulated and on the morning of the 12th we marched out and gave up the town."

He does not mention that one onlooker saw "tears coursing

down the cheeks of General Moultrie" while Leslie's Royal English Fusiliers and some Hessian Grenadiers planted the British colors by the gate on the ramparts, and Lincoln limped out at the head of his ragged army of defenders. "They were indulged," says a British observer, "with beating a drum and to bring out their colors cased. They laid down their arms between their abatis and surrendered prisoners of war." About 5,000 Americans and armed citizens were lost to the cause of independence in the greatest British triumph of the war.

The first word of the Charleston disaster reached New Jersey on May 29, 1780, via a New York newspaper. Washington, still at Morristown, was at first inclined to doubt the truth of the report, but the evidence was too clear. He sent the *Gazette* on to the President of Congress, with a comment: "Certain I am that unless Congress speaks in a more decisive tone; unless they are vested with powers competent to the great purposes of this war, or assume them as a right; and unless they, and the States respectively, act with more energy than they have hitherto done, our cause is lost."

Chapter 19

Congress promptly demonstrated its inability to learn, either by experience or advice. On June 13 it named the ubiquitous Gates to succeed Lincoln in the Southern command, and it did so without consulting the commander in chief or giving him a chance to propose his own candidate for the post. Nathanael Greene had been too long wasted and unhappy as quartermaster. He had more than once threatened to resign from the army altogether to escape unwarranted censure which amounted to persecution. He had also been threatened with dismissal for the insubordinate tone of his protests to Congress. He was by now obviously overdue in the field, where his leadership and popularity were badly needed.

Lafayette returned to Morristown from France in May, 1780, bringing with him the promise of reinforcements under the command of the Comte de Rochambeau, a grandee veteran of the European wars. But before Rochambeau could arrive, Clinton and Arbuthnot returned to New York from their triumph at Charleston. Clinton had brought Leslie with him and left Cornwallis in the South "with sufficient force to keep it against the world"—expecting him to consolidate a supposedly uncontested British rule over the Carolinas, which, after Lincoln's surrender, were defended only by scattered guerrilla, or partisan, forces under Marion, Sumter, and Pickens.

Washington's usual distracting need for troops and equipment now became a nearly fatal handicap again, and he feared that the French general would refuse to believe that the ragtag regiments which were all he could produce were capable of conducting a campaign alongside the fresh, well-drilled and accoutered soldiers of Louis XVI. At the same time he was obliged to relinquish everything he could spare in detachments to equip Gates, who was required to confront Cornwallis in the Carolinas.

Gates set out southward on June 26 to overtake and outrank de Kalb, who had been given a small force of Maryland and Delaware troops with which to reinforce Lincoln at Charleston. Fortunately they had not arrived there in time to be swallowed up in the surrender with the rest of Lincoln's men. After Lincoln had been taken prisoner the Southern command devolved on de Kalb, who could only continue doggedly on his line of march through North Carolina in the hope of being joined along the way by an effective partisan force with which to harry Cornwallis. He was encamped at Buffalo Ford on the Deep River in North Carolina on the road to Camden when Gates caught up with him on July 25. De Kalb felt only relief, uncomplicated by any jealousy of rank, at being ordered to turn over the command to the *soi-disant* victor of Saratoga.

The heartening news of Rochambeau's arrival at Newport reached the Jersey headquarters on July 14. Although Heath was in command there since the British evacuation, Lafayette was at once dispatched with letters of welcome and a first outline of Washington's cherished plan for a combined operation from Rhode Island against New York, where Clinton was reestablished in the glow of his Southern victory. Convoyed to Rhode Island by Admiral de Ternay, the French force comprised only the first division of the corps of 12,000 soldiers promised by King Louis to aid the United States in its struggle for independence from France's old enemy, England.

The French landed at Newport on a foggy, dismal day which by evening was enlivened by fireworks, illuminations, and the pealing of bells in honor of the new allied forces. The elegant white French uniforms, faced with pastel shades of rose, blue, lavender and gold, the silk regimental colors, the polished buttons and accouterments, and the ballroom bearing and manners of the newcomers were regarded with amazement but no derision by the tattered American contingent occupying the fortified posts and camps which were thrown open to the visitors.

The Jersey camps soon began to bustle with preparations for joining Rochambeau's force by a general move across the Hudson. The troops were ordered to begin a thorough sprucing up and tightening of discipline, which was an almost hopeless undertaking in view of the state of the commissary and the worthlessness of whatever money could be scraped up to spend.

Then, as usual, came the inevitable reversal of Washington's reviving hopes. On July 13, before the French were even well settled in, the British Admiral Graves arrived off Sandy Hook to reinforce Arbuthnot at New York, and by the end of the month the British fleet had blockaded the French in Narragansett Bay. Clinton appeared to be loading transports at New York for an immediate attack on Rhode Island, and Washington was not able even to muster an adequate detachment to support Rochambeau at Newport. It was a new humiliation to be borne with his usual equanimity, while he did the next best thing—he moved troops across the Hudson as though intending to attack New York in

Clinton's rear. The feint succeeded, causing Clinton to turn his transports around to reoccupy the city in force. Washington then fell back to his Jersey posts.

Admiral de Ternay, a sick, aging man, was haunted by the example of D'Estaing in Rhode Island and showed no stomach for a fight there with the odds against him. He was further depressed to learn that the second division of the French force was blockaded at Brest by a British navy squadron and could not be expected to reach America before autumn, when it would be too late in the year for any military undertaking.

Rochambeau began entrenching, as though for a long stay where he was. He considered the youthful Lafayette an inadequate representative of the American commander in chief, and the Marquis returned a little crestfallen to the American camp. Washington perceived that only an interview between himself and the crusty French veteran would clarify a virtual stalemate.

At this critical point calamity struck again, and Gates's long run of good luck at last failed to conceal his incapacities. The inevitable disaster overtook him at Camden in South Carolina on August 16, 1780.

Little had been heard of Gates in the five or six weeks since he led the march southward to join de Kalb in the attempt to head off Cornwallis before he could reach Virginia. The first incredible rumors of the engagement at Camden indicated a total defeat and destruction of Gates's army by Cornwallis. Confirmation of the disaster reached Washington at Hackensack on the fourth of September in the midst of his preparations for the meeting with Rochambeau which had been arranged to take place at Hartford, halfway between their respective headquarters.

A council of war assembled around him to consider the situation which must now be presented to the imposing French general who had already formed an unfavorable estimate of his American colleagues. Gradually the horrific details of the debacle at Camden trickled in at Hackensack. Against the advice of his staff and to the amazement of his field officers, Gates had attempted a night surprise against the British base established at Camden under Rawdon. This maneuver entailed a dark march through sultry heat along roads that were deep with sand or soggy with swamp water—by ill-trained men who had been sub-sisting on green field corn and unripe peaches, with an occasional ration of fresh unsalted beef. This debilitating diet was not reme-died by a last-minute issue of molasses in place of the rum ration that had not arrived.

Gates's natural-born incompetence was then supplemented by a monstrous coincidence of timing. The British army, informed of his presence in the neighborhood, had been set in motion at the same hour of the same night with the same objective—a surprise attack at dawn. It met the Continental force head on, about 2:00 A.M., where the road across Saunders Creek ran along a narrow rise between two swamps in a pine forest. There was a sudden blaze of pistol and musket fire, and the chilling British huzzah mingled with random shouts and shrieks from the American ranks as the British gunfire took toll. Then, as if by mutual consent, the shooting ceased and both armies paused blindly in the dark.

When daylight came, it could be seen that the lines were very close together and that the position would give the advantage to the British, whose flanks were better protected by swampy land. Long before the sun was visible in the humid morning haze the British drums were beating to arms. The American drums hastily replied, and de Kalb rode out to take a position in front of his Maryland and Delaware brigades.

Gates and his staff withdrew to the rear of the American lines, and Gates learned to his astonishment that Cornwallis himself had arrived from Charleston and was leading the British and that Tarleton's formidable green-clad dragoons had also joined the Camden garrison. Gates's adjutant, Colonel Otho Williams of Maryland, remained with de Kalb in the front line and left an eyewitness account of what followed.

The smoke of battle would not rise on the dank, still air of the swamp, and it was therefore impossible to see the effect of the gunfire on either side—except that nothing was going to stop the British. Soon the artillery of both armies was playing furiously, and the din was laced through with the rattle of drums and the sharp sweet notes of the cavalry bugles. With his own brigade firm as a rock at his back, de Kalb actually began to push forward in vicious hand-to-hand fighting, his cheery orders still coming with the rhythmic precision of the parade ground, though he was soon bleeding from two wounds. Then he was down, entangled beneath his horse, and his aide was seen to help him to his feet and bind up a sword-cut on the Baron's head with his own sash, while imploring him to retire from the field. De Kalb brushed him aside and led a bayonet charge on foot over heaps of slain and took fifty kilted prisoners from the British 71st, a Highland light infantry regiment.

But Tarleton's green dragoons came thundering in, and Stevens's Virginians took to the swamp. De Kalb lost his footing and went down again, while on all sides of him frantic officers laid the flat of their swords to American infantrymen who fled "like leaves before the wind," and de Kalb's devoted aide tried to protect his prostrate general with his own body, crying out his name against the rattle and pound of the cavalry charge that swept over them.

Gates was "carried away," as he later explained, from his strong position in the rear by the flight of his militia. He was mounted on a fleet Virginia horse which brought him to Charlotte by nightfall, and some of his officers managed to keep up with him. He had arranged no rendezvous in the event of a retreat, and when Williams found his way to Charlotte in his wake, Gates had already departed for Hillsboro on a fresh horse. Those who were left of the companies who had escaped death or capture by taking to the swamps straggled on to Hillsboro after him. They were exhausted and beaten and hungry, but Gates was all the commander they had, and they rallied to him.

The militia had broken too soon, the Continentals had stood fast too long. Cornwallis was free to remove his wounded and prisoners to Camden, where de Kalb died of eleven wounds. The colonies had lost an army by capture at Charleston and another at Camden by annihilation. It looked now as though they had lost the war.

The council at headquarters in Jersey could only stare at each other in speechless dismay. Two armies had been swallowed up in the Carolinas, along with irreplaceable officers. Lincoln was a prisoner. Gates was a discredited fugitive. De Kalb was dead. The British could reinforce Cornwallis by sea for a northward drive that would be almost unopposed. What, if anything, could be done to meet the threat of a British army, supported by control of the Chesapeake, running free across the undefended Virginia countryside till it reached New Jersey from the south, while Clinton remained in a position to close in from New York on the north? The French, frozen by the British blockade in the Rhode Island fortifications behind Clinton, would be of little use then, and Congress's hasty plans for calling up new bodies of militia, which only melted away homeward as soon as they were half trained, were wasteful and of no lasting value. And now a tough old British sea-dog, Admiral Rodney, had joined another twelve sail of the line and their attendant frigates to Clinton's strength at New York, so that the safe arrival at Newport of the French second division became more unlikely every day.

The question of Clinton's next move, now that Admiral Rodney was also present on the chessboard, occupied everyone's mind. Speculation was divided between the possibility of an all-out British attack on the French at Newport, or the likelihood of another seaborne expedition aimed at the mouth of the Cape Fear River in North Carolina, where Wilmington stood to suffer Savannah's fate, or possibly Portsmouth on the James in Virginia.

The loss of face before their French allies was humiliating beyond expression, but the scheduled first meeting between Washington and Rochambeau at Hartford must still be carried off with dignity and determination. There was yet another complication. The hard feelings between Greene and Congress had worsened during the summer and in August resulted in Greene's final resignation as quartermaster and the appointment of the acerbic Timothy Pickering to succeed him.

Among Washington's preparations for the conference at Hartford was the choice of an officer best fitted to deputize for him in Jersey, in case Clinton made a sudden stab in that direction. On September 16 he spelled it out for Greene and for everyone else concerned.

"In my absence the command of the army devolves upon you," he wrote the erstwhile quartermaster. "I have such entire confidence in your prudence and abilities that I leave the conduct of it to your discretion, with only one observation: that with our present prospects it is not our business to seek an action, nor to accept one, except upon advantageous terms."

The army was to be collected and moved to the old campground at Tappan, closer to the banks of the Hudson—an exercise which, thanks to Steuben's training, could now be accomplished with a minimum of confusion and delay. Greene's marching orders issued for September 19, after Washington's departure, illustrated the professionalism which the German drillmaster had managed to impose upon what might have been a disorganized mob of undisciplined, ill-equipped, and discouraged men.

Every drumbeat and bugle call had its meaning and was understood by all, as the orders were passed from brigade to brigade and regiment to regiment. It was only a day's march, and by nightfall Greene was able to report to Washington that he had relocated at Tappan and that "nothing material has happened in the army since your Excellency left camp."

On the evening of September 26, 1780, as Greene was about to put down his pen and choose a book to relax his mind for a night's repose, a letter was brought to him by a steaming express rider from the Hudson, where Washington had arrived at West Point on his way back from the Hartford conference. It was in Hamilton's handwriting and presumably contained an account of the momentous meeting between Washington and Rochambeau, at which the French-speaking aides would have been present. Greene expected from it some intimation of when the headquarters party would be arriving at the Tappan camp. He opened it eagerly and read:

"There has just been unfolded at this place a scene of the blackest treason. Arnold has fled to the enemy. André, the British Adjutant-general, is in our possession as a spy. His capture unravelled the mystery. West Point was to have been the sacrifice. All the dispositions have been made for the purpose, and 'tis possible, though not probable, tonight may see the execution.

"I advise you putting the army under marching orders, and detaching a brigade immediately this way."

Greene allowed himself no time for stupefaction but sacrificed the rest of the night making out orders and writing a letter to the President of Congress to accompany Hamilton's, which he forwarded by another express rider to Philadelphia. Between three and four o'clock of that morning Washington's instructions arrived, putting the whole army under marching orders. Greene had already sent off two brigades in consequence of Hamilton's letter.

The following day Washington, looking a little more impassive than usual, arrived at the Tappan camp with the prisoner. The court for André's trial sat in the old Dutch church in Tappan village, and Greene was given the painful duty of presiding. Clinton made every possible effort to save the life of his agent, who had recklessly transgressed his orders by wearing civilian dress as a disguise, while carrying incriminating papers proving espionage. The execution was delayed while Greene was required to receive Clinton's deputy in futile negotiations for André's release. A legend exists that Greene held firm to the stipulation that if he gave up André the British must give up Arnold. But true to the tradition that no deserter was ever returned to his own certain execution, the idea of an exchange, Arnold for André, met only with an indignant British refusal, and the last stern duty remained to be performed.

Washington and his staff were not present in the hollow square at the execution of André, though the muffled drums and marching feet of the grim ceremony must have been audible at the general's desk where he and Hamilton continued doggedly to work at his interminable correspondence. But Greene had to be there, as his duty required, on horseback in the group of stony-faced officers who had sat with him in judgment at the trial—to return André's punctilious salute as the young British major, clad in his gorgeous scarlet regimentals, passed by on his way to the gallows.

Chapter 20

The sensation in Rhode Island can be imagined, when Kitty
Greene revealed to the governor the story of Arnold's perfidy as
told to her in a letter from her husband. Arnold had been there
among them with Spencer in the early spring of 1777, after Clinton's landing at Newport. He was remembered at Providence as a
spirited and popular figure, and the Assembly had nothing but
admiration for him. From Providence he had gone to his heroic
conduct at Saratoga, where he received the wound that earned
him the inactive post as commandant at Philadelphia after the
British evacuation. His behavior there, as evidence of his gradual
moral deterioration, was not generally known as far away as
Rhode Island. In spite of the criticism leveled at his extravagance
and his marriage to the Tory belle Peggy Shippen, his request
for a transfer from Philadelphia to the strategic command at
West Point had been granted by Washington as proof of the
commander in chief's misplaced confidence in Arnold's basic
integrity.

It might well be considered as a sign of "divine protection" of
the American cause, as Greene had piously suggested, that Arnold's intended betrayal of West Point did not include a kidnap
plot during Washington's Hartford journey. An attempt to seize
the commander in chief then would have been a perfectly feasible
venture from Clinton's New York base. The scheme to deliver

West Point to the British failed of completion by only a matter of hours and a fortunate coincidence, while Washington himself was on the spot and defenseless. It was not the first time, nor the last, that the least imaginative historian is forced to pause and ask himself: How did we win this war?

Washington's own reaction at West Point can hardly be contemplated. Lincoln, Gates, Arnold—a record of failure and incompetence and treachery that would have broken a less resolute and inspired leader. One can only wonder again at the source of his strength of will to persevere in the teeth of one disabling catastrophe after another. Without doubt the presence of the few staunch and openhearted men like Knox and Nathanael Greene who were left to him played a part in his incredible ability to endure.

His arrival at the tidy, if troubled, camp at Tappan must have seemed to him like release from nightmare, after the starchy interview with Rochambeau at Hartford, where, with Lafayette as interpreter, Washington, Rochambeau, and de Ternay remained closeted together all day. One of Rochambeau's French aides reported with Gallic skepticism: "They separated quite charmed with one another, at least they said so."

Behind the closed door three possible courses of action were discussed, but none was decided upon. According to Washington, "We could only combine possible plans on the supposition of possible events, and engage mutually to do everything in our powers against the next campaign." So it was in his chronic state of disappointed, patient fortitude that he had encountered the hours of tension and tragedy at West Point, where he had found Peggy Shippen Arnold in hysterics and a group of white-faced officers professing their own criminal ignorance of the plot. But there was to be a grim satisfaction in his choice of a successor to Arnold at West Point—one totally reliable deputy, the Quaker general Greene.

With the approach of another autumn it was time again to think of winter quarters. Washington favored a position somewhere in the New York Highlands, for the sake of maintaining communications with Newport as well as proximity to West Point, which had given them all such a scare. A detachment was being garrisoned there, and on October 7, 1780, Greene was writing to Kitty, who had been complaining again of the long separations army life imposed upon them: "I am this moment going to begin my march for West Point, which place, and the troops on the east side of the North River, I am to have command of. It is yet uncertain what disposition will be made for the winter. Perhaps I may spend the winter there, perhaps not. The situation is not much to my liking, there being little prospect of glory or comfort; and therefore I am almost afraid to give you an invitation to come and see me. The situation and many circumstances are against it; nevertheless I leave it altogether with you. Mrs. Knox, too, hopes to pass the winter there."

Marching his two brigades up the west bank of the Hudson, he arrived at West Point on October 8 and found conditions there so poor for man and beast that he protested to a friend in Congress that "the total want of every species of supplies I fear will prove fatal to us." Nevertheless, he sent an escort named Hubbard to conduct the always impatient Kitty to West Point and began to count the days which would bring the end of October when she might be expected to arrive.

He then received a disturbing letter from Knox, written at the Jersey camp Greene had just left: "I am informed (not from Headquarters) that General Gates is recalled to answer to the Congress some matters respecting the geography of the Southern States, and that his Excellency is directed to send some general in his stead. Who will that person be? You may ask me the same question, but I protest I know not, for I have had no opportunity of deriving knowledge where it is to be found, since I heard of Gates's recall. Poor fellow! The heat of the Southern climate has blasted the laurels of Saratoga which were thought from their splendor to be evergreen!"

Now that the damage had been done, at Camden, Congress was finally willing to listen to a proposal from the commander in chief. Washington seized the opportunity to show his own confidence in Greene, in a way which would act as a public declaration that the various Congressional complaints against Greene's administration of the quartermaster department were false and unfounded. The time had also come to deprive himself of his own right arm, but as usual he did not flinch from necessity. In an-

nouncing the appointment to Greene he wrote as a friend rather
than as a commanding officer:

"Congress having been pleased to authorize me to appoint an
officer to take command of the Southern Army, in the room of
General Gates, I have thought proper to choose you for this purpose. You will, therefore, proceed without delay to the Southern
Army now in North Carolina, and take command accordingly.

"Uninformed as I am of the enemy's force in that quarter, or
of our own, and the resources which it will be in our power to
command for carrying on the war, I can give you no particular
instructions, but must leave you to govern yourself entirely according to your own prudence and judgment, and the circumstances in which you find yourself.

"I am aware that the nature of the command will offer you
embarrassments of a singular and complicated nature; but I rely
upon your abilities and exertions for everything your means will
enable you to effect. I give you a letter to Congress, informing
them of your appointment and requesting them to give you such
powers and such support as your situation and the good of the
service demand. You will take their orders at Philadelphia in your
way southward.

"I propose to them to send Baron Steuben to the southward
with you. His talents, knowledge of service, zeal, and activity will
make him very useful to you in all respects, and particularly in
the formation and regulation of the raw troops who will princi-
pally compose the Southern Army. You will give him a command
suitable to his rank, besides employing him as Inspector-general.
If Congress approves it, he will take your orders at Philadelphia.
I have put Major [Henry] Lee's corps under marching orders,
and as soon as he is ready shall detach him to join you.

"I suppose that General Heath, if not already at West Point, is
on his way there from Rhode Island. I write to him to take command of the post. I have only to add, that I wish for your earliest
arrival here. . . ."

Greene had longed more than once during the unhappy days
of his quartermastering for an opportunity to distinguish himself
in the field, and now that he received, out of the blue, an independent command it came as a very mixed blessing. Hubbard

could have no more than reached Kitty at Coventry with the invitation to join him at West Point for another winter of domestic companionship, however uncomfortable the surroundings. She could hardly travel faster now, even if urged to make haste. She always made haste to come to him, and it would be unwise to upset her along the way with what would be for her very unwelcome news. The children sometimes delayed her, whether she brought them with her or arranged to leave them behind with his brothers, and now there was the baby born at Morristown last winter to be considered. What would his tempestuous Kitty say to this latest blow?

He had left Rhode Island the last time in considerable distress of mind over the disastrous D'Estaing episode, hurrying back to Washington's side at Middlebrook. She had been able to join him belatedly there, and they had all contrived some gaiety in spite of the ravages of the war. Since then she had shared with him the hardships of the second Morristown winter—the worst of all— after making a reckless journey to reach that camp in time for the birth of her fourth child. Little Nat was born at Morristown during a blizzard at the end of January, 1780, and the whole army partook of his father's pride when the ordeal was safely over. Pathetic little gifts, lovingly contrived by the numb fingers of men who were faint with hunger, had been brought to the Greenes' door. Kitty had cried over them and cried again because there was nothing to offer in return except her gratitude and compassion.

His second son was the first child at whose birth Greene had been present. Now, at West Point, as he contemplated a suddenly more uncertain future than before, he realized that quite apart from Kitty's present disappointment and his own at the abrupt change in their immediate prospects, his Rhode Island affairs had been left too long in the hands of his brothers, loyal though such stewardship might be. He had the children's future to think of, if not his own. He must somehow provide.

After a sleepless night, while his mind roved uneasily around the possibility of obtaining some brief reprieve, he took up his pen to reply to the commander in chief:

"Your excellency's letter appointing me to the command of the

Southern Army was delivered to me last evening," he wrote slowly, unhappy to add even the shadow of his reluctance to Washington's burdens. "I will prepare myself for the command as soon as I can. But as I have been five years and upwards in service, during which time I have paid no attention to the settlement of my domestic concerns, if it was possible I should be glad to spend a few days at home before I set out to the southward, especially as it is altogether uncertain how long my command may continue, or what deaths or accidents may happen during my absence.

"General Heath arrived here last evening, and will take command this morning. I shall make him fully acquainted with all the dispositions I have made, and will give him my opinion what is best to be done to carry into execution your Excellency's instructions for putting the garrison here into a proper state of defense and prepare it for the approaching winter. . . ."

Contemplating Greene's unusual hesitation and private anxieties, Washington's mind no doubt went back to that June day in Philadelphia five years before when the command of the whole Continental army had been laid on his shoulders. He had not seen fit then to allow himself the luxury of a brief return to Mount Vernon to put his own affairs in order and bid his wife goodbye for a long absence. Nor had he had any opportunity since then to visit his home on the Potomac, being compelled by his sense of duty and the daily pressures of his office to leave Mount Vernon in the hands of his cousin Lund.

He did not see fit now to grant Greene the indulgence he had steadfastly denied himself. British troops had already embarked from New York, probably for Charleston, and were believed to be under orders to cooperate with Cornwallis, who since Camden had advanced as far as Charlotte in North Carolina. He replied inflexibly that he wished to see Greene at the Jersey headquarters without further delay. Before his letter could arrive at West Point, Greene had sensibly given over thoughts of going home and wrote Washington that he realized that "the time it would take, and the state of the Southern Department, would not admit of the indulgence." He could not resist a mention of the main cause of his request for delay, knowing that it would find understanding and compassion in Washington's own loneliness. "When I marched here from Tappan," he added, "I wrote to Mrs. Greene to come to camp, and I expect her here every hour. Should I set out before her arrival, the disappointment of not seeing me, added to the shock of my going southward, I am very apprehensive will have some disagreeable effect on her health, especially as her apprehensions were all alive before there was the least probability of it. My baggage sets out in the morning, and my stay here shall not be more than a day longer, whether Mrs. Greene arrives or not."

That was easy to say, out of his desire to spare Washington worry of any kind. But there had been no word from Kitty or from Hubbard, and so far she had no more reason than usual to keep him informed of her progress toward camp. He could only stiffen himself to write the now overdue letter to Kitty which he well knew would be read in a storm of tears and anger.

But the willful hope of her arrival in time would not die. On the evening of the twentieth Greene crossed the river and rode out as far as Peekskill on the chance of meeting her coming in. The road was empty, and the few travelers he encountered were sure they had not passed her along the way. Back at West Point, he sat down to compose one last farewell letter, to be entrusted to the colonel of the garrison and forwarded to her as soon as her whereabouts could be learned:

"My dear Angel—

"I am this moment setting off for the southward, having kept expresses flying all night to see if I could hear anything of you. But as there was not the least intelligence of your being on the road, necessity obliges me to depart. As I shall ride very fast, and make a stop of only one or two days at Headquarters, and about the same time at Philadelphia, it will be impossible for you to catch up with me. Therefore, whatever things you have for me, you will please to forward by the express who will await you.

"I have been almost distracted, I wanted to see you so much before I set out. My fears of being ordered southward was what made me hurry away Hubbard at such an early hour. God grant you patience and fortitude to bear the disappointment. My apprehensions for your safety distresses me exceedingly. If heaven preserves us until we meet, our felicity will repay all the painful moments of a long separation. I am forever and forever yours, most sincerely and affectionately, NATH. GREENE."

He spent a short time at Washington's Preakness headquarters, which were located in the handsome brick Dey house off the Pompton road. Here, in unaccustomed comfort, he sat again around the council table with Washington, Hamilton, Wayne, and Knox, receiving from the commander in chief the latest instructions prepared for him. He was directed to pause at Philadelphia to deliver letters to Congress and receive from them such powers and orders as his situation required.

At Philadelphia a letter from the sympathetic colonel at West Point contained only an account of the conflicting reports on her failure to reach West Point or to communicate with him there. It did not do to speculate that some mischance might have befallen her during the journey. The only conclusion must be that she was still safe at Coventry, having despaired of getting to him in time.

The mystery of her delay remains to this day, resting on the habitual failure of communications in those chancy times and the frequent miscarriage of letters sent out in the vicinity of enemy patrols.

Greene's previous sojourns in Philadelphia had mostly been spent in acrimonious discussions of quartermaster business. This time his reception was a little different, and for once Congress was prompt to pass a series of resolutions in aid of his new department's needs. It remained to be seen what the good intentions of Congress would be worth a short while hence.

He hoped to assemble and equip a "flying camp" of eight hundred light horse and 1,000 infantry. With this modest force and the always unpredictable militia, he hoped to make life so difficult for the enemy as to hinder their advance and subsistence north of Charlotte. Knox had promised him artillery, and at the end of October he wrote from Philadelphia urging its immediate dispatch, adding that his army so far was "rather a shadow than a substance, having merely an imaginary existence."

Unlike Gates, he believed that cavalry could be useful in the partisan warfare which was all he expected to be able to perform. He requested the promotion of Major Henry Lee to colonel and one of Lee's captains to major to form and lead a mounted legion of light horse, which was soon to become famous for its ability to nip at the heels of the clumsy British columns and to beat the British foraging parties to vital sources of supply.

Greene was hopelessly short of arms, artificers, blankets, clothing, and hospital supplies, all of which it was useless to expect to obtain from the Southern states he was trying to save. He appealed to the Philadelphia merchants themselves for contributions on a deferred payment basis. The merchants in a body excused themselves on the ground that they had already promised more than they could deliver. It was discovered that three "small, decent caps" could be made out of three old-fashioned cocked or flopped hats and the pieces thereof and that short coats could be contrived out of the tattered long ones. For shoes there was no substitute. He was frantic for wagons.

While he was at Philadelphia the first good news arrived since long before the debacle at Camden. Some mountain riflemen led by Southern officers nobody in Philadelphia had ever heard of had caught Major Ferguson's Tory force of regulars and militia at King's Mountain near the Up Country border of North and South Carolina and in a savage battle had very nearly wiped them out, with terrible losses to the British, including Major Ferguson himself. The intimidated Patriots of the Up Country might now be expected to rally to Greene's support.

At the last moment of his Philadelphia stay it developed that the sum furnished by Congress for his traveling expenses was typically insufficient for his needs, since it must be divided between himself and Steuben, who was to make the journey with him. He asked for more, and it was grudgingly granted, up to a fantastic $180,000, in depreciated bills not worth a fraction of their face value.

On November 3, 1780, two years after Lincoln, Greene left Philadelphia with a last backward glance for Kitty and took the road leading southward into history.

Chapter 21

A man could hardly have asked for better company than Greene had that wintry morning on the road out of Philadelphia.

Steuben's title of "Baron" was said to be his own invention, but there was nothing else counterfeit about the stout, genial Prussian who was two years older than Washington and claimed to have served as aide-de-camp to Frederick the Great. Retired and at his ease, he had encountered Franklin and Deane at Paris and was persuaded by French sympathizers with the American cause to abandon his European career and undertake to reorganize and discipline Washington's ragtag army. It was as a volunteer adventurer at the age of forty-seven that he had arrived at the temporary capital at York during the terrible winter of 1777–78 and was named inspector general with the rank of major general and sent on to Valley Forge in place of the unpopular Conway.

His New York aide, Benjamin Walker, had by now managed to pick up considerable German and had somehow imparted to the Baron and to his French aide an adequate amount of laughable English. Steuben still considered him indispensable and never tired of recalling Walker's first diffident entrance into the linguistic deadlock on the parade ground at Valley Forge. "If I had seen an angel from heaven I could not have been more rejoiced!" Steuben would relate, wheezing with his infectious laughter.

Walker became a devoted companion to "the Baron," as he was affectionately known to all, and rode at his side that November morning in 1780, along with the secretary-aide, Captain Duponceau, who had accompanied him to America.

Duponceau was too shortsighted to be a soldier, but he could see a pretty girl at any distance and was good at the endless paper work that came to Steuben's desk. It was his habit also to lend his secretarial services freely to Washington's overworked staff while at headquarters. His health was always poor, and he had just recovered from one of his prostrating illnesses when he rejoined Steuben at Philadelphia in the autumn of 1780. In his journal he recorded his own surprise when, in the evenings at the end of the day's travel, the conversation turned on literature, and Greene showed familiarity with the Latin classics and was observed to be carrying with him a Latin volume for his bedtime reading. Greene's aides were Major Burnett and Colonel Morris.

At Annapolis they found the Maryland Legislature in session, and Greene laid before them a detailed statement of his needs and the necessity of giving prompt attention to those of the states farther south which he was trying to save. The responsibility of reminding the members of their promises and forwarding the supplies they collected was left with General Gist, the Baltimore merchant who had led the Maryland regiment at the battle of Long Island and who with Smallwood had supported de Kalb at Camden. Gist had only escaped capture that day by taking to the swamp with other fugitives when Tarleton's terrible dragoons thundered in. He had not rejoined Gates at Charlotte after the battle.

They found Baltimore full of rumors, most of them falsely optimistic—except one, which said that the British were in possession of the James River. On the twelfth of November they were hospitably received at Mount Vernon by Washington's proxy, his cousin Lund, and Mrs. Washington. The commander in chief's wife was on the verge of her annual departure for winter headquarters, which were located this year at New Windsor on the Hudson above West Point.

At Fredericksburg, where they expected to find Weedon, who kept a tavern there before he joined the army in time for the retreat from Manhattan, his wife welcomed them cordially. They learned from her that her husband was out with the militia called up to confront the British, who were said to have occupied Portsmouth. Pressing on, they arrived at Richmond on the sixteenth.

Everything there was confusion and alarm, for though the British expedition under General Leslie at Portsmouth had re-embarked, their ships still lay in Hampton Roads. The reason for their sudden withdrawal from the mouth of the James was still uncertain, for the little force of ill-equipped militia gathered on the west bank by Weedon and the parson-general Muhlenberg were hardly intimidating to British regulars.

Thomas Jefferson was now governor of Virginia, and Greene addressed him in urgent detail on the gravity of the situation and the importance of his being supplied by the Southern states with the wherewithal for their defense. Jefferson managed, by stupendous effort, to collect all of thirty wagons instead of the hundred requested. The draft of Virginia militia had fallen short by two thirds, and the men who appeared lacked clothing, weapons and ammunition.

During the six days he spent in Richmond Greene was busy with his correspondence, reminding everyone from New Windsor to Annapolis of their promises and of his increasing needs. Even in the midst of daily disappointments and exertions, his mind would return to the little family he had left behind him, and from Richmond he sent a letter to Washington to be forwarded to Mrs. Greene "by the first safe conveyance."

While at Richmond he reluctantly detached Steuben to take command of whatever forces could be raised in Virginia, with instructions for the inspection and forwarding of stores from there, the appointment of a deputy quartermaster, and other matters of military organization in which the old professional was so capable. And at this time he acquired two young unemployed Virginia officers as aides—William Pearce and Nathaniel Pendleton.

Riding on, he was informed at Petersburg that the enemy had returned to Portsmouth, and he notified Steuben to take charge of the defense of Virginia. At Hillsboro, where the North Carolina Legislature sat and where they had received Gates's first calamitous report of his broken army, Greene could learn only that Gates had gone, some said to Salisbury, some said as far as Charlotte, which had been abandoned by Cornwallis after King's Mountain in an unexpected withdrawal of his whole army southward to Winnsboro. "No information of any kind can be obtained here," Greene wrote to Steuben on November 27, "which determines me to move on without loss of time."

And so, continuing the fantastic search for a misplaced army, he reached Charlotte on December 2 and went straight to Gates's headquarters in the little square. What he found there requires the introduction of some hitherto unexplored characters, not all of whom were strangers to him, and who were to become his trusted companions during the crucial weeks ahead.

The arrival of Greene at Charlotte was anticipated with some uneasiness by the officers at Gates's headquarters, who would not have been surprised if Gates had made some sort of embarrassing scene when he was required to transfer the command to Greene, with whom he had never been friendly. On the contrary, Gates received his successor with dignity and composure—and perhaps with some secret relief. At least there was no outward sign of the conceit and arrogance of rank which had hitherto marred his reputation and popularity. Greene's conduct in the trying circumstances was as always modest, courteous, and tactful. Their first meeting, in the words of Gates's adjutant general, Colonel Otho Williams, was "an elegant lesson of propriety, exhibited on a most delicate occasion."

A Maryland man himself, Williams was a competent judge of good manners, being a model eighteenth-century gentleman, tall, handsome, accomplished, and much beloved by his fellow officers and the men under his command. He had been taken prisoner at Fort Washington in 1776, and after fourteen months in the appalling provost jail in New York he had been exchanged and promoted colonel of the 6th Marylands, who fought at Monmouth and more recently had stood firm in support of de Kalb at Camden. He shared with another Marylander, Colonel John Eager Howard, the command of the two Maryland battalions that had been pieced together out of the leftovers from Camden to form a regiment of Continental veterans.

Howard, born to wealth and large estates outside Baltimore, and bred a Tory, had abandoned all his comfortable prospects to turn soldier and had distinguished himself with the 5th Marylands at Monmouth and Germantown. He had accompanied de Kalb's march southward and, like Williams, had taken heavy casualties at Camden in de Kalb's heroic stand. Howard's "equanimity" in battle was famous, as was his reliance on Steuben's favorite weapon, the bayonet, which his men were trained to use with cool ferocity. After Gates's departure from Charlotte for Philadelphia, Williams became adjutant general to Greene, and his written record of the ensuing campaign is a stirring account of daily hardship and courage.

Greene was gratified by the presence at Charlotte of William Washington, the burly young kinsman of the commander in chief, last seen in Jersey before he was sent with his cavalry troop to support Lincoln in South Carolina in 1779. Being outside the city of Charleston at the time of its surrender, the previous May, young Washington had since then survived several sharp brushes with Tarleton's green-coated dragoons and was now able to bring his small mounted force to join Greene at Charlotte.

Also awaiting Greene's arrival was that almost legendary leader of fighting men, the mighty Virginian Dan Morgan. Like General Washington, Morgan had seen the old Indian wars and had served under Braddock. Half his teeth had been shot away by a bullet that passed through his left cheek. After taking an active part in the fighting in Canada and at Saratoga and Monmouth, he so suffered from rheumatism that he had resigned from the army in the summer of 1779 and retired to his Virginia home called Soldier's Rest, up near what is now Berryville. He remained inactive there for twelve months, enjoying the companionship of his wife and children. Then Charleston fell, and Gates, of whom he had never had a high opinion, lost Camden. Morgan collected a few followers, presented himself at Gates's roadside headquarters, and asked simply what he could do. Gates had had the sense to welcome him, and gave him the command of a newly formed light infantry corps with which to harry British outposts.

Among the new acquaintances Greene was to make at Charlotte was Isaac Huger, the South Carolinian whose grandfather's French name was now pronounced "U-gee" and who with his four brothers had been in the Southern battle line since the beginning of the war. Isaac had been with William Washington in the famous skirmish with Tarleton at Monck's Corner, and so was like-wise not in Charleston at the surrender. One of the few Southern officers to escape captivity, he had come in to offer his services to Gates at Charlotte before Greene arrived.

With the Virginia Colonel Edward Carrington, who had joined him at Richmond as quartermaster, the energetic Thad-deus Kosciuszko as chief engineer, and William Davie of North Carolina replacing Gates's inefficient commissary, Greene set about creating an army out of odds and ends and furnishing it with makeshift equipment for the coming winter. When asked by Greene to exchange the saddle and the saber for commissary duty, Davie protested that he was a fighting man and knew noth-ing about money or keeping accounts. Greene, to whom the ar-gument had a familiar sound, replied dryly that Davie would be troubled with neither money nor accounts, as there was not a dollar in the military chest and no prospect of obtaining any. He chose the rest of his subordinates with care, most of them strang-ers, though Kosciuszko was already known to him from his work on the defenses at West Point.

The troops he found at Charlotte were destitute of bare necessities, especially clothing, and there were many invalids. A hospital attended by a veteran army surgeon, Dr. Read, and a prisoners' camp with a palisade were to be established at Salisbury in the army's rear. Magazines and ironworks with blacksmiths were to be set up at specified mills along the many rivers and kept stocked with bar iron, lead, cartridge makings, and spare camp-kitchen equipment.

His worst embarrassment was the want of "hard money" in-stead of the worthless paper issued by Congress, the value of which had sunk to a hundred to one. Salt, too, was in urgent demand for the army and could not be bought with paper money. The women who could be induced to make up cloth into shirts and pantaloons for the army preferred to take their pay in salt.

Since the fall of Charleston three great partisan leaders—Marion, Pickens, and Sumter—had developed a genius for dis-rupting British communications and supply by daring hit-and-run tactics, which often secured prisoners or information with which they disappeared again into the wilderness. Of these three, Thomas Sumter was nearest to the camp at Charlotte and had been in touch with Gates before Camden. Sumter had then captured a British post at Hanging Rock and secured a large stock of British stores and loot, which so encumbered his baggage and engaged his attention that he failed to reinforce Gates as expected.

Always independent, and jealous of his rank as senior South Carolina general, Sumter had become the reckless, headlong leader of a courageous band of mounted raiders and always found it convenient not to have received communications he did not intend to take any notice of. Gates's defeat at Camden seemed to justify Sumter's determination not to become involved in the operations of the main American force. Nicknamed "the Gamecock," he wore in his hat a defiant cock's feather, and his blue coat had red facings and gold epaulets, marking him among his miscellaneously clad followers, while his tall, striding figure was a picturesque rallying point for the outlaw spirits of the Up Country. Many of these had seen their homes burned over the heads of their helpless families, as Sumter's own plantation house in the High Hills of Santee had been destroyed by Tarleton's ruthless dragoons a few days after the Charleston surrender. Sumter had ridden away from it earlier in the same day to meet and organize the first defensive unit to be formed in the prostrate state.

Since Camden he had fought British mounted detachments at Fishing Creek and at Fishdam. On November 22, at Blackstock's plantation on the Tyger River, he used buckshot—a spreading charge of pea-sized lead pellets—against Tarleton's dragoons at close range and emptied twenty saddles. Tarleton fell back in disarray, through a narrow fenced lane under sharpshooter fire from the log outbuildings of the plantation. "Both men and horses fell so fast that the way was nearly stopped up," an American witness wrote, "the retreat stumbling over dead horses and men." It was during this retreat that Tarleton performed one of those heroic actions which must have happened on both sides more frequently than recorded. With bullets whistling around him, he wheeled his horse to where a wounded fellow officer lay helpless, lifted the man into his own saddle, crawled up behind him, and carried him off the field.

Sumter spurred out after the retreating enemy and was caught in the fire of Tarleton's rear guard. A bullet passed through his right shoulder to his left side, where it lodged. He attempted stoically to give no sign of being hurt and remained in his saddle to return to his command post in the gathering dusk. As he dismounted, one of his aides heard the dripping of blood on the dry November leaves underfoot and cried out that the general was wounded. "Say nothing about it," Sumter bade him sharply. But his disabled right arm hung limp from his shoulder, and he asked the aide to return his sword to the scabbard for him and call a man to take his horse. He knew that the morale of his militia depended on his presence among them and was determined to stay on his feet but soon fainted from pain and loss of blood. They carried him into Blackstock's log house nearby, and he confessed then to his devoted black body-servant, Soldier Tom, that he was badly wounded.

The camp surgeon was summoned from his work on the battle-field and saw at once that Sumter was bleeding to death. Cutting away the blood-soaked coat with a kitchen knife, he found that the bullet had nicked the backbone and would have to be removed. When he began probing for it—without an anaesthetic—the general gripped the bedpost and writhed in silent agony. By the time his wounds were staunched and covered with a field-dressing, Sumter was barely conscious. His aides contrived a rough litter out of a raw bullock's hide lashed to long poles and slung between two horses, and he was thus conveyed in darkness with only a small bodyguard back to his camp in the Waxhaws district.

"Sumter is defeated, his corps dispersed, and himself dangerously wounded," Tarleton reported from the field to Cornwallis, and added somewhat incoherently, "But my Lord I have lost men —50 killed and wounded—every officer I have, killed or wounded —the enemy attacked and forced me to action before the cannon and light infantry could be brought up—I did not mean to attack Sumter, only to harass him and lie close to him till I could bring up the rest of the corps, as he would never pass the Tyger if I had attacked. . . ."

Sumter had obviously rattled the British—so much so that rewards had been offered to the local Tories for his betrayal and even for his murder in his tent. When Cornwallis heard that Sumter was "speechless, and certainly past all hope," he wrote Rawdon that he rejoiced to be rid of "the greatest plague in this country" and added, "I wish your friend Marion was as quiet."

Tarleton forwarded a hopeful report that Sumter was dead. But in a house near Tuskegee Ford on the Tyger River only about twenty miles from Charlotte, guarded by a few of his militia and nursed by Soldier Tom, racked with pain and burning with fever, Sumter was recovering. Dr. Read rode out from the hospital at Salisbury to dress the wound and was nearly captured by Tory scouts on his way back. Sumter had refused to be moved to the hospital, which probably saved him, too, from capture on the road. Since he was still too weak to go to Charlotte, Greene went to him, accompanied by Governor Rutledge, who had ridden into camp in his casual way the day before.

After the defeat at Camden, Rutledge had gone north to Hillsboro, as though abandoning a hopeless state of affairs in South Carolina. Thereafter he drifted in and out of the partisan camps, always secretly in touch with Charleston through an underground pipeline of communication maintained by faithful slave messengers from his mother, who continued to reside in occupied Charleston by the perilous courtesy of the conqueror. He became known as the best recruiting sergeant in South Carolina, riding alone into the Up Country settlements, throwing his horse's bridle over a hitching post and speaking in the public square, always in danger of capture by traitorous Tories. Much depended on his continued freedom to circulate as a rallying point for the intimidated Patriot population. Greene recognized the value of his mere presence among the always scary militia, and Rutledge was often to be found in Greene's camp.

Their visit to Sumter found him chafing at his lack of strength, and the inflammation from his wound had made it difficult for him to use his arms. They listened to the latest reports from his private intelligence service, which said that General Leslie had returned to Charleston with reinforcements and was marching up the Santee Road to join Cornwallis at Winnsboro, after which a new campaign might be expected to start. It was doubtless as a result of this interview with the house-bound Sumter that Morgan was soon detached from the army at Charlotte to the Catawba River venture which would lead to the battle at the Cowpens in January.

Francis Marion, less reckless than Sumter, more cautious and clever, operated with a small mounted troop out of the swamps north of British-held Georgetown near the coast. His headquarters at Snow's Island in the PeeDee swamp were hidden and almost inaccessible. His only comforts there were a canvas tent-fly slung between two live oaks and a badly scorched blanket laid beneath it, his horse always tethered within reach. He had appeared once at Gates's camp, before Camden, taken the measure of the man, and departed again, repelled by Gates's open indifference to cavalry in any form. He had last been seen soon after the Camden defeat, when he swooped down on a British convoy of prisoners at Nelson's Ferry on the Santee, surprised the guards into surrender, freed the captives to return to the army without paroles, and disappeared again toward Snow's Island.

Greene lost no time in attempting to get in touch with Marion.

"I arrived at this place the day before yesterday, to take command of the Southern Army," he introduced himself from Charlotte on December 4. "I have not the honor of your acquaintance but am no stranger to your character and merit. Your services in the lower part of South Carolina, in awing the Tories and preventing the enemy from extending their limits, have been very important, and it is my earnest desire that you continue where you are until further advice from me.

"It is of the highest importance that I get the earliest information of any reinforcements that may arrive at Charleston, or leave the town to join Cornwallis. I wish you, therefore, to fix some plan for procuring such information, and for conveying it to me with all possible dispatch. The spy should be taught to be particular in his inquiries, and to get the names of the corps, strength, and commanding officer's name, place from whence they come and where they are going. It will be best to fix upon somebody in town to do this, and have a runner between you and him to give you the intelligence, as a person cannot make these inquiries without being suspected, who lives out of town. The utmost secrecy will be necessary in this business. Whatever sums of money are advanced for these purposes will be repaid. . . ."

Spying was never a palatable job, the risks were often horrifying, and the penalty for discovery was a miserable death. But way south with his legion—a mixed force of cavalry and light infantry.

Less spectacular, but not less enterprising, was Andrew Pickens, a veteran of some Up Country skirmishing with the Cherokee Indians around the frontier settlement called 96. He had appeared with a few followers outside Augusta in 1779, scattering Tories who were attempting to join the British garrison which was then commanded by Sir Archibald Campbell.

Since the Charleston surrender Pickens had been immobilized at home by having "taken protection" and signed a parole. But when his plantation near 96 was burned by British Major Dunlop and a troop of Northern Tories, Pickens considered that his "protection" had been violated by the other side and took to the field again, accompanied by a small party of equally outraged neighbors of the district—all of them said to be fighting with a rope around their necks as a result of "defecting" from their paroles. His followers were mounted on their own horses and received neither payment nor clothing from the government, until their needs became so acute that Pickens was forced to apply to Greene for relief. Operating north and west of Augusta, Pickens was somewhat removed from immediate usefulness to Greene at Charlotte.

Greene labored incessantly at organizing his departments under their new heads, while encountering appalling difficulties each day—such as a total lack of lint and bandages in the hospital supplies and medical stores. Boards for barracks and the necessary nails, provisions like flour and salt, boats and wagons for their transport, all had to be collected wherever they could be found, often by impressment, which he always considered regrettable. At the same time he attacked the demoralization of Gates's defeated troops, resulting from the weeks of inactivity and discouragement before his arrival. Discipline was tightened to such a degree that after announcing his intention of making an example of the next man to desert, he had one tried and hanged in sight of the whole army. They were duly impressed. "New lords, new laws," they agreed philosophically, and desertions fell off very fast.

Meanwhile, the camp was brightened by a bloodless exploit by Colonel Washington at Rugeley's Mills, sometimes called Clermont Plantation, about twelve miles above Camden. Colonel

Rugeley was a Tory who in expectation of promotion had raised a stockade and abatis around his house and collected a hundred or so men under his personal command to defend it as an outpost to the British garrison at Camden. Washington's story, which split the sides of the Charlotte camp when it reached there, is solemnly related in the memoirs of Lighthorse Harry Lee, who was not, to his regret, present with Washington's troop that day.

When Washington rode in at Clermont with a small force and summoned the place to surrender he received a rude answer. Not strong enough in numbers and without artillery to storm the stockade, he withdrew to the edge of the woods and threw up breastworks as though for a siege. He then "shaped the trunk of a tree in imitation of a field-piece or cannon," mounted it on wagon wheels, and brought it up "in military style" just peeking out of the woods at the edge of Rugeley's clearing, as though in preparation to bombard the fortified house. To add weight to his "device," he sent in a flag to warn the garrison of their impending destruction, which could only be avoided by immediate surrender. "Not being prepared to resist artillery," Lee related soberly, "Colonel Rugeley seized promptly the opportunity, and with his garrison surrendered at discretion!"

Lee then went on to draw the military moral, which was deeply impressed upon his youthful mind, as he was to demonstrate at Fort Watson and Augusta the following summer. "No circumstances can more strongly demonstrate the propriety of using every effort in war," he pointed out. "This stratagem of Washington's, though conceived and executed with little hope of success, was completely successful, and enabled him to effect an object which at first view most men would have abandoned as clearly unattainable."

Cornwallis, now ailing at his camp at Winnsboro, also commented on the affair at Clermont. "Colonel Rugeley will never be made a brigadier," he wrote briefly to Tarleton.

Greene was as amused as anybody and assigned the popular Washington to Morgan's force when he detached Morgan in the middle of December to roam the Broad and Tyger River country to the west and north of Winnsboro and keep Cornwallis in a state of alarm for his isolated posts at 96 and Augusta. Morgan took with him John Eager Howard's Maryland Continentals, who had no fear of the British bayonet. Dividing his scanty army was a bold decision which went against Greene's book-learned principles of war, but he was convinced it would be worth the risk involved. It seemed to him that a threat by Morgan to the British rear would hearten the inhabitants of the Tory-dominated Up Country and provide them with a rallying point, while enabling Morgan to draw on supplies and stores in a country that had not already been stripped by either army.

Greene now prepared to put the remainder of his army into winter quarters, at a site chosen by Kosciuszko. With little more than a thousand men, most of them Continentals, including Williams's Marylanders, Greene evacuated Charlotte on December 16 and marched through cold rain, mud, and frost to where Hicks Creek joined the PeeDee at Cheraw Hill, just over the South Carolina border. Here he intended to establish what he fondly called "a camp of repose," though there would be anything but idleness there.

While the men felled trees and constructed their shelters, Greene spent long hours at his little traveling desk organizing his departments. He wrote endless appeals to the governors and legislatures of the Southern states for more men, wagons, horses, forage, clothing, flour, and salt. He tightened discipline again and gave attention to sanitation and whatever hospital accommodation could be devised. He made friends with the officers new to his command by inviting them to his dinner table in turns, to learn their own opinions and habits of mind. Before the spring campaign could begin he had won the respect and confidence of all.

"I am now at the falls of the PeeDee," he wrote Washington at the end of the year, "and the region of my future operations must be above the falls of the rivers, until I can control the movements of my adversary. Below the falls the rivers are deep, and their banks are covered with impassable swamps across which, at long intervals, roads have been constructed, which afford the only avenues of retreat. I cannot afford to get entangled among the difficulties they present, until I can turn upon my adversary and fight him when I please."

Thus clearly he foresaw and set the pattern of the desperate months to come, during which time he would elude and wear

down the confused and outmaneuvered British regulars until he
was at last ready to turn and fight on ground of his own
choosing.

Chapter 22

Having followed Greene from the North into the new territory
which was to be the scene of his future endeavor, it is necessary
now to pick up the loose ends which the British were compelled
to weave into their own plan of campaign against this unexpected
opponent. This entails a certain amount of back-tracking into the
previous summer when Cornwallis had everything going his
way.

After his victory at Camden in August, Cornwallis had advanced into North Carolina as far as Charlotte, while Gates fled
on to Hillsboro. During the march from Camden to Charlotte the
British regulars were so plagued by sickness in the summer heat
and by shortages of food and forage that the general paused for
two weeks on the way, on the high ground of the Waxhaws district, to allow his soldiers to recover from their Low Country
fevers, wounds, and internal ailments. He did not reach and occupy Charlotte until late in September. By that time Tarleton too
had been prostrated by the prevailing fever, depriving Cornwallis
of his best scouting and cavalry leadership. Although he had intended to proceed against Hillsboro in time to scatter Gates and

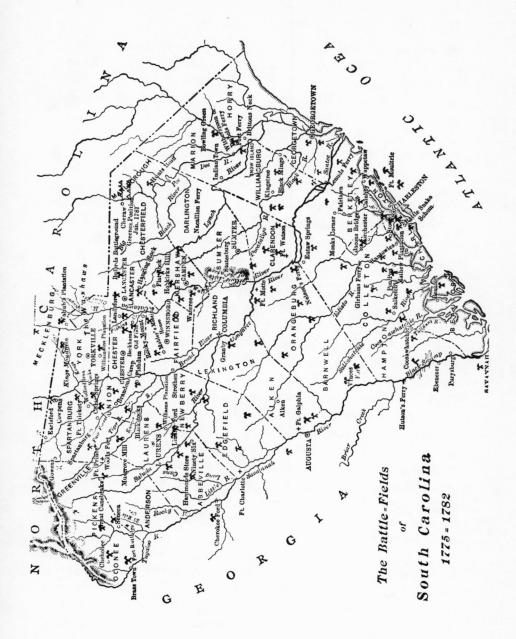

The Battle-Fields
of
South Carolina
1775=1782

the Legislature and establish his winter supply base there, at a shorter distance than Camden from his coastal communications, he was compelled to sit down in Charlotte and wait for cooler weather and a general recuperation of men and transport animals.

The news, as it trickled in to him there, showed a steady deterioration in his prospects, even before he received the first accounts of Ferguson's defeat at King's Mountain on October 7— news that had reached Greene in Philadelphia on his way south.

Major Patrick Ferguson was one of the best of the British professional soldiers and had been nearly four years in the American war, after seeing service on the Continent and in the West Indies. Slenderly built, with a deceptively gentle manner, he was nicknamed The Bulldog. A notable marksman himself, he had invented a breech-loading rifle that was useful in all weather and had the advantage that, unlike the regulation musket, it could be reloaded from a prone position and possessed a greater range and accuracy. To test it, Ferguson had been given a special corps armed with this new gun. It was mainly thanks to the stubborn, shortsighted Howe that the weapon had not been produced in quantity and issued to the entire British army.

Arriving with Clinton at Charleston the previous January, Ferguson had recruited a corps of local Tory riflemen and commanded them in the back-country around 96, until he received intelligence after Camden that the "over-mountain men," or frontier militia, were embodying against him up to almost triple his own strength. He at once began to fade back toward the protection of Corwallis's army, then at Charlotte, and requested reinforcements.

On the way, he came to King's Mountain, a rocky spur of the Blue Ridge, and camped on a plateau at its summit, where he prepared to meet an assault by the Mountain Men, who were a mixed force of tough pioneer "outlaws" without a general officer to lead them. They had learned of Ferguson's position and were advancing toward him in increasing numbers, through dismal country and dismal weather. They drove in his pickets and swarmed up the slope toward his camp on the summit in a slow, determined encircling movement, taking shelter behind rocks and trees and firing as they climbed.

Shooting downhill, Ferguson was at a disadvantage; his fire went high, whistling through the trees above the heads of the Americans, while the mountaineers' bullets found their mark with deadly effect. Ferguson twice threw back the attack, exposing himself recklessly to hearten his men, and was soon surrounded by what seemed to be volcanic fire causing many casualties. Because of a shattered right elbow from the action at Brandywine, Ferguson carried his sword in his left hand and held between his teeth the silver whistle with which he signaled his men. When the piercing shriek of Ferguson's whistle suddenly ceased, he was discovered with several musket balls in his body, still hanging from his stirrup by one foot. His men lifted him clear and propped him against a tree trunk, where he died. Hopelessly his outnumbered followers showed a white flag and surrendered. Their losses were almost five times those of the Mountain Men.

There is a picturesque sidelight on the story of Ferguson at King's Mountain, in a persistent legend that he was attended at the camp by no less than two devoted mistresses, "nominally cooks," and both "fine-looking young women." One of them was red-haired and was known as Virginia Sal. She is further said to have been the first casualty when the shooting began and is supposed by a tradition of the region to have been buried in the same grave with Ferguson.

It was a battle Cornwallis could ill afford to lose. When the defeat became known, his recruiting of Tory militia continued to fail his expectations at both ends of the British front, from Georgetown to 96, owing largely to the vigilance of the partisan leaders who kept the Tory population in a state of caution and indecision.

While still at Charlotte Cornwallis was himself struck down by the violent fever afflicting both officers and men, which prostrated him for weeks. Heavy autumn rains brought transport almost to a standstill and drenched everything perishable that was not under shelter. The garrison he had left at Camden sent word that it was running short of provisions. These grim circumstances, combined with the King's Mountain losses, forced Cornwallis to abandon his hopes of plucking Hillsboro out from under Gates as a triumphant climax to his 1780 campaign.

Reluctantly he ordered the evacuation of Charlotte and on October 14 began to retreat his army to Winnsboro in South

Carolina, midway between Camden and the Up Country post of 96. Here he hoped to maintain a headquarters with reasonably safe communications down the rivers to his Charleston base.

His continuing illness compelled him to turn over the command to young Lord Rawdon, while he himself made the retreat from Charlotte to Winnsboro lying in a jolting, springless wagon dragged by exhausted teams over flooded roads with mud up to the axles. Food along the march was so scarce that the general was "only sustained by opium and port wine"—surely a miracle of survival.

Arriving at Winnsboro late in October, Cornwallis was still too weak to hold a pen, but he made a remarkable recovery by sheer will power and was soon able to contemplate his unhappy situation. Since Ferguson's defeat in a battle he was not supposed to have undertaken at all, everything had gone wrong for the British. Cornwallis sent Rawdon back to command the garrison at Camden and withdrew Major Wemyss from his unsuccessful campaign against Marion in the Georgetown area near the coast. Wemyss had become the second most hated man in the British army, next to Tarleton, for his ruthless burning and plundering of plantations and abuse of the population. Gates was still at Hillsboro, and Sumter was operating independently along the Broad River, when Cornwallis sent Wemyss after Sumter, abandoning the pursuit of Marion.

At Fishdam on the Broad River, November 12, a week before Blackstock's, Wemyss galloped into Sumter's pickets and was severely wounded at the first fire. His lieutenant, who took command when Wemyss fell, broke off the action and retreated, leaving his disabled commander on the field with the other wounded, where Sumter found him the next day and took him prisoner. It was said that when Sumter found in Wemyss's pocket a list of the plantation houses that had been looted and destroyed during Wemyss's march, he threw it into the fire, knowing that such a record if discovered by his Patriot followers would have constituted the captive major's death warrant. Wemyss, whose wound crippled him for life, was sent to Charleston on parole and never returned to the army.

As soon as Tarleton recovered from the fever sufficiently to ride, Cornwallis sent him out to avenge Wemyss and to push Sumter toward the British post at 96. But Sumter was not to be caught between two British forces and had turned to fight at Blackstock's on November 22. It was here at Blackstock's that he had received the wound that would put him out of action till the following spring.

The next British setback had occurred at Rugeley's Mill on December 4, when William Washington's boyish hoax with the log cannon turned Colonel Rugeley into a laughingstock. Rawdon at Camden, famous for his temper and unable to see the joke, was still in a rage when he received the unwelcome news of the formidable Greene's arrival at Charlotte on December 3 to replace Gates.

The explanation of Leslie's mysterious disappearance from the James River coast was of course his orders from Cornwallis to land reinforcements at Charleston, from where they could be brought up the Santee Road to join the main army at Winnsboro —the only British force in the South which had not been damaged or outwitted by the partisans.

Meanwhile the British army had to eat, and it was stripping the countryside roundabout Camden and Winnsboro. Supplies of clothing and food sent by Clinton from New York to Charleston, where Colonel Nisbet Balfour was the British commandant, had then to find their way up from the coast to the interior. The roads were impassable because of flooding and winter mud. The chronic scarcity of wagons and teams afflicted the British equally with the Americans, until Balfour had desperate recourse to flatboats on the numerous waterways. The River Santee flowed from North Carolina (where it was called the Catawba) past Camden (where it changed its name to the Wateree). Thirty miles south of Camden it was joined by the Congaree (which was composed of the Broad and the Saluda) flowing from west of Winnsboro. At the Congaree forks stood McCord's Ferry and a road to Camden began. Below McCord's until it met the ocean between Georgetown and Charleston the river was known as the Santee.

To defend the water route it was necessary to establish and garrison strategic outposts along the banks, and these became known as Forts Granby, Motte, and Watson. As the winter wore on, Cornwallis's army in their huts at Winnsboro were as shabby and sick as their American counterparts at Cheraw, until some supplies finally arrived from Charleston in early December.

As Greene intended, Cornwallis had been compelled to weaken himself by sending out detachments of his own to cope with Greene's patrols. Among these, Tarleton's dragoons were now in pursuit of Morgan, who had crossed the Broad River westward on Christmas Day. He had been joined by Pickens and James McCall, both of whom led men who had good reason to retaliate against the Tories then marauding and murdering in the Patriot settlements around Fairfort Creek, in the vicious encounters that civil war always produces.

In Tarleton's wake, Cornwallis broke camp at Winnsboro and marched toward a junction with Leslie's reinforcements from Charleston, who were reported to be struggling through the Santee swamps on their way to Camden. Morgan's information on the enemy's movements was reliable, and he resolved to tackle Tarleton while the fight would be on reasonably even terms, detachment against detachment, before Cornwallis could add his own force to Tarleton's strength.

With Pickens's and McCall's fresh militia, Howard's Maryland Continentals, and William Washington's cavalry, Morgan chose his ground, not far from the already historic King's Mountain, at a place called Hannah's Cowpens, once a pasture for backwoods cattle. He camped there, breakfasted at his leisure, and was ready to confront Tarleton on the morning of January 19, 1781.

It was a quick, brief, savage engagement, lasting barely an hour. William Washington's charge broke through the British line, Howard's men went in with their bayonets, and Pickens's riflemen obeyed the unsportsmanlike order to "pick off the epaulet men," taking deadly aim at the officers. The confusion in the British ranks which followed the resulting loss of command was a deciding factor in the battle.

The British were stunned and bewildered by the violence of the attack, and when the avenging American cry of "Tarleton's quarter!" was heard, many redcoats familiar with Tarleton's reputation for murdering helpless men who had already thrown down their arms in surrender, fled headlong, or called for the quarter their leader never gave. Morgan and his officers were obliged to throw themselves between their own men and the defeated enemy to prevent an imitation of the wholesale slaughter for which Tarleton was famous.

One of Morgan's men left his record of the day: "Just as we got to our horses, they overtook us and began to make a few hacks at some, without doing much injury. Now, I thought, my hide is in the loft! But they, in their haste, had pretty much scattered, perhaps thinking they would have another Fishing Creek frolic, but in a few moments Colonel Washington's cavalry was among them like a whirlwind, and the poor fellows began to keel from their saddles without being able to remount. The shock was so sudden and violent that they could not stand it and immediately betook themselves to flight. There was no time to rally, and they appeared to be as hard to stop as a drove of wild Choctaw steers going to Pennsylvania market. In a few minutes the clashing of swords was out of hearing and out of sight."

It was here at the Cowpens that the smoldering feud between Washington and Tarleton blazed up again in hand-to-hand single combat, with sidearms and cavalry sabers, during which Washington's less well-tempered steel broke in half. In the very thick of the fight Tarleton discharged his pistol into Washington's knee, wounding his horse at the same time, and received from Washington's broken sword a deep slash on his right hand. The aide riding at Tarleton's side was aiming a saber blow at Washington when Washington's bugler, "too small to wield a sword," saved him by firing a pistol into the aide's arm.

Like the fight at King's Mountain, the battle at the Cowpens was an unexpected affirmation of the unbeatable American spirit. Only the British baggage guard at the rear and Tarleton himself with a handful of dragoons escaped. William Washington pursued them until nearly dark, and on his return drove before him a hundred straggling prisoners which he had collected as he rode.

"The troops I have the honor to command have gained a complete victory over a detachment from the British army commanded by Lieutenant-colonel Tarleton," Morgan reported soberly to Greene. "Twenty-nine commissioned officers have fell into our hands, two standards, three field-pieces, thirty-five wagons, a travelling-forge, and all their music are ours. [The drummers, buglers, and their instruments.] Their baggage, which was immense, they have in a great measure destroyed."

It was said that when the defeated dragoons went into bivouac that night, Tarleton in an anguish of humiliation and grief cast himself down upon the wet ground and lay there all night, sleepless and speechless, counting his losses. The next day he rode with his remnants into Cornwallis's camp on Turkey Creek, where Leslie was due to arrive with the reinforcements from Charleston. Questions were asked, and recriminations followed. Why and how could such a defeat have happened to the famous Green Dragoon, who had now lost face forever, even in his own estimation?

There was jealousy of Tarleton among the senior officers of the British line, who had been superseded by what they considered partiality shown by Cornwallis in Tarleton's favor. In the American camp after the battle, Tarleton's precipitate behavior was criticized by Major MacArthur of the 71st, who had surrendered his sword to Colonel Howard of the Marylands. Nothing better than this defeat could have been expected, he told Howard, when troops were commanded by "a rash, foolish boy." It was not the end of Tarleton's brutal career, but the mystique of his legendary prowess was damaged forever.

Word of Morgan's success was nearly a week reaching the camp at Cheraw. Otho Williams, who had seen Gates's whole army in flight from Tarleton's Green Dragoons, wrote his congratulations to Morgan. "We have had a *feu de joie*," he reported, "drunk all your healths, swore you were the finest fellows on earth, and love you, if possible, more than ever. The General has, I think, made his compliments in very handsome terms. Enclosed is a copy of his Orders. It was written immediately after we received the news, and during the operation of some cherry bounce."

Morgan, exhausted and suffering from sciatica, dared not sit down to enjoy his triumph. The only road to reunion with Greene led over the fords of the Catawba River, flowing between them on the east. And Cornwallis, awaiting the arrival of Leslie, was only thirty miles away and would certainly attempt to cut off the victorious Americans. Morgan ordered an immediate retreat northward to Ramsour's Mills on the Little, or western Catawba, over mired roads and swollen watercourses, expecting every hour to hear that Cornwallis was at his heels.

But Cornwallis delayed a precious twenty-four hours to pull Tarleton together and allow Leslie to come up with him. He did not reach Ramsour's Mills till January 24, two days after Morgan had crossed the river there to camp on the east bank of the main Catawba at Sherrill's Ford. The winter rains poured down, while all the rivers and creeks rose and overflowed, and the roads became bottomless. Morgan's agony of sciatica held his horse's pace to a walk, and while at Sherrill's he learned from his scouts that Cornwallis lingered at Ramsour's to burn his baggage and wagons, in a desperate effort to speed up his pursuit by turning his whole army into light infantry carrying their necessities in their packs.

The magnificent British brigadier Charles O'Hara of the Guards, who had just arrived for the first time in the South with Leslie, was much impressed by this drastic action on Cornwallis's part, particularly when he saw the Earl himself set an example by tossing his personal baggage and comforts into the flames. Only enough wagons were retained to carry the ammunition, hospital stores, and a supply of salt, with a few empties for the use of possible sick and wounded. "In this situation, without baggage, necessaries, or provisions of any sort for officer or soldier, in the most barren, inhospitable, unhealthy part of North America, opposed to the most savage, inveterate, perfidious, cruel enemy, with zeal and bayonets only, it was resolved to follow Greene's army to the end of the world," O'Hara wrote home incredulously as the chase got under way.

Morgan, encamped on the far, or east, bank of the torrential Catawba, set a watch on its fords above and below Sherrill's, all of them now impassable with high water, and awaited further orders from Greene. During the pause, he had all the fords blocked with felled trees and picket posts, except the main crossing next below Sherrill's, called Beattie's, which he kept open and guarded by a force of North Carolina militia under General William Davidson, who was also made responsible for Cowan's, a private and less useful crossing downstream from Beattie's.

In the midst of the rejoicing at Cheraw over Morgan's victory, Greene had foreseen some difficulties and the need for speedy action on his own part. First, to hinder Cornwallis he must re-unite his army and place himself between the enemy and their goal, which at present would be Virginia, where the traitor Arnold had established a British base at Portsmouth and was raiding along the James River banks. Between Cornwallis and Arnold lay miles of flooding streams and muddy roads, and at the Virginia border the Dan River rushed headlong eastward before turning south into North Carolina, where it became the Roanoke and entered Albemarle Sound. Once across the Dan, Cornwallis would have a clear road to Petersburg and the James.

To contest this British maneuver there was only a small force in Virginia led by Lafayette, which Washington had detached southward in the hope that it might be sufficiently augmented by Steuben to reinforce Greene if he could reach the James ahead of Cornwallis. Carolina distances and climate were inconceivable equally at New Windsor on the Hudson and at New York. Greene was heartened by Lafayette's move but was well aware of the odds against cooperation between them.

At Cheraw he called in all his detachments and collected all the stores within reach. He sent out new appeals to the governors for militia and to Steuben for recruits—to which Steuben replied grimly that the state of Virginia seemed to be full of officers on furlough and all behaving as though the war was on another planet.

Greene put his army under marching orders, with Isaac Huger in command, for Salisbury seventy miles to the northward on the Yadkin River (as the upper PeeDee was called) between Charlotte and Hillsboro. He wrote to advise Marion, who with Lee was still operating around Georgetown, that he relied on his continued activity in the rear of the enemy near the coast, but ordered Lee to leave Marion and overtake Huger on the march to Salisbury. Finally, with a single aide, Burnett, and a sergeant's guard of horsemen, he set out into the downpour to place himself at the head of Morgan's detachment on the Catawba in Cornwallis's path.

Five days later he arrived at Beattie's Ford, having crossed a hundred and fifty miles of countryside infested with militant

VIEW OF THE GREAT FALLS OF THE CATAWBA.

Tories, through a pouring rain all the way. Morgan, Washington, and Davidson were at Beattie's awaiting him, and they all held a brief conference seated on a convenient log.

While the fords were flooded it would be impossible for Cornwallis to march, and if he could be kept west of the Catawba until more Carolina militia came in, encouraged by the Cowpens victory, Greene hoped that one more such crippling fight might force him to fall back to his Santee line below Camden. While Greene was still at Beattie's the British vanguard appeared on the hill on the opposite side of the river, and the three generals came to some rather hurried decisions on the spot. Morgan's advance guard was already on the road to Salisbury, where Huger and

Williams were headed with the main army from Cheraw. Leaving Davidson to hold Beattie's and Cowan's, the other two rode off toward Salisbury, intending to withdraw their entire force eastward beyond the Yadkin.

But the rain suddenly slackened, and the Catawba began to fall, though the current was swift above a treacherous rocky bottom. A steep wooded bank provided cover for Davidson's men. At daybreak on February 1 Cornwallis sent Webster's 33rd Foot to annoy Davidson at Beattie's and himself led the main force on to Cowan's, which his scouts had reported to be more lightly guarded. As always, the Earl showed the way and was first into the deep water on his spirited gray horse. He was followed by O'Hara's Guards and Tarleton's dragoons. Midway in the stream his horse was struck by a bullet from Davidson's snipers firing from the opposite bank, but the animal struggled ashore before falling dead.

The British ranks behind him were breast-high in cold, rushing water, with heavy knapsacks on their backs, sixty rounds of powder and ball tied to their necks, and their firelocks and bayonets fixed to their shoulders. They were unable to fire a shot till they reached the bank, while Davidson's marksmen picked them off one by one as they struggled in the water. A local eyewitness reported that "the river was full of 'em, a-snortin' and a-hollerin' and a-drownin'." Strong men and horses were carried downstream or drowned by the current. Leslie lost his horse in the river, and O'Hara's rolled him over and over among jagged rocks. A bombardier with a three-pound cannon was swept "heels over head" for forty yards downstream.

The dogged tenacity and discipline of the British regulars were demonstrated again when once out of the river they advanced under hot fire up a bank so steep they had to pull up by the bushes. When Davidson rushed in to steady his men, he received a bullet through the heart and dropped from his saddle. His militia then broke and "made straight shirt-tails" in their flight toward Salisbury, pursued by Tarleton's dripping dragoons.

The Salisbury road was already clogged with civilian refugees who had heard the gunfire at the fords. At Tarrant's Tavern, halfway to Salisbury, many of them and some militia had paused for refreshment—bewildered country people in a jumble of privately owned saddle horses and wagons loaded with household goods. Whiskey was being dispensed from buckets until someone raised a cry that Tarleton was coming—and the green dragoons charged down the road sabering unarmed civilians and runaway militia impartially.

At Salisbury Greene waited till nightfall, hoping to gather in some militia which did not appear, and there the news of Davidson's death reached him. He had sent an express rider to intercept Huger and change the meeting place from Salisbury farther eastward to Guildford Courthouse, halfway to Hillsboro. He dispatched another messenger to overtake Morgan and order all boats and other craft to be commandeered for miles up and down the Yadkin, in case Trading Ford beyond Salisbury was still flooded.

He hoped to hold Cornwallis at the Yadkin until the men from Cheraw could be rested and organized for a fight. He caught up with Morgan himself that night, to find Trading Ford impassable on foot. Thanks to his foresight in collecting boats, they got Morgan's men across the river just as O'Hara brought up the British advance guard to the west bank. There was a brief engagement there, and Morgan's rear guard had to scramble across under fire, leaving behind them a few wagons and a handful of militia, who at sight of the redcoats "split and squandered" into flight.

The next day, when Cornwallis arrived at Trading Ford with his whole army, it was raining hard again in the mountains upstream, and the torrential Yadkin roared between him and the American camp on the far bank, where all the boats were moored. Cornwallis ordered up his artillery and cannonaded the camp.

Greene had taken up his quarters in a small wooden cabin screened from the river by the nature of the rocky ground. There he sat imperturbably writing up his dispatches while Cornwallis's artillery found the range, and "the clapboards were flying from it in all directions," Dr. Read recorded. "But still the General wrote on, nor seemed to notice anything but his dispatches. His pen never rested, except when a new visitor arrived, and then the answer was given with calmness and precision, and the pen immediately resumed."

Aware that Greene had not been able to collect North Carolina militia and had not received the expected reinforcements from Virginia, Cornwallis was determined to prevent him from bettering his prospects. He had a choice of trying to cut off Huger by crossing the Yadkin downstream and striking his line of march before he could reach the rendezvous at Guildford Courthouse— or making a dash for the Dan himself by crossing the Yadkin above Trading Ford and placing himself between Greene and Virginia. "It being my business to force him to fight," he wrote, "I made great expedition to get between Greene and the fords of the Dan."

But to reach the ford above Trading required a long detour to the north around a flooded loop of the Yadkin, depending on unreliable guides who had falsely assured him it could be done with ease. Instead, it was slow, muddy going along miserable back-country roads, while Greene possessed the main road to Guildford Courthouse. There he was finally reunited to Huger and Williams, who had been joined along the way by Lee as ordered. Accompanied by his officers, Greene studied the ground roundabout Guildford Courthouse as a possible place to make a stand. They were nearly a hundred miles from the Dan River, which lay between them and Virginia. It was February and the roads were bottomless red clay, into which the horses' hoofs and the wagon wheels sank deep, and the men went in to their ankles at every step. At this point Greene received a letter from Washington on the Hudson. "My hopes," wrote the commander in chief, "rest on my knowledge of your talents."

A council of war was held on February 9, 1781, at Greene's headquarters at Guildford Courthouse. It was attended by Huger, Williams, Howard, Colonel Washington, Lee, Carrington, and Morgan. Morgan was by now in such a state of pain and exhaustion that Greene reluctantly allowed him to depart for home. The new arrivals from Cheraw were "in a most dismal condition for want of clothing, especially shoes," and they had marched over frozen rutted roads where wagons broke down and horses foundered. Many were nearly naked and nursed bleeding, frostbitten feet. Cornwallis, they knew, was not much better off, for his regulars were worn by weeks of marching in the same hideous weather, and Leslie's had come all the way up from Charleston before that. Since the enforced conflagration at Ramsour's Mills they had been without even the minimum comforts of their usual baggage.

But Cornwallis was only twenty-five miles from Guildford Courthouse on Greene's left, as near to the shallow crossings of the upper Dan as Greene was. Without doubt Cornwallis would try to push them downstream toward the deeper water where the fords and ferries would still be flooded and useless, hoping to force an engagement there, with their backs to the river.

Greene's officers were unanimously of the opinion that he was not strong enough to confront Cornwallis at Guildford Courthouse, and so he made the unwilling decision, as Cornwallis had anticipated, to continue his retreat toward the Dan. This move meant leaving the defense of North and South Carolina in the hands of Sumter, who was slowly recovering from his Blackstock's wound, Marion on the PeeDee, and Pickens, now in command of the North Carolina militia since Davidson's death at Cowan's Ford.

Greene sent his heavy baggage ahead to the Virginia border, where Kosciuszko would prepare the way for a crossing of the Dan into the fertile, friendly countryside in Halifax County. Carrington, the Virginia quartermaster, had himself crossed the Dan southward with de Kalb the previous year and was familiar with its vicinity, having at that time examined it and the Roanoke for a safe retreat route. He was confident that enough boats could be assembled to cross Greene's army at Irwin's and Boyd's ferries, lower down the river than the fords available to Cornwallis on his present course. Some homemade boats had come up from Cheraw with Huger. Carrington was dispatched with them ahead of the army, charged with the collection of all available craft on the Dan, to be brought in at Irwin's. Express riders were rushed off in all directions to appeal for militia and to gather more boats to carry the army into Virginia beyond the Dan.

Geography and the weather were now to become the dominant factors in the long cat-and-mouse game of strategic retreat that would make Greene famous.

Chapter 23

It would be the 1776 Jersey maneuvers all over again, in much worse terrain, and Greene was glad of the previous example in endurance, when they had all followed the indomitable figure of Washington to such unexpected success at Trenton. Now it was Greene who must exert whatever powers of leadership and inspiration he could summon up, in faithful imitation of the commander in chief.

Lacking Morgan's experienced hand with light troops for a quick maneuver, Greene gave the job to Williams, who accepted it cheerfully, concealing his own misgivings. The assignment took him out to the left on an oblique line to throw himself between Cornwallis and Greene's main column, driving in the British scouts and screening Greene's line of march. The main army moved out on February 10 along the road to Irwin's Ferry.

Greene had not had his clothes off overnight since he joined Morgan on the Catawba, and he slept in the saddle. At night while the army rested on the damp frosty ground he wrote and dictated letters by the light of a sputtering lantern. For three days the armies moved almost parallel to each other, Greene on the right, or eastward side, Cornwallis on his left. Williams skirmished between them, traveling the worst possible byways and back roads, shepherding the main army from a little to its rear and in front of Cornwallis. Lee's mounted legion guarded the

American rear, and the two armies were often so close together that Cornwallis's advance guard under O'Hara, and Lee on Greene's rear, were in frequent contact.

The greatest vigilance was necessary on both sides to prevent a night surprise. Patrols and pickets had to be so numerous that in the American army each man got only six hour's sleep out of forty-eight. Neither army dared to halt long, and so killing was the pace that an early breakfast, usually of cornmeal or bacon, was the only hot food issued during the day.

In this way the armies covered an exhausting average of thirty miles a day. The few tents they still possessed were never used during the brief encampments, and the men crouched each night, wet and shivering, around their bivouac fires with one blanket between three of them, so that by routine one of each trio stayed on his legs to tend the fire.

Cornwallis was sustained by his misapprehension that he held the only route by which Greene could cross the Dan. He was unaware that Carrington had collected boats at Irwin's Ferry on the south bank at the end of Greene's line of march and that Kosciuszko was already at work erecting breastworks on the north bank to cover the crossing.

On the third day Lee and Tarleton met face to face, Tarleton having pressed forward. A sharp engagement occurred, during which Lee's bugler, a boy in his teens, well mounted because it was his duty to keep always at the colonel's side, was brutally sabered by a British dragoon. The fellow was at once taken prisoner and was about to be hanged from the nearest tree when the sudden appearance of a supporting body of British cavalry interrupted the execution and the dying boy was carried away in the arms of one of Lee's troopers. His body was eventually left unburied in the woods by the side of the road as the desperate march continued.

Later the same day another encounter took place at a narrow bridge, where Lee escaped capture only by a hard gallop from a byway into the road leading to Irwin's Ferry in Greene's immediate wake. That night as the cold, drizzling darkness drew in, Lee's men saw watch fires ahead, and their hearts sank. Cornwallis had swerved into the road behind them, on the right track at last, and if Greene had halted at the fires the enemy was in a position to pinch the whole American army between the river and the British van. A hasty resolution was formed in Lee's camp to make a last bloody stand to buy time for Greene to load his troops into the boats and escape once more.

It was not required. The fires only marked Greene's halt of the night before and had been kept burning by friendly country people to cheer Williams's arrival on the ground. Lee bivouacked that night almost within musket shot of the British pursuit, and at dawn the grim race began again.

About noon a loud shout went up from the American force ahead of them—a muddy courier had brought the news back from Greene to Williams, who passed it on to Lee—the main body of Greene's army had crossed the Dan at Irwin's Ferry the preceding night.

Williams was ordered to file off to the right on the road to Boyd's Ferry, where the boats now waited, leaving Lee to maneuver in front of the enemy before following him. Williams reached the near shore at sunset and was soon transported to the Virginia side. The boats then returned for Lee, who was to send his infantry after Williams and remain behind with his cavalry till nearly dark before galloping for the riverbank at Boyd's.

Carrington was waiting for him there with the boats which had just returned from landing the infantry in Virginia. Under his direction the horses were turned into the river and made to swim for it, while the weary troopers embarked in the boats with their arms and equipment. Lee and Carrington were the last two men to step ashore on the far side of the Dan on the night of February 14. Behind them the British came to a standstill. The Dan could not be forded. The boats were all on the north bank. Cornwallis had lost the race.

He rested his disappointed army for four days, and then on February 19 turned back toward Hillsboro, nursing a fading hope that the North Carolina Tories would rally to the British standard there. He had not captured the rebel army, though he had driven it out of the Carolinas. He had allowed himself to be drawn beyond the limit of his communications with his nearest source of supply at Wilmington, North Carolina. At Ramsour's Mills he had destroyed his baggage and the rum ration, to strip down for the race to the Dan. He could not last much longer without falling back down the Cape Fear River, which flowed into the sea at Wilmington, to make use of his resources there.

Greene had no intention of abandoning the Carolinas to the possession of the enemy. He had saved his heavy baggage and most of his stores, for what they were worth, and he could now receive reinforcements and supplies from the friendly Virginians while he rested and refreshed his triumphant army. Militia began coming in, along with a few hardy Virginia officers—Stevens, Lawson, Campbell, and others—not well equipped but willing and not already fatigued by the long flight to the Dan.

Young Colonel Lee, to his own satisfaction, was the first to take the field again. As Cornwallis moved away toward Hillsboro, Lee recrossed the Dan southward with his mounted legion to operate with Pickens and his small force of North Carolina militia in the vicinity of the Haw River, which flowed between Guildford Courthouse and Hillsboro to become the Cape Fear River above Wilmington. They were under orders to suppress every attempt by local Tories to rally to Cornwallis at Hillsboro.

Lee still had unfinished business with Tarleton, who had crossed the Haw westward to rouse up the Tories in that neighborhood and induce them to join the British camp at Hillsboro. Lee and Pickens followed him, and what came to be known as "the Pyle massacre" occurred on February 25, when Lee encountered a small force of Tories led by Colonel Pyle on their way to Hillsboro. Pyle mistook the weathered green coats of Lee's legion for the British green of Tarleton's famous dragoons, whom he had expected to find. His recognition of Pickens's Up Country militia came too late, and in the confusion of a sudden onslaught, where Lee had the advantage of surprise and no quarter was given, several hundred of the luckless Tories were slain.

Lee and Pickens, with no fatalities among their men, did not pursue Pyle's fugitive survivors but held to their course, hoping to overtake Tarleton himself. But he had heard of the fight in time to regain the safety of the Hillsboro camp. The Tories were now thoroughly discouraged, and the British army was suffering from its lack of baggage, from exposure, and from constant daily hunger. Cornwallis reluctantly withdrew from Hillsboro and the river road to Wilmington and crossed the Haw westward toward Guildford Courthouse in a last obstinate attempt to come to grips with Greene, who had returned to North Carolina only three days behind Lee.

Once again the deadly game of tag began, but now it went in circles, marching and countermarching, over and around the streams called Troublesome Creek and Reedy Fork and Allamance. Tents were set up only to shelter stacked muskets and ammunition, to keep them dry for instant use. Greene shifted his ground every day, so that no one ever knew where the next overnight camp would be. But he was never far from Guildford Courthouse, which stood on the brow of a little hill above a clearing, overlooking the main road to Salisbury, which was only a muddy track winding through woods and across a rivulet in a valley—ground which he had thoroughly reconnoitered before setting out for the Dan. This was his chosen battleground, but he was determined not to be drawn into action until all his reinforcements were in.

Indefatigable, almost sleepless, always cheerful and composed, while his staff and the dogged men who kept up with him threw themselves down anywhere for exhausted slumber, Greene sat each night at his portable desk, lighted by a single lantern, writing his endless dispatches and orders. At dawn, after an hour or two on his camp bed, he made the rounds of the camp, his mere approach straightening the backs of the sentries at their posts, heartening his wet, hungry, homesick militia with a word of praise or sympathy, smiling at the entreaties of his officers that he should allow himself more rest. There is a legend that he once discovered a young major drowsing in his blanket and rebuked him with a sharp inquiry how he could sleep with the enemy so near. "But, General, I knew you were awake!" the man replied. To Greene, that was a compliment.

And so the dreary military dance went on, with Lee and Pickens always hovering on Cornwallis's flanks, Williams and Washington maneuvering in front and to the rear. There were constant little skirmishes, false alarms, close shaves, quick escapes. Cornwallis had to provoke a fight now, and he had to report a British success to his superiors in New York and London before he became a laughingstock in the countryside whose support was essential to his success. His men had suffered from the same bad weather and privations that Greene's had endured, and they were mercenaries and professionals serving for pay which had not arrived for weeks. They were without the flame of patriotism to sustain them, and they would put up with only so much misery before deserting or balking.

Greene had less to lose by an unsuccessful engagement and could better afford the continued delay. He was determined to deal a crippling blow when the opportunity came and force Cornwallis to fall back to Wilmington to recuperate. At last he felt ready to risk it, with his reinforcements all gathered in. He was top-heavy with militia, who would run after firing the first round, as they always did. But he had a backlog of Continental veterans to rely on, and his cavalry was in better shape and better mounted than Cornwallis's and in his opinion better led, for Lee was cautious and clever where Tarleton was headlong and angry.

On March 4 Greene left his camp at High Rock Ford on the Haw and arrived at Guildford Courthouse in time for a last survey of the ground before darkness fell. His army slept on their arms on the field where they knew they were to fight the next day.

Frost covered the ground during the night, and the morning sun rose bright and warm, for it was already spring in the Carolinas. Breakfast was eaten tranquilly, the men clustered in silent little groups, each busy with his own thoughts, as they awaited the signal to take their battle stations. The drums beat at six o'clock, tents were struck, and the baggage was moved to the rear. Lee had gone out earlier to reconnoiter along the road. Before long he encountered Tarleton and sent back a courier at the gallop to report the British army on the march. Cornwallis had taken up the challenge.

The faces around the council table in the Courthouse were grave but confident. The gravity was caused by something more than respect for Cornwallis, and it was voiced by Colonel Williams as spokesman, just before the council dispersed. The staff had desired him to say that it was their most urgent wish that the general would not expose himself in the coming action and to remind him how much depended on his continued presence in good health in the field. There was not one of them who could not be replaced, said Williams, but if they lost him they would have no remount.

There was a moment's silence before Greene replied, for he was much touched. Then he remarked that if they wanted him to fight the battle from behind the lines they should have hung on to Gates—he was their man for that. "If I am indispensable, and no man is that, the hand of the Lord will cover me," he told them. "To your posts, gentlemen."

The day was turning unseasonably warm as he rode down to inspect the front lines, consisting of the North Carolina militia, posted behind the illusory protection of a rail fence. His voice rang out strongly in the tense silence as the men crouched over their rifles, dreading the British bayonet.

"Three rounds, my lads—three rounds, and then you may fall back," he promised them, knowing they would fall back anyway.

Even while they grinned and cheered him, feeling better for the sight of him, vicious firing began in the distance, where Lee's advance party was skirmishing with Tarleton's. The battle had begun.

Chapter 24

There have been many colorful accounts of the battle of Guildford Courthouse, including "Lighthorse Harry" Lee's own, in the memoirs written in the third person and published soon after his death in 1818. But most of them become incoherent and contradictory as the day wore on and the pattern fell apart, until now it is only by the use of a complicated diagram that an overall picture can be drawn, and this can easily become tedious.

The start of an eighteenth-century battle was rather like a deadly minuet, with regiments of bright uniforms drawn up in full sight of each other, awaiting in cold-blooded, disciplined courage the drumbeat and the bugle call which signaled the start of the carnage; moving forward then into action at a steady pace that was measured by the drums at 120 steps to the minute; closing the ranks and stepping over prostrate bodies without faltering as the volleys from enemy muskets and artillery mowed down the comrades on the right and left hand; and finally the shock of hand-to-hand combat, bayonet thrust and horse pistol, clubbed musket and grunting, sweating, cursing physical contact.

Then the cavalry, usually posted on the flanks, would come thundering in, bugles blowing, sabers swinging, pistols popping, until it seems a miracle that anyone at all survived. Casualty figures were amazingly low, at times, though many of those listed as wounded would die for lack of care, sanitation, and common comfort. Amputations and disfigurement were almost inevitable if a man lost his footing and fell.

Guildford Courthouse began as a typical "set piece" battle, with no surprise attack and no siege operations, the outcome resting on British discipline and American fervor. Greene had had time after dawn to arrange his little army in three parallel lines across the road up which the British must advance. A little in front of the first line Captain Singleton blocked the road with two light pieces of artillery.

It was almost noon, and the day was growing hot before the British van swung into view along the road. Singleton immediately opened fire on them with his two guns. The British artillery was at once pushed forward, and Cornwallis drew up his men under a brisk cannonade from both sides. Mindful of their drumbeats, the scarlet-coated regulars deployed methodically in quickstep to the right and left, ignoring their casualties.

As anticipated by Greene, the first-line North Carolina militia scattered under the charge of Leslie's Highlanders, which came with the unnerving British huzzah and the bayonets thrown forward. The Virginians in the second line opened ranks and let the Carolinians through, taunting them as they fled, and then faced the British onslaught bravely, cutting great gaps in the red lines with a well-directed volley. But Webster's 33rd Regiment broke through "as though a door had opened behind the fugitives," and O'Hara's Guards followed Webster.

The Continentals of the third line were heavily engaged when Washington's bugles sounded and his cavalry swept in, saber arms flailing, and it all dissolved into the shrieking, clanking, iron-shod carnage of a cavalry charge against infantry. When he had passed, the British rallied doggedly and the Continentals had a glimpse of Greene as he rode among them in the gunpowder murk. "Steady, now!" he called to them. "Stand firm, and you can finish it! Our fire is taking effect!"

It was Cornwallis himself who decided the day. His horse had been killed under him, and he was remounted on a dragoon's animal when he emerged from the woods on the right to see his best troops mixed with their stubborn opponents in what threatened to become a British rout. Relying on the seasoned troops he commanded, he ordered his artillery to open at close range, firing ruthlessly into the Guards and the 33rd in order to check the advance of the Marylands. O'Hara, who was wounded, protested frantically that they were destroying their own men. Cornwallis ignored him and watched grimly as the Marylands reeled back and the Guards formed again among their dead and dying and stood to face the staggering enemy. More than one British officer turned away sick at the sight, but Cornwallis called it stern necessity, and the British cannon spoke again and again, mowing down red coats and blue impartially.

Meanwhile Greene had ridden forward to get a better view of what appeared to promise an American victory, galloping into a badly damaged but still collected enemy, until his aide Burnett with a horrified shout caught his bridle and turned the horse back toward the Courthouse behind the American lines. Greene was stunned and sickened by the callous discipline of command that had caused the British general to cannonade his own men in order to head the enemy, but he had seen enough to know that he had crippled Cornwallis's army. It was not a spectacular victory he had won, and he could not keep the field, but he was safe to leave it to the British remnants. Determined not to increase his own losses needlessly, he ordered a retreat to his old encampment at Troublesome Creek.

After a hot, sunny spring day, the night fell rainy and cold over the battlefield—"the dead unburied," Lee recorded in his memoirs, "the wounded unsheltered, and the groans of the dying and the shrieks of the living shed a deeper shade over the gloom of nature. The victorious [British] troops, without tents and without food, participated in sufferings which they could not believe. The ensuing morning was spent in performing the last offices to the dead, and providing some comfort for the wounded. In executing these sad duties, the British general regarded with equal attention friends and foes. As soon as this service was over, Lord Cornwallis put his army in motion eastward. All his wounded incapable of moving (about 70 in number) he left to the humanity of General Greene."

Cornwallis had spent the night in a private anguish of his own, while his casualty reports came in. Stuart, Grant, O'Hara, Webster, Tarleton—all wounded or killed and more than five hundred lost in the ranks. He had had barely enough men to begin the battle. What could he hope for now?

Greene led the dreary night withdrawal under the pelting rain, to reach Troublesome Creek as day was breaking. From there he at once sent back a white flag with a surgeon to attend the wounded still on the field. His losses were less crippling than Cornwallis's. Stevens and Huger were wounded, and most of the militia had gone home "to kiss their wives and sweethearts." The troops were worn out with marching and fighting, but they were in fine spirits nevertheless, for they knew they had acquitted themselves well and had accomplished an organized retirement instead of a headlong flight. In a letter to a friend in Congress Greene reported that they had "blundered through without meeting any capital misfortune. We were obliged to give up the ground, and left our artillery; but the enemy has been so soundly beaten that they dare not move towards us since the action, notwithstanding that we lay within ten miles of them for ten days. We have little to eat, less to drink, and lodge in the woods in the midst of smoke. Our fatigue is great. I was so much overcome night before last that I fainted."

Cornwallis had no choice but to retreat to Wilmington, where Colonel James Craig had taken possession in January, being assigned to the task of keeping open a seacoast base for Cornwallis as he prepared to follow Greene "to the end of the world." Cornwallis was now hampered by the sick and wounded he carried with him. Many of these died along the road of privation, poor food, rough travel, and the pitiless fever that accompanied a wound. The greatest loss in this way was the popular and amiable Webster of the 33rd, a close personal friend of Cornwallis throughout the Jersey campaign and through bloody Camden to the fatal wound at Guildford and a grave in the village of Elizabethtown, only a few miles short of the comparative comfort of Wilmington. Tarleton too had been hit, but both he and O'Hara recovered to take the field again.

Greene followed the retreating British column as far as Ramsay's Mill on the Haw, where he abandoned hope of overtaking Cornwallis for another damaging fight on his own terms. Finding himself now the pursued instead of the pursuer, Cornwallis had departed his camp on the Haw so hastily that he had left whole quarters of freshly slaughtered beef still hanging. These were seized by Greene's hungry Continentals, who found even the British garbage worth rummaging in. Greene wrote Washington that he was determined to carry the war back to South Carolina, "which would be unexpected to the enemy and force him to follow or give up all his posts in that State." Ensuring himself a safe retreat, he sent his baggage back to Charlotte, where he could count on the support of the inhabitants.

In December of the previous year Greene had arrived at Charlotte to find the British in full possession of South Carolina and Georgia, which they held by a line of small garrisoned posts extending along the rivers from Charleston to Augusta and 96. North Carolina and Virginia above this line were wide open to attack by Cornwallis from the south. Since then, by dividing his limited forces Greene had compelled Cornwallis to do the same, and had lured him from his Santee bases on an exhausting pursuit that finally ended on a battleground of Greene's own choosing. Guildford Courthouse was two hundred miles from Cornwallis's coastal communications with New York, and he had been left encumbered with sick and wounded "in the midst of timid friends and bitter enemies." In the first three months of 1781, therefore, what would prove to be the turning point of the war had been achieved by the Quaker book-soldier from Rhode Island, against Britain's battle-hardened regulars led by their best general in the field.

Clinton, kicking his heels in New York, was fully aware that Cornwallis's failure to overrun North Carolina and occupy Virginia, which was the real goal, would have serious consequences, both in America and at Whitehall in London, for it was being said in Parliament that "another such victory would destroy the British army."

Arnold had been in Virginia since December, but he got no farther than the James River, where he had sat down to fortify Portsmouth. Steuben, who had been left by Greene to protect Virginia with an inadequate force while he tried to collect recruits, could do little to dislodge Arnold without the help of a French fleet in the Chesapeake. Owing to more misunderstandings and miscalculations at Newport, Rochambeau had been unable to supply naval aid. The force Washington sent to Virginia under Lafayette in February had had to disembark at Head of Elk in Maryland, while Lafayette rode on to a conference with Steuben at Williamsburg in Virginia. While they were still discussing their situation, the British veteran General William Phillips, recently exchanged for Lincoln, arrived at Portsmouth to outrank Arnold.

It was apparently a part of the British strategy emanating from New York that Cornwallis should leave the conquered Carolinas prostrate behind him and proceed to a junction with Arnold and Phillips on the James—although he was at that moment retreating toward Wilmington after his mauling at Guildford Courthouse. An account of that battle first reached Steuben at Richmond by the hand of Colonel Morris, direct from Greene, with a request for reinforcements to be sent to him quickly to aid him in the pursuit of Cornwallis to the coast. Steuben went to Chesterfield Courthouse to gather recruits and ammunition to send to North Carolina, himself remaining in Virginia to join forces with Lafayette. Their combined army was soon augmented by Wayne with his Pennsylvanians.

On the third of April the men at Greene's camp at Ramsay's

Mill were ordered to "wash and clean themselves, get their arms in good order, and be prepared to march at short warning." Before breaking camp Greene wrote to Sumter, who was recruiting on the Catawba, to say that he expected to be in the neighborhood of Camden by the middle of May and asked him to join him there with militia (which Sumter could not be depended upon to do). He also sent orders to Pickens to invest 96 "if he felt able" (which he did not) or at least to prevent reinforcements from reaching Rawdon at Camden. Lee was ordered to find Marion on the PeeDee and cooperate with him against the Santee forts— with a literary allusion, perfectly understood by Lee, to the example of Scipio Africanus, a hero of the Punic wars who razed the city of Carthage. "I am conscious that no general ever commanded troops worse appointed or worse supplied than those who form your present army," he added sympathetically.

It is worth pausing here, in the midst of a grim chronicle of war, for a digression set down in Lee's own illuminating account of his part in the operations after Guildford Courthouse. On his march to the junction with Marion he camped for a night with his corps of light infantry and cavalry in a field on the bank of Drowning Creek, a branch of the Little PeeDee where, he relates, "a very extraordinary occurrence took place."

Between two and three o'clock in the morning, the Officer of the Day was informed that strange noises had been heard in front of the picket stationed near the creek—noises resembling that of a body of men moving toward the camp. A bugle called in the horse patrols as was the custom on the approach of the enemy. The troops were summoned to arms and arrayed for defense, while the sentinel who had fired nervously into the rustling darkness around him was questioned, and maintained that he had heard the stealthy movements of enemy horsemen. Lee was sure that no enemy was anywhere in the neighborhood, unless Cornwallis had sent out a detachment from Wilmington to intercept him, which was very unlikely. He was inclined to dismiss the alarm as the product of the picket's scary imagination—until, in quite another quarter of the camp's perimeter, another picket fired and gave the same explanation—he had heard something approaching him across the inky swamp he faced. Lee took this report more seriously and changed formation to confront it when a third picket's gun went off from still a different direction. Again the corps changed front, in an endeavor to keep the fires between them and the unknown menace, which seemed now to surround them, while a creepy sensation of being haunted began to grow upon the officers. A fourth alarm, from the picket on guard at the main road which was their intended route the following day, seemed to leave no doubt that they had somehow been reconnoitered and encircled.

Marion was two days' march away. Greene was already several days' march toward Camden. Whatever it was, they were alone with it and must fight their way out of some kind of ambuscade. Lee passed among the men with low, heartening words, formed up in two columns, horse and foot, and waited anxiously for the break of day. At dawn they moved out cautiously into the road in marching order, infantry in front, baggage in the center, cavalry in the rear, expecting every moment an explosion of enemy fire. Nothing happened. The cream of the joke is in Lee's own poker-faced passage of explanation:

"In this state of suspense we might have continued long, had not the van officer directed his attention to the ground, for the purpose of examining the trail of our active foe, when to his astonishment he found the tracks of a large pack of wolves. It was evident that the presumed enemy was a troop of these wild beasts, collected together, and anxious to pass along their usual route. Finding it obstructed by our camp, they turned from point to point to pass across the field; being everywhere fired on, they widened their circuit until they reached the road from which they had been originally turned.

"Our agitation vanished and was succeeded by facetious glee. Nowhere do wit and humor abound more than in camps; and no occurrence was more apt to elicit it than the one we had just experienced. Never was a day's march more pleasant, being one continued scene of good humor, interspersed with innocent flashes of wit. For a time the restraint of discipline ceased. Every character, not excepting the commandant's, was hit; and very salutary counsel was often imparted under cover of a joke. Each considered himself a dupe, all laughing at a credulity which any attempt to remove during the scene would have been treated as insulting temerity. The pickets, the patrols, the sentinels, and the

Officer of the Day were marked as particular objects of derision. How wonderful that not one of them could distinguish between the movements of wolves and soldiers! They were charged with disgraceful ignorance, shameful stupidity, even rank cowardice. Vain was the attempt of the abused individuals to defend their character and conduct; it was the interest of the many to fix the supposed stigma on the few, and the general verdict was against them. Reaching a settlement, the corps halted, and for a while the remembrance of the ludicrous occurrence of the night yielded to the solicitude of everyone to provide his breakfast."

Inevitably the story leaked out, amid irrepressible humor, to the inhabitants of the little settlement, who were able to give a further explanation. The corps had unknowingly encamped on a spot close to where a store of provisions for the army had been collected and then abandoned as being too distant from the line of march. As it became putrid from neglect, the wolves had been drawn to it for some nights past. When access to their nightly feast was interrupted, they had circled hungrily around the camp trying to find a way through to their usual meal.

Doubtless when Lee eventually caught up with Marion in the PeeDee swamp on the fourteenth of April, the story of the spooky enemy at Drowning Creek was received by Marion's pack of knowledgeable swamp-foxes with hilarity and much friendly derision. Marion welcomed Lee as a partner in the enterprise against the river forts, and there was no quibble about rank between them.

The handsome, buoyant, polished Virginia horse-soldier, who often went into action with his hair fashionably powdered white, and the gaunt, swarthy, taciturn swamp-country partisan had somehow understood and liked each other at first sight, when Lee was sent down from Cheraw the previous December. His subsequent recall to join Huger on the march from Cheraw to the Guildford Courthouse junction had seemed at the time an unwelcome interruption to their mutual fun with the British in the Low Country, but now they were together again, happily bound on a new mission.

It must have been rather a rollicking expedition that left Marion's swamp hideaway and set out in bright spring weather for the British stronghold on the Santee which was first on their list as being the nearest—matching stories as they rode, of the now famous retreat to the Dan at which Lee had assisted and of the river raids and bushwhacking which had occupied Marion during the past winter.

The fortified stockade known as Fort Watson had been erected on an ancient Indian burial mound which rose some fifty feet on Wright's Bluff overlooking Nelson's Ferry on the Santee. Lieutenant-Colonel John Watson Tadwell-Watson, of His Majesty's Third Regiment of Guards—the magnificent "Buffs"—had built his redoubt according to all the rules, complete with fosse, or ditch, parapet, abatis, and ports for guns. Its only lack was a fresh-water supply within the fortifications.

Marion had received intelligence that Colonel Watson was at that moment absent from the fort which bore his name, having left it in the command of a Lieutenant Mackay on orders from Rawdon to bring up reinforcements from Georgetown to the garrison at Camden. Colonel Watson was not unknown to Marion, for in March of that year, while Lee was parrying O'Hara on the race for the Virginia border, Marion and Watson had encountered each other at the causeway in Wiboo swamp.

After some wicked hand-to-hand fighting with the famous Buffs, Marion had been forced to call back his ragged horsemen from in front of Watson's redcoat charge. As usual, he was able to evaporate into the swamp. But as Marion backed away, Watson followed, and there was another skirmish at a ford on the Black River, where Marion's sharpshooters took a merciless toll among the Guards, who were forced to fight waist-deep in black swamp water.

This time it was Watson who withdrew—he had never in his life seen such shooting, he said. From the Witherspoon plantation he sent a child with a letter to Marion requesting safe passage for his wounded to Charleston. Marion, whose white flag Watson had already violated by detaining the man who bore it, granted the pass for Watson's wounded with an acid lecture on civilized warfare, which did not, he pointed out, include the burning of homesteads and the terrorizing of women. After still another engagement, on the Sampit River, Watson complained in writing that

Marion's men "will not fight and sleep like gentlemen, but like savages are eternally firing and whooping around us by night, and by day waylaying and popping at us from behind every tree!"

Marion and Lee, advised that Watson was somewhere behind them on his way up from Georgetown to join Rawdon, pitched their camp among flowering haws near Wright's Bluff and began their siege of Watson's unfortunate deputy. First they cut off Mackay's access to his water supply by posting sharpshooters to pick off anyone who emerged on that errand. Mackay then dug a ditch along which his men could run to the spring unseen. There would not be time, with Watson on the march, to starve Mackay into surrender, and Marion had no cannon.

Inaction did not suit him, accustomed as he was to hit-and-run tactics. Here he was compelled to sit down in the open and wait for a stubborn opponent to give up. He became irritable and fretted for a cannon with which to finish Mackay's business and move on to the next job. His men sensed his mood and began to desert. Then a well-read newcomer to the corps proposed a fantastic solution which was practiced, he said, in classic warfare but which seemed almost as farfetched as the Trojan horse. Hezekiah Maham wanted to build a hollow log tower, tall enough to overlook the rampart of the fort, with a platform on the top and a timber parapet to shield marksmen who could be stationed there to fire into the fort from above it.

Marion heard him skeptically, Lee with excitement, and horsemen were dispatched to bring in all the axes available from every neighboring plantation. The chopping and felling of trees went on all night, and the logs were stacked conveniently out of sight from the fort. After another night's work Mackay found himself helplessly looking *up* at a crow's-nest of riflemen whose bullets whizzed into his breastworks, while his buckshot sank harmlessly into the green logs protecting Marion's marksmen. He surrendered. The terms offered by Lee and Marion for the sake of a quick settlement were unexpectedly generous. The officers were permitted to keep their swords, sign paroles, and remove their personal baggage to Charleston, where they would await regular exchange.

Cornwallis was then discovered to be leaving Wilmington for an unknown destination. By Greene's orders Marion and Lee remained at a plantation behind Wright's Bluff watching for Tarleton, who would soon be heard from in case Cornwallis meant to relieve Rawdon at Camden—and meanwhile Watson slipped past them, "his men much fatigued and hungry," but safely on the road to Camden. Marion was furious and felt deprived of his rightful prey. Lee, playing diplomat, wrote to Greene suggesting a letter of appreciation to the sensitive partisan, whose successes had been, Lee pointed out, neglected by his superiors. This Greene was quick to supply.

But Lee was not lacking in energy and zeal, and he bombarded Greene with reports of their joint activities, their unfortunate lack of a field piece at Fort Watson, and their need of additional riflemen, which Greene could not spare for the river-forts sideshow. Sometimes he replied rather crisply, from his camp at Twenty-five Mile Creek: "You write as if I had an army of fifty thousand men. Surely you cannot be unacquainted with our real situation. I am as strongly impressed with the necessity of pushing our operations on the west side of the Santee as you can be, but the means are wanting. If we cannot accomplish great things, we must content ourselves with having avoided a misfortune."

After the disastrous retreat from Guildford Courthouse Cornwallis had remained at Wilmington eighteen days, while his army licked its wounds and he debated his difficult choice—to back up Rawdon at Camden, or go north to meet Phillips, whom he supposed to be marching toward him from the James with reinforcements from New York. He chose Phillips, and with this fatal decision on April 25 he left the scene of Greene's Southern campaign and crossed the Dan northward into Virginia, intending with the aid of Phillips to dislodge Lafayette and Steuben from the Richmond area.

The sudden death of Phillips from fever at Petersburg before Cornwallis's arrival, and the reinforcement of Lafayette by Wayne and his Pennsylvanians, forced Cornwallis into the Virginia campaign which in October would drive him to the hopeless stand at Yorktown.

Behind him, Rawdon remained to take up the challenge that Greene was now about to direct against the main British post at Camden.

Chapter 25

It was Greene's hope to take Rawdon by surprise, but before he arrived outside Camden on April 20, willing tale-bearers in the hostile Tory countryside had warned the British garrison of his approach. Surprise having become impossible, "various madcaps" in Greene's camp were eager for a storm attack at once. Reconnoitering cautiously, he found the Camden works too formidable to be carried by even the most gallant assault tactics and retired a few miles to a strong position at Hobkirk's Hill, hoping that Rawdon would come out and attack him there. His chosen ground was a narrow wooded sand-ridge overlooking two small streams running through the swamp. Greene camped that night in battle order, with his veterans in front, William Washington's horse troop on their right, and the artillery in the road.

At daybreak of April 25 the American camp was occupied by the arrival of some stores and the cooking of breakfast, amid some grumbling because the promised issue of rum had not yet materialized, when firing was heard from their pickets in the woods on the left. The American drums beat to arms and the troops seized their weapons and formed ranks. Some light infantry was hurried off under Kirkwood, a Cowpens veteran, to support the pickets, and was slowly forced back, volley on volley, toward the hill where the main army waited, many of them breakfastless, for the sound of their own guns signaling the start of the action.

Rawdon came on handsomely, displaying on a very narrow front, and Greene's quick attempt to flank him failed after the death of a militia officer threw his companies into disorder. Early in the battle, when the British cavalry had seemed to falter, Rawdon galloped up to the weak spot and was quickly surrounded by Washington's dragoons and his sword was demanded as a token of his surrender. But Rawdon was "a man of uncommon address." A swift glance around revealed confusion among the Marylands, where a hasty word of command had been misunderstood. Rawdon saw his own dragoons rallying to his relief, and he bowed politely to his captors, appearing to acquiesce; but managed to fumble the delivery of his sword as though having difficulty in unhooking it, until his own men were among Washington's, forcing them to withdraw—a narrow escape for Rawdon and a costly loss to the Americans.

Greene exposed himself recklessly and led his men "like a captain of the grenadiers." In an attempt to save his cannon from capture, after the artillery horses had been killed, he dismounted and with his bridle in one hand and a dragrope in the other, by his voice and example revived the courage of the panicked artillerymen whose teams were useless. At the decisive moment Washington's troopers galloped in, each horseman with a prisoner up behind him. The captives were quickly thrown off, and the guns were saved by the cavalry horses.

The Americans retired from the field skirmishing and in good order. They paused about three miles away to recoup, as the fainthearted British pursuit was soon given over. Greene camped that night only five miles from the field, and the parole and countersign for the night were "Persevere" and "Fortitude." To Steuben Greene wrote: "This repulse, if repulse it may be called, will make no alteration in our general plan of operations. We fight, get beat, rise, and fight again."

As usual, the British claimed a victory and exaggerated Greene's defeat. When Lafayette in Virginia heard the facts he summed up by the comment that "like all of Greene's 'reverses' it would in the end contribute only to the ruin of the enemy." It was at best an inconclusive victory for Rawdon, who could only return to his Camden fortifications and await the anticipated arrival of Colonel Watson from down river with reinforcements, while

Greene made camp at Saunders Creek, on almost the same spot where Gates had met his resounding defeat the previous year.

The incorrigible Sumter was nowhere to be seen, as was his habit. He sent in some supplies to Greene's camp, but he could never bend his independent spirit to subordinate command under Greene and found many excuses not to join the main army. Greene was afraid to press him lest he take offense and resign altogether, and so left him to pursue his main usefulness, which was to encourage the spirit of resistance in the countryside and control the roving bands of Tories who did violence to friend and foe alike.

The battle at Hobkirk's Hill made very little change in the relative circumstances of Rawdon and Greene. Both had suffered losses, provisions were short, and Rawdon's vital communications with Charleston were threatened by a virtual blockade of Camden by Greene. Subsistence was Greene's own main problem now. Carrington, in charge of the commissariat, was indefatigable, but transportation was scarce and deliveries at headquarters were irregular. Greene could only recall his own past difficulties as quartermaster and strive for patience. As usual, his forces were dwindling as terms of militia service expired, and new levies were slow to come in.

Colonel Davie, the Salisbury lawyer who had served on Greene's staff during the long retreat and at the two engagements since then, enjoyed Greene's confidence. On the night of May 9 he found the Quaker general bent over a map spread on the table in his quarters at the Colonel's Creek camp. "I have sent for you," he quoted Greene as saying, "to inform you that Lord Rawdon is preparing to evacuate Camden. That place was the key of the enemy's line of posts, and they will now all fall or be evacuated. I shall march immediately to the Congaree. Arrange your convoys to follow us and let me know what expresses and detachments you need."

Rawdon's decision to leave Camden was apparently sudden and based on information or orders brought by Watson from the coast, for Cornwallis was now known to be heading for Virginia and, as Greene rightly suspected, a junction with Arnold and Phillips on the James. The evacuation of Camden meant outright British retreat from all the country north of the Congaree. Balfour, commanding at Charleston, seems to have gone into panic after the loss of Fort Watson. When Cornwallis reached Halifax in Virginia he was overtaken by a wail of defeatism from Balfour: "I must inform your Excellency that the general state of the country is most distressing and that the enemy's parties are everywhere. The communications by land with Savannah no longer exist; Colonel Browne is invested at Augusta, and Colonel Cruger is in the most critical position at 96. Indeed, I should betray the duty I owe your Excellency did I not represent the defection of this province as so universal that I know of no mode short of *depopulation* to retain it."

Rawdon had sent orders to Cruger at 96 to join Browne at Augusta and to Maxwell at Fort Granby on the Congaree to fall back to Orangeburgh on the North Edisto River nearer Charleston. Neither of these orders reached their destination, thanks to partisan watchfulness, and the garrisons continued to hold their isolated positions.

In his open acknowledgment of failure, Rawdon's tactics were as usual ruthless. Before he left the little town of Camden he burned the jail, the courthouse, and the mill, along with some private houses and stores; he even sacrificed the greater part of his own army's baggage. On the tenth of May he set out for the Congaree in the hope of rescuing Fort Motte, at that moment under siege by Marion and Lee.

Chapter 26

Greene entered the smoking ruins of Camden soon after Rawdon's departure. He had been delayed by the hope of receiving some overdue Virginia militia, which did not arrive. He was therefore just too late to attack the garrison as it moved out, encumbered by its sick and wounded. He followed Rawdon toward the Congaree, where Lee and Marion were already besieging their second objective, Fort Motte.

This post, near McCord's Ferry, was the principal depot of the supply convoys from Charleston to Camden and 96. The British had taken possession of a comfortable mansion, the summer home of the wealthy widow Motte, who had been Rebecca Brewton of Charleston. The house occupied "a commanding position" above the river, and Major McPherson's garrison had dug a trench and raised a parapet on its inner margin close to the walls of the dwelling. Mrs. Motte, an unwilling hostess, had refused to occupy a room in the building appropriated by the British, and had retired with her daughters to live in her overseer's farmhouse on a little hill to the north of the fortified house. Here she welcomed the arrival of Lee and Marion on the eighth of May. They posted themselves around her farmhouse and put relays of work parties to digging parallels.

While this work was going forward, the American officers were liberally entertained at Mrs. Motte's hospitable dinner table, spread with whatever delicacies she had managed to conceal from her unwelcome British visitors. She even administered to the invalids and wounded who traveled with the American corps.

When summoned to surrender, McPherson declared his intention of resisting, in the conviction that Rawdon on his retreat from Camden would arrive in time to save him. A message from Greene urged the besiegers to make haste before Rawdon could cross the river and informed them of his own move to support them. That night Rawdon's campfires could be seen from both the fort and the farmhouse, but he was still on the wrong side of the river and would have to march downstream to Nelson's Ferry before he could gain the other bank.

There was no time to batter down the mansion with a single cannon, or to complete the digging of their approach trenches. But there was another expedient well known to Marion's rugged band of followers—the old Indian trick of shooting flame-tipped arrows into dry timbers, so that the house would burn down over the heads of its defenders.

It fell to the courtly and charming Lee to disclose to Mrs. Motte the hard decision which had been arrived at by himself and Marion. She heard him without flinching and declared herself willing to see her home and possessions sacrificed to her country. Observing that the hastily contrived arrows they planned to use were inadequate, she produced from a storeroom a bundle of arrows and a fine bow, which had been brought back as a curiosity from the East Indies years before by her brother, who was a sea captain. She presented them to Lee. One of Marion's men drew the bow and sent lighted torches into the tinder-dry shingles. Mrs. Motte watched unmoved while the flames crept along the roof.

McPherson ordered a couple of soldiers up to knock off the flaming shingles and extinguish the fire. Marion's riflemen drove them down with their mission unaccomplished, and McPherson showed a white flag. Marion's guns fell silent while the fire was put out. Not a drop of blood had been shed.

Greene arrived shortly afterward, having crossed at Friday's Ferry with a cavalry escort. He heard the theatrical account of the siege with laughter and apologies to Mrs. Motte, who invited them all to dinner at the farmhouse. The victorious officers and their British captives all sat down together at her table, in a brief, civilized interlude. Marion's Colonel Horry and McPherson's Captain Ferguson told each other stories about the fight at Nelson's Ferry after Camden, when both had been present. Lee recorded in his memoirs that Mrs. Motte's demeanor "and the engaging amiability of her manners left it doubtful which set of officers were the defenders of her country."

It was Greene's first opportunity to take the elusive Marion by the hand and express his personal appreciation of his services in the partisan warfare that had worn down Cornwallis and Rawdon and driven them from the ground above the Santee. It was reunion too with Lee, who was regarded with an almost paternal affection by both General Washington and Greene.

After this social interlude with no hard feelings on either side, the members of Fort Motte's garrison were dispatched on parole to join Rawdon, whose retreat had now reached Nelson's Ferry on the Santee. Greene ordered Lee off the same night for Fort Granby, which lay above them at the fork of the Broad and Saluda rivers, and with Augusta and 96 was all that remained of the British Up Country posts.

Sumter was still acting independently and refusing to recognize Greene's authority, operating always within his own personal web of spies and informers and leading what amounted to a separate small army of his own recruiting. After having established a siege of Fort Granby himself, he had posted a militia force there to watch the garrison while he embarked on what he later confessed was a "somewhat whimsical" expedition to attack Orangeburgh on the North Edisto, west of Fort Motte. The small British garrison there had fortified the brick jail and were still in ignorance of Rawdon's decision to abandon all the Up Country posts and retreat to Charleston. Orangeburgh surrendered promptly on May 11 to the single six-pounder Sumter carried with him, and he took possession of its supplies and nearly one hundred prisoners.

Before Sumter could return to his interrupted siege of Fort Granby, Lee had arrived there by Greene's orders and with his victorious troops from Fort Motte brushed aside the militia Sumter had left on guard. To get a quick surrender Lee offered the commandant the same overgenerous terms which had worked at Fort Watson. They were accepted on May 15, and Lee even furnished Major Maxwell with an escort down to Nelson's Ferry.

Unaware of Fort Granby's surrender to Lee in his absence, Sumter reached the post he considered already his own on the following day and was incensed when his militia men reported Lee's high-handed behavior. Lee had departed toward his next assignment at Augusta, where Pickens was already walking up and down waiting for him. Sumter wrote a huffy letter to Greene, complaining of his old wound and the "discontent" among his militia, and enclosing his commission and resignation. To a man of Greene's equable nature the Carolina brigadiers seemed a testy lot.

Tactful and patient as always with his temperamental subordinates, Greene sent Sumter a soothing reply, including some judicious flattery, expressed sympathy for the discomfort of the wound which still tormented him, and reminded him that Greene himself as a Continental officer had no authority to accept Sumter's resignation. This was a matter for Governor Rutledge to act upon, and Rutledge was not available. "I therefore take the liberty to return to you your commission, and to inform you that I cannot think of accepting it, and beg you to resume your command," he added and suggested the value of a move on Sumter's part to raze the captured British posts along the rivers.

Mollified, Sumter established himself at Fort Granby, from where he could observe any further moves by the British up or down the rivers. Sumter was less dedicated than Marion, less disciplined than Lee, and unfit now to collaborate in the critical mopping-up campaign which lay ahead of Greene's army.

Greene's crying need was always horses, and Tarleton with Cornwallis in Virginia was now in a position to impress and carry off the fine blood stock that Jefferson had evaded handing over to Greene while the army lay at Halifax after crossing the Dan. Marion always seemed able to mount his men respectably, and Greene's repeated requests to him for horses had caused some resentment between them. Marion had refused to dismount any of his own men in order to supply horses for the main army, lest his volunteer followers desert him in a body. However, this touchiness of Marion's and Greene's resulting annoyance had been smoothed over at the Fort Motte meeting before Marion set off to lay siege to Georgetown, which would soon be in his hands.

Forts Watson, Motte, and Granby, as well as Orangeburgh, had all fallen within a month since Greene returned to the Camden area. News of his successes had reached the commander in chief at New Windsor on the Hudson, and he wrote his congratulations. Joseph Reed at Philadelphia, who still maintained a correspondence with his friend from the Cambridge days, wrote Greene that Congress was discussing a proposal to strike a medal for him, but for want of money this was never done. Governor Rutledge was in Philadelphia again, trying to get appropriations and supplies for the Southern army, and he could tell at first hand of his own experiences in Greene's camp, where he was always a welcome guest.

Gratified, but by no means inflated by this belated recognition, Greene wrote Rutledge that it was time to think of reestablishing civil government in his state, with the implication that the governor should come home and set about it. He then addressed himself to the very considerable problem represented by the remaining British post at 96, which was still a rallying point for the Up Country Tory trouble-makers.

Chapter 27

It has been suggested that if Greene had followed Rawdon's discouraged march southward from Camden in the oncoming heat of the Low Country summer, and had somehow overtaken and defeated him short of his Charleston base, the post of 96 would have shriveled up and died on the vine, along with Augusta. But it is always easy to say what should have been done. It was only after careful weighing of alternatives that he had sent Lee to support Pickens at Augusta and turned northeast with his own column to follow the Saluda toward the little settlement of 96—so-called because it lay ninety-six miles from the old frontier fort of Prince George on the Keowee River in the Cherokee country.

It was a healthful, fertile region that had been devastated by the perpetual local warfare between the Tory and Patriot inhabitants. The single street of log houses bisected the square area enclosed by a stockade, ditch, and abatis, which had been constructed to protect its small population from the Cherokee incursions. Outside the fortified square on the left, in a little valley, was the spring that formed the settlement's only water supply. This was overlooked and protected on the far side by a solid blockhouse. Within the village stockade was a fortified jail building.

96 was garrisoned by a mixed New York and North Carolina veteran Tory force commanded by the energetic and courageous Colonel Cruger, who in 1764 had been the mayor of New York City and had taken sides with the British from the beginning of the war. His garrison had erected at the east corner of the stockade a star-shaped redoubt with sixteen angles, a ditch, abatis, and ports for three small cannon.

Cut off from communication with Rawdon at Camden and Balfour at Charleston by the active partisan patrols of Pickens and Sumter, Cruger learned from a countryman that Lee had got between him and Browne at Augusta and that Greene was advancing upon him up the Saluda. He began at once to strengthen his works by digging traverses and covered ways for the movement of troops inside the stockade and to the spring, and he put up small blockhouses at the corners. He laid in a stock of provisions, sent his wife to live in a farmhouse outside the village, and awaited events.

On May 22, Greene arrived. The weather was dark and rainy, and with Kosciuszko Greene reconnoitered during the first night after their arrival, until they were fired on from the Star. They

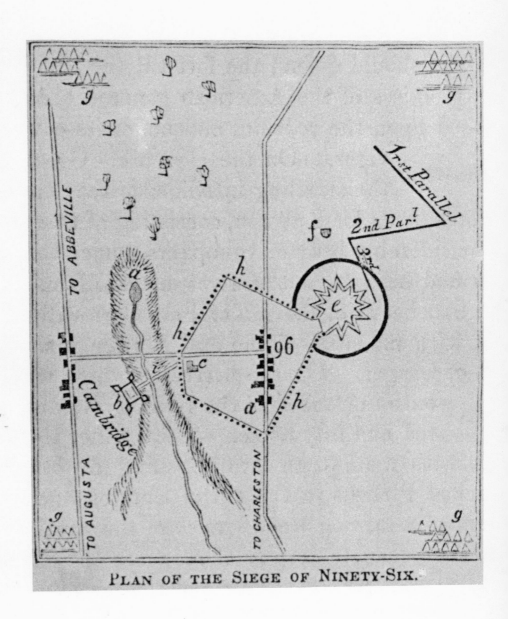

PLAN OF THE SIEGE OF NINETY-SIX.

decided upon it as the chief object of attack, believing that if it fell they would have access to the rest of the fortifications. It would seem to have been through his own choice and not incompetence that Greene followed the advice of his professional engineer and began the formal siege procedure instead of first cutting off access to the spring by attacking the blockhouse which guarded it.

The slow work of digging approach parallels consumed a week, while the work parties were protected by armed comrades who stood by to discourage the daring sallies of the besieged, resulting in many a bloody little skirmish in and around the trench. On June 3 Greene summoned the Star to surrender and received a pompous refusal from Cruger. The digging went on.

While Greene was immobilized outside 96, Marion attacked and captured Georgetown and leveled the British defense works there. On June 5 Lee and Pickens accomplished the surrender of Augusta, the only British garrison left in Georgia except Savannah. Lee then joined Greene at 96 and launched an attack toward the spring, being convinced that Greene could have shortened the siege by making that his first endeavor. Lee blamed Kosciuszko for lack of "the spark" in his professional methods of engineering by parallel, to which Greene had consented. Within a few days Lee had almost cut off access to the spring, so that every pail of water had to be won at great risk under fire or under cover of darkness. Lee then had recourse to the same device that had been successful at Fort Watson and Augusta—the Maham tower of crisscrossed logs overtopping the defenses. But Cruger was able to raise his parapets by piling sandbags inside them and could not be reached from above.

One evening a mounted countryman drifted into Greene's lines, conversing casually, a not unusual occurrence. Suddenly he put spurs to his horse and dashed into the fortified area, where he was received by the British as though he had been expected. He brought the garrison a message from Rawdon that with reinforcements from Charleston he was marching from his rest camp at Monck's Corner to Cruger's relief.

Greene was already uneasily aware of Rawdon's turnabout and had warned the partisan forces to "harass and retard" Rawdon's forced march up the Santee Road. But Marion was too far away at Georgetown, and Sumter missed fire again or never got the orders. Greene's men at 96—especially Lee—were eager for a try at the stockade before Rawdon could arrive. With some misgivings Greene authorized a premature "forlorn hope" assault on the main works of the Star. Enemy fire pinned down the first attacking party in the ditch and took a dreadful toll, while the abatis held against all attempts to burn or scale it, until Greene, always mindful of his losses, ordered a retirement. Most of the wounded were brought back safely to camp, under a galling fire. The assault failed, and although Greene had reason to be proud of the attempt he had no choice but to retire before Rawdon's advance.

The siege of 96 had lasted twenty-eight days and cost 185 American lives. "I have only to lament that such brave men fell in an unsuccessful attempt," Greene wrote Congress from his next camp east of the Saluda. "The troops have undergone incredible hardships in the siege. It is mortifying to leave a garrison so nearly reduced. I will recover South Carolina or die in the attempt." In a letter to Lafayette, now entertaining Cornwallis in Virginia, he said that his next endeavor would be to force the British to evacuate 96 and retreat into the Low Country, where the intense summer heat could be a valuable ally.

While encamped in the vicinity of Winnsboro, which had once been Cornwallis's stronghold, he planned his next cautious moves. Loyalists there were "as thick as the trees" and so bold that they even stole from the camp. It appeared that Governor Jefferson was responsible for countermanding the Virginia militia ordered southward, preferring to retain it for service against Cornwallis's army now overrunning Virginia. Greene sent Lee and Washington to maneuver in front of Rawdon's advance, screening his own intentions, and wrote again to Sumter for similar action. It is here that another of the lively legends of this picturesque war occurs.

As related by Benson Lossing, who traveled in the vicinity within living memory of the events, Rawdon's return to the Congaree had so alerted the Tory population that express riders carrying dispatches between the American units around Camden and Winnsboro encountered ambush and capture. Greene therefore met with some unwillingness among the men who would normally have undertaken the delivery of a letter to Sumter, then believed to be somewhere around Hanging Rock. To Greene's surprise and amusement, the daughter of a local planter volunteered to find Sumter and deliver the letter.

Emily Geiger was not yet eighteen years old, but she was a country girl, a competent horsewoman since childhood, and acquainted with the neighborhood roads. Impressed by her spirit and patriotism, Greene consented to allow her to undertake the mission, stipulating that if she was stopped and questioned she was to describe her journey as a family emergency. But lest she lose the letter, or have it taken from her, he required her to memorize its contents, which revealed his own position and intentions with a request for Sumter's cooperation. They gave her a good horse and she was off, with the letter concealed in her bosom.

Passing through a dry swamp area, she was intercepted by some Tory scouts, who would have made short work of an express rider on the same errand. Because she came from the direction of Greene's camp, even Emily was under suspicion, despite her youth and girlish indignation at being interrupted in what she insisted was private business for her family. She was conveyed under arrest to the nearest house and shut up in a room by herself, having strenuously resisted an attempt by her captors to search her. With singular delicacy they agreed to await the arrival of a woman from the next plantation.

"No sooner was she left alone," says Lossing, "than she ate up Greene's letter, piece by piece." When the matron arrived and searched Emily to the skin, she found nothing, and with many apologies Emily was then released to resume her journey. She reached Sumter's camp and recited the message, and it is probable that for once Sumter could not deny that he had received Greene's orders, though he was soon off on another of his independent forays toward Monck's Corner, recently vacated by Rawdon's rest camp.

Rawdon had entered 96 on June 21, plagued by illness and lack of provisions, his climate-worn regulars falling by the roadside to die there of hunger and fever in the pitiless heat. For Rawdon the game was up, and as soon as he arrived he gave orders to Cruger to prepare to evacuate 96. He knew that to abandon the village now was to leave its Tory population defenseless before the certain vengeance of those Patriots who had suffered persecution committed under British protection during Cruger's occupation.

The conflict between Tories and Patriots in the district had long been bitter and brutal, and scarcely a plantation on either side had escaped pillage or massacre. When Rawdon's intention to evacuate 96 became known, some of the Tories chose to accompany him and Cruger when they withdrew southward toward Charleston. Just as the Philadelphia Tories had followed Clinton to New York, this sorry train of wretched exiles from 96 had still the faint hope of gaining possession of some confiscated estates in the coastal land where British rule was still maintained. Many died of Low Country infections, and the survivors would establish a miserable settlement derisively known as Rawdontown, outside Charleston, until even that city surrendered to the new republic whose ultimate victory they had been unable to believe in. Behind them, 96 was abandoned to fire and sword in renewed conflict between those who had chosen to remain there.

Greene, meanwhile, had been constantly on the move, always in touch with Charlotte, where he had set up a hospital base with stores of forage and provisions. Dismantling mills and stripping the countryside as he went, he made pursuit by the ill-found enemy impossible, as the same deadly game of tag they had played with Cornwallis seemed about to begin again with Rawdon as the opponent.

On June 23 Greene was encamped on the bank of the Bush River, where his troops were ordered to clean their arms and accouterment, to wash their clothes, and to cook their provisions as quickly as possible. Rolls were called frequently to prevent desertion and no passes were granted. He still believed that another action forced on an exhausted enemy might prove decisive, if only he could collect enough men in time.

When he received word that Rawdon was heading back toward Orangeburgh he abandoned the project with some regret. A letter intercepted by William Washington's patrol revealed that Watson had been forced by ill health to retire from the command of the Buffs and return to England. He had been succeeded by Colonel Alexander Stuart, fresh from Ireland with a new contingent of regulars and ignorant of what the South Carolina climate could do.

The British Stuarts of this Southern campaign have never been properly sorted out, for spelling and Christian names. This was not the same man who had been wounded at Guildford Courthouse. He wrote Rawdon to say that he was already on his way up the river road to relieve the floundering retreat from 96.

Dreading another turnabout by Rawdon with the new reinforcements, Greene sent word to Marion to prevent the junction between Stuart and Rawdon, which nevertheless took place at Orangeburgh when Rawdon arrived there. Greene left Huger in command while he detached himself and rode ahead of the army to join Lee, who was always nipping at Rawdon's heels. The enemy were too well covered by the Edisto River and the fortified buildings at Orangeburgh, of which they were now in possession again, to be attacked on ground which was unfavorable to cavalry.

Having at least accomplished the enforced evacuation of 96, Greene thought it safer to attack the lower outposts at Monck's Corner and Dorchester—"which were nothing but churches occupied," he wrote Congress. Such a move on his part, he hoped, would force Rawdon out of his secure position at Orangeburgh in order to protect the approach to Charleston. Marion and Sumter, cooperating with each other for once, and with Lee, were detached for this purpose. But once again, according to the accounts of Lee and Greene, Sumter let them down.

Greene wrote to Pickens on July 23: "Had not Sumter detached his force too much, and had he not mistaken a covering party for an advance of the attack, he would have taken the garrison at Monck's Corner, amounting to 600 men. The enemy evacuated that post, burnt the church and the stores, and fled towards Charleston. They were pursued about two hours after they had been gone by Lieutenant-Colonel Lee's Legion, who came up with them near Shubrick's plantation, took their baggage and all their rear guards, amounting to between fifty and sixty men, and obliged the whole party to shelter themselves in Shubrick's house, where the generals Sumter and Marion made an attack upon them. But for want of cannon, which had not been ordered on, they failed. The enemy suffered greatly. Our loss was inconsiderable, though the troops were much exposed. The reason was, the enemy were all raw Irishmen, who knew little or nothing about firing."

So much for Stuart's reinforcements.

It was now late July, and the summer heat of the Low Country was taking its deadly toll, even among Greene's casually clad veterans and Marion's swamp-bred natives. The British, buttoned into their scarlet woolen uniforms and carrying heavy packs and accouterment, were suffering beyond description, and the tormented wounded of both sides had been too long without rest or tending.

Greene returned Sumter to the Congaree, where Fort Granby stood, and assigned Marion to Nelson's Ferry on the Santee, once guarded by Fort Watson. Lee's legion accompanied Greene with the main army to a "camp of repose" in the idyllically named High Hills of Santee across the river from what had been Fort Motte.

Chapter 28

The Hills of Santee are an irregular chain of sandy heights some twenty-four miles long, rising about two hundred feet above the left bank of the Wateree River north of its junction with the Congaree to form the Santee, flowing southward to Georgetown.

The air of the hills seemed divinely pure and breezy, the water clear and cool, the land fruitful and green, after the noxious, fever-ridden swamps in which the army had been operating so long.

Greene, sitting eternally at his portable writing desk in his tent, composed his urgent appeals to the leading citizens in civil government for a draft of reinforcements, for cavalry horses, for forage and staple supplies. Communications were incredibly bad when contemplated from an age of telegraph and wireless. The solitary horse express with his dispatch bag was subject to all the hazards of lonely roads, bad weather, and ambush. The mails were similarly vulnerable, and letters of a private nature were often intercepted by the enemy, with no indication to either side that they were missing. General Washington did not write freely to Greene, who was under a like handicap, and even after Washington was actually on his way south from the Hudson, accompanied by Rochambeau, to begin the decisive Virginia campaign which would end at Yorktown, Greene believed that the main Northern army was still engaged in laying siege to Clinton at New York.

On the twentieth of August he wrote to Washington from the camp above the Wateree: "I am much at a loss what are Lord Cornwallis's intentions in Virginia. I am also totally ignorant what is going on at New York, having heard nothing from your Excellency since June, which leads me to believe that your dispatches are intercepted. I wait with impatience for intelligence by which I mean to govern my own operations. If things are flattering in the North, I will hazard less in the South; but if otherwise, we must risk more here."

But still no intimation of Washington's enterprise reached him, and on August 22, without waiting for the cooler weather which was soon to begin, he struck camp at 4:00 P.M. and ordered the *March* to be beaten at 5:00. His last act on the High Hills was to pardon a deserter who had returned to camp of his own accord and who was "released and sent to his duty in the Line."

Like Watson, Rawdon had been broken by his experience in the Carolina swamps. He left Stuart in command of the recovered post at Orangeburgh in July and returned to Charleston, intending to sail for England to recoup his health. Before Rawdon left Charleston, he concerned himself—along with Balfour, the brutal commandant at Charleston—in the summary execution of Colonel Hayne. Hayne was a highly respected citizen of Charleston who at the time of the surrender had with many others been given his parole and retired to his home. But later being summoned to join the British army by compulsion, he escaped to an American camp and was commissioned colonel of a Patriot militia force. During a reckless raid at the Quarter House too near Charleston he was captured by the British and sentenced to be hanged—an illegal verdict whether he was considered as a British subject or as a prisoner who had broken his parole. His was much the same action as that of Pickens, but Hayne was caught. It was a particularly tragic situation, as his wife had recently died and he had small children who would be orphaned if the death sentence was carried out on their father. He was nevertheless hanged by the joint orders of Balfour and Rawdon, even after the citizens of Charleston petitioned for his pardon. Greene heard of the execution with great indignation and issued a proclamation of his intention to make reprisals. He refused to take vengeance by hanging an innocent Tory prisoner then in his possession for the crime of two other men and let it be known that he desired only to see Rawdon at the end of a rope. Rawdon got away to a distinguished inheritance in England but was so haunted by the Hayne case that he wrote a letter to Henry Lee many years later attempting to justify his conduct.

On first taking over the command from Rawdon, Stuart had advanced from Orangeburgh to a camp site near McCord's Ferry, anxious to show himself capable of succeeding where the great Rawdon had failed. As the crow flies, his camp on the Congaree was only about sixteen miles from Greene's, but between them lay both the Wateree and the Congaree, and the junction of the rivers was overflowing from recent rains so that a vast lake was formed, out of which rose tall live oaks bearded with Spanish moss and cane brakes bent by the swift current. Greene was compelled to undertake a seventy-mile circuit of difficult marching through the heavy riverside atmosphere and could only move in the cooler hours of early morning and late afternoon, to conserve the health of his men.

At Friday's Ferry he learned that Stuart was below McCord's, hoping to be met there by a convoy from Charleston. Greene crossed the Congaree and camped on familiar ground near the Motte plantation. Here Marion joined him from an expedition to the Edisto. Sumter, in his independent way, had disbanded some of his always unpredictable force and retired from the scene. The repercussions from this move put William Henderson in command of the remainder of Sumter's corps, as Greene moved on downriver, compelling Stuart to retire before him. It was part of Greene's design to "recover the country" so far as possible without bloodshed, by pushing the enemy down to the sea below Charleston.

Lee, always reconnoitering ahead, brought word that Stuart was setting up a post at Eutaw Springs a few miles below Orangeburgh. Shedding his heavy baggage along his line of possible retreat, Greene followed slowly, his force augmented by Marion and Henderson, and about equal to Stuart's, which was around 2,000 men.

The eighth of September broke clear and hot. Greene was on horseback at his bivouac at Burdell's plantation before daylight, ranging his army in two columns, led by Marion and Pickens. Williams and Howard were on the left with their Marylanders, Lee on the flank, and William Washington, accompanied by the South Carolina veteran Wade Hampton, in the rear. The artillery, such as it was, moved with the columns.

Stuart at his Eutaw Springs camp was ignorant of Greene's approach, for his intelligence had all been waylaid by Lee's vigilant detachments. The British "rooting parties" of unarmed men had been sent out as usual to gather the ubiquitous sweet potatoes for breakfast when a deserter came in to report the American army close at hand. Stuart sprang to attention, to make the most of a favorable position for defensive action.

A stout three-story brick house with garret windows overlooked a clearing, which was the only open ground, and a garden behind the house was surrounded by a palisade enclosing a barn and smaller outbuildings which afforded cover. The approach on all sides was embarrassed by a ravine where Eutaw Creek flowed from a cold spring that bubbled up around cypress knees overhung by tall trees draped with moss and bordered by the almost impenetrable shrub called black-jack. Deep woods surrounded the clearing, across which the road to Charleston forked off from

EUTAW SPRING.

the road to Nelson's Ferry. The British army tents were spread across the roads in the clearing, under the windows of the house.

Stuart drew up his line in a solid formation in front of the camp and left his tents standing. The 3rd Regiment—the famous Buffs again—formed the right, Cruger from 96 had the center, and Major John Marjoribanks (Marshbanks) with his light infantry were in the thicket on the left. The artillery was distributed along the lines and Coffin's cavalry was held watchfully in reserve.

The Americans moved forward cautiously, still hoping to take Stuart by surprise. They were soon grateful for what shade was cast by the tangled underbrush along the road, which had been cut through the woods. About eight o'clock Lee, in the van as usual, made contact with a scouting detachment from the camp and broke them by a fierce charge, before which they scattered, "every man for himself," leaving prisoners and wounded in the hands of the Americans. It was beginning well.

Greene had ridden up to the firing, as was his habit, when he was advised by a breathless aide that the enemy had got to his rear. It is recorded that without even a glance behind him he ordered this officer to ride into them and say that they would be cut to pieces by his cavalry if they did not immediately surrender. The aide obeyed. The enemy surrendered. The general rode on into his battle, following Lee, who pressed forward toward the main body at the camp, as the firing there became hotter. Williams's fieldpieces covered Marion and Pickens, who held their militia steady.

Before long the two front lines were in deadly contact—the colonial hunters' deliberate aim against the practiced, regular volleys of the British musketry—until the American center began to give way. Greene had a second line, but soon the whole British force was engaged as Stuart threw in his few reserves. After Williams and Howard brought up their Maryland bayonets, the British began to cave in, until they were fleeing in all directions, through the woods and along the Charleston road in wild disorder. It seemed that for once Greene would be able to claim a real victory and hold a battlefield, but that satisfaction was snatched from him when the Americans reached the British tents and baggage, where ample food and drink lay defenseless before starving men. They broke ranks and scattered into the tents and marquees to fall upon all available refreshments.

A small British party had fled into the brick house, with Lee's dismounted troopers so close behind them that there was even a hand-to-hand struggle for possession of the half-shut door. It was finally slammed in the faces of the Americans, leaving several British soldiers outside to be taken prisoners. Firing from the upper windows, the defenders forced the Americans to fall back out of range, taking the prisoners with them.

Meanwhile, gallant Marjoribanks in the black-jack thicket was defending his position against Washington's cavalry, which under heavy fire from the windows attempted to wheel by sections into a small open space around the springs in Marjoribanks's rear.

Washington's horse was shot under him, and while he lay entangled he was wounded and taken prisoner. Wade Hampton collected the remnants of Washington's troop and tried to continue the movement against Marjoribanks, now exposed by the British retreat, and trying to gain the shelter of the house, whose brick walls had withstood the light American artillery. Although wounded, he succeeded in beating off Hampton's charge and seized two American cannon, which were dragged under the walls of the house.

Except for a few heedless revelers among the tents, the American line was re-formed in the border of the woods. Greene found it not seriously damaged, the cavalry having suffered most without being demoralized. But Stuart had also re-formed and was prepared to renew the battle around his devastated tents.

The heat of the day was now intense, and the wounded lay groaning in the fierce sun which parched the throats of even able-bodied men in the smoke and dust of the battlefield. The clear cool waters of the springs behind the garden of the house were running red with the blood of the British wounded who had dragged themselves there to quench their thirst and fill canteens for their comrades who were unable to reach it. Once more Greene had to resign himself to let ground fairly won remain in the possession of a shattered but stubborn enemy. His bivouac of the night before was the only place where fresh water could be found in sufficient quantity for the needs of his men, his wounded, and his prisoners. He sent Lee to Stuart with a white flag and the proposal that both armies should unite in burying their dead and removing the wounded to what comfort could be found for them.

Once more Greene's weary march began toward the previous night's encampment. The walking wounded leaned exhausted against their staggering comrades, who were faithful to the task of supporting a friend to safety. Many rough litters were devised from cut boughs and poles to convey men who were unable to keep on their feet. Powder-blackened faces were streaked with sweat, and discarded bloodstained clothing was strewn along the road back to Burdell's.

Greene's aide, Pendleton, was ordered to ride through the woods in search of stragglers and helpless wounded and came upon the Virginian Campbell being carried on a litter in a dying condition, attended by his son. Among them all marched the prisoners, sullen or secretly relieved to be out of it, numbering up to a quarter of the total of their captors.

It was Guildford Courthouse all over again. Stuart's losses were terrible, and he followed the Americans no farther than the edge of the clearing. Both sides claimed the victory, but although too crippled to take advantage of a weary enemy the British were left in possession of the field. Williams agreed with Greene that it was "by far the most bloody and obstinate" engagement of the campaign.

At Burdell's they found fresh water to drink and bathe their wounds, and the cook-fires were soon burning under the iron camp kettles. Greene's duties pressed upon him—first to write out the most urgent orders and reports, and then to visit the wounded, who raised pain-twisted smiles as he passed and reached out grimy hands for his quick clasp—a trying obligation which he always performed to the last suffering man.

Marion and Lee had been assigned to watch Stuart, who broke up his remaining stores at his demolished camp and left seventy wounded behind him when he began his stumbling retreat down the Charleston road. He was pursued and harried by the tireless partisans, who swooped in to cut off small parties of stragglers, or to capture a couple of wagons loaded with vital supplies and inflict more wounds to be tended in the heat and dust of the road. Major Marjoribanks, whose courageous stand outside the brick house had saved the British from a humiliating retreat on Charleston, died of his wounds on the march and was buried beside the road, where a lonely headboard carried his name.

John Eager Howard, Henderson, Pickens, and Marion's friend Hugh Horry were all wounded, and Colonel Washington was a prisoner. Lee and Williams were still unscathed.

News of the battle at Eutaw Springs was carried to Congress by Greene's Virginia aide, Captain Pearce, and enhanced Greene's reputation. Knox wrote that "without an army, without means, without anything, he has performed wonders." Even the British acknowledged a certain genius in the Quaker general who had held Britain's finest to a standstill. "The more he is beaten," one of Stuart's officers complained, "the farther he advances in the end. He has been indefatigable in collecting troops and leading them to be defeated."

Chapter 29

Greene's battered army crossed the Santee at Nelson's Ferry on September 12 on its way back to the benign Hills of Santee, where the chain of hospitals began, extending all the way to Charlotte. He had by now nearly as many enemy wounded as his own. Added to these were all the men incapacitated by the deadly fevers and usual camp ailments of the late summer season in the Low Country. Hospital stores dispatched from Virginia by Steuben had been intercepted and destroyed by Tarleton, operating for Cornwallis along the James.

From Governor Nelson there arrived fragmentary news that Washington was actually in Virginia with his Continentals, accompanied by Rochambeau and the French troops of the Northern army, all concentrated against Cornwallis, who was now expected to make a swift retreat through North Carolina to Charleston. Greene was ordered to intercept him before he could unite with Stuart and begin a new campaign in the South.

But even while Greene gathered himself to confront Cornwallis again on the old ground, he received a letter from Washington to say that the British general had gone to bay at Yorktown. He was hemmed in on the water side by a French fleet under De-Grasse which would prevent his rescue or reinforcement by the British navy and was cut off on the landward side by the combined armies of Washington and Rochambeau. The siege of Yorktown began on September 28, and Greene received periodic bulletins of its progress until October 18 brought the final capitulation of the British army in Virginia.

The camp on the High Hills celebrated that event without restraint when the General Orders told the glorious story. And what would be next? they asked themselves at the High Hills headquarters. Surely Charleston would be next, with DeGrasse offshore and a veteran army under Washington across the neck. Greene had already written to Washington urging him to bring his army to Charleston after the Virginia campaign. To reinforce his request he had sent the letter to Yorktown by Lee, who arrived there in time to witness Cornwallis's surrender.

But the old French pattern prevailed. DeGrasse declared that he was due in the West Indies and sailed away, having rendered greater service than D'Estaing had ever done. New York still remained in Clinton's possession, and Washington felt constrained to retrace his steps northward to the old Hudson position. Rochambeau was preparing to winter in Virginia before returning with his troops to France. Charleston was still up to Greene. But he was promised substantial reinforcements from Yorktown, in the shape of veteran troops under that seasoned campaigner St. Clair and some Pennsylvania units led by St. Clair's perpetual rival and Greene's old friend from the Monmouth days—Anthony Wayne.

In October Greene was writing Congress of his compassionate tour of the hospitals, where sugar and salt and coffee could only be obtained roundabout from New Bern, bartered there for tobacco. "Our sick and wounded have suffered greatly," he reported. "The extent of our hospitals, the malignity of the disorders, and increasing sick since the battle of Eutaw, the little means we have to provide for them, and the great number of our physicians who fell sick in service, have left our sick and wounded in a most deplorable condition. Numbers of our brave fellows who have bled in the cause of their country have been eat up with maggots and perished in that miserable situation. Hospital stores and medicines have been exceedingly scarce; not an ounce of bark [quinine] have we in the department at this time. But fortunately the cold weather is coming on and the malignity of the fevers begins to abate. To afford the sick and wounded all the relief in my power, I visited the hospitals from this camp to Charlotte."

And back again, indefatigable, resolute, riding in his sleep, patient, good-humored, and kind. But now his own health was beginning to show signs of intolerable strain. His best aide, Burnett, broke down entirely and was sent north for a change of air, carrying urgent messages to the Board of War and the Superintendent of Finance, Robert Morris. There was no hard money available for the purchase of supplies, and even the worthless Continental currency had disappeared, while state issues were of no value outside the state itself.

The troops had received no pay for two years and were as usual distressed for want of essential clothing and were often without even the temporary comfort of "spirits" to sustain them. Greene was miserably tried by the widespread destitution on all sides, and the personal disappointment of what looked to Congress like a more successful campaign than he knew its reality to be.

Charleston and Savannah, besides New York, were still in British possession. Major Craig, who was in command at Wilmington when Cornwallis came limping in after his Pyrrhic victory at Guildford Courthouse, abandoned his post there when he heard of the surrender at Yorktown and scuttled into Charleston. The city was already overcrowded with British and Tory defenders, and Craig was promptly detached to John's Island to protect the cattle pastured there. The inland water route was now the British command's only communication with Savannah. On November 7 Leslie superseded Stuart at Charleston.

It was plain to Greene that an outright siege of Charleston could not be attempted with the meager force presently under his command and that he must await the arrival of the promised reinforcements from Virginia. Harry Lee had returned from Yorktown to the headquarters in the hills to describe in enthusiastic detail the stirring events he had witnessed during the siege.

Young Laurens had also rejoined Greene's family to see the finish
of the campaign in his native state.

After waiting for an overdue supply of ammunition, which
when it finally came was less than his expectation, Greene broke
camp in the hills for the second time and on November 18
marched south again across the Congaree in pursuit of his plan to
reoccupy the territory as near to Charleston as possible. A message from Marion said that Stuart had withdrawn still farther
within that shrinking perimeter to the vicinity of Goose Creek,
which uncovered a British garrison at Dorchester on the Ashley
River. Anxious to gather in still another British outpost, Greene
left Huger and Williams to follow him with the main army while
he set out ahead with a "flying party" composed of Lee's, Hampton's, and a mounted detachment of Maryland and Delaware
Continentals.

Notwithstanding all their precautions for secrecy, such as
traveling by unfrequented swamp paths and "securing" any stray
inhabitants they encountered who might inform the garrison of
their approach, Dorchester was nevertheless warned and threw
out patrols. One of these was caught and almost annihilated by
Wade Hampton's South Carolina cavalry on December 1. But
Greene had been recognized by some of the survivors, and his
presence was reported in the town, whose defenders therefore
assumed that the entire American army was upon them.

That night the garrison at Dorchester hastily destroyed their
stores, threw their cannon into the river, and under cover of darkness decamped still farther to the post known as the Quarter
House, only seven miles from Charleston. Leslie was working
night and day on fortifications inside the city and stocking up
provisions on John's Island, which was an island only because of a
narrow inlet called the Wappoo River which flowed between it
and the mainland. Pressing his advantage, Greene picked up
Huger and Williams at Four Holes Bridge and led the way
through interminable swamp beneath towering cypress trees to a
plantation on the far side of the Edisto River called the Round O,
which he reached on the seventh of December.

Kosciuszko had chosen the ground at the Round O in a fertile,
relatively unplundered region among some of the earliest estab-

lishments in South Carolina. Lee described the district as "elegant," lying in the midst of once luxurious rice plantations and adorned with pretty women of the first families.

The enterprise of the British army in South Carolina seemed to have been broken by the battle at Eutaw Springs, and neither Leslie nor Stuart showed any inclination to resume operations against the Americans encamped on their very doorstep. Marion was posted between the Cooper and the Ashley rivers at the top of the neck, Sumter was at Orangeburg to curb the Tories upriver, Hampton was midway at Four Holes, and Lee and Laurens roved between, maintaining communications.

A rumor of heavy reinforcements expected at Charleston from New York and Ireland caused Greene considerable uneasiness before his own reinforcements from Yorktown could arrive. When the new British contingent was reported as numbering less than five hundred, he was much relieved. "I have not been frightened," he wrote with his oblique humor, "but as Dr. Skinner says, I have been confoundedly scared." With the prospect of adding Wayne and St. Clair to his command, he encouraged Governor Rutledge to convene the General Assembly, which would reestablish civil authority in South Carolina and relieve him of the obligations of maintaining martial law.

It had been Rutledge's intention to convene the Legislature at Camden, a safe distance from the British at Charleston, but Greene pressed him to make use of the relatively plentiful region of the Edisto, which could be fully covered by the present disposition of the American army. It was not long since the governor and council of North Carolina had been captured at Hillsboro by a roving band of militant Tories, and the same risk would exist for Rutledge at Camden. He therefore heeded Greene's advice and chose the village of Jacksonboro on the west bank of the Edisto, which after the fashion of Carolina rivers changed its name midway and was here known as the Pon Pon. Jacksonboro consisted of a courthouse, a jail, and a few small houses. Its impudent proximity to Charleston reasserted the recovery of the state from British rule.

The Legislature which met at Jacksonboro on January 18, 1782, was a notable gathering, though many of its 1778 membership were missing. The soldiers who came in from the field to sit again as senators and representatives had been armed only by necessity and were anxious to have done with military life and return to their damaged properties and private enterprise. Besides the military, the Legislature was attended by prisoners of war recently released or exchanged from their captivity in the British camps at St. Augustine and from crowded prison ships where they had been confined in such miserable squalor that many of them were broken in health for the rest of their lives.

A more distinguished body of men had never before met in the state of South Carolina. Many of them had suffered cruel and unjust treatment in support of their beliefs. The rest, still wearing their rusty uniforms, had endured privation and hardship during the bitter campaigns which at Eutaw had finally come to the pause which presaged the end. Marion and Sumter attended as senators.

Paper was so scarce that they had to wait to secure a small supply before their records could be kept. No journal of either House has survived. The courthouse and the jail served as the chambers where they met. They found personal accommodations at nearby plantations, or begged shelter at the army cantonments. But they met, with quick, hard handclasps for old friends and anxious accounting for faces which would never be seen again.

Governor Rutledge was there to address the Legislature, and Greene moved the army down from the Round O to Skirving's plantation, six miles from Jacksonboro on the south bank of the Edisto, or Pon Pon. This move placed him between Jacksonboro and Craig's British troops on John's Island. Lee and Laurens were amicably joined in guarding the swampy ground that lay between the camp and the island. A daring raid on British boats lying at anchor in the Wappoo River was attempted by these two irrepressibles and failed dangerously through the mistake of a guide. Greene was compelled to ride to their rescue, and they returned somewhat crestfallen to their routine observation posts.

Rutledge had conducted himself with dignity and discretion as the representative in exile of his captive state, both in Philadelphia where he went to plead its cause with Congress and with the armies in the field where he often shared the hard daily life of its defenders. His opening address reviewed the sad history of the interim and welcomed back the aging or ailing Patriots who had suffered through it. He concluded with an eloquent tribute to the conduct of General Greene and the troops under him and urged a suitable expression of gratitude and appreciation by his hearers.

Both Houses responded generously and unanimously voted their thanks on behalf of the state which Greene had so stubbornly defended. More concretely, they originated a bill "for vesting in General Greene, in consideration of his important services, the sum of 10,000 guineas," to be expended in the purchase on his behalf of a suitable homestead at which to establish himself and his growing family after the war. A committee was appointed to locate and secure for him a handsome plantation from among those confiscated by the state from Tory owners, and it chose a place on the Pon Pon River not far from his current camp.

Such generosity touched him deeply, for he was always haunted with worry about the future support of Kitty and the children when the war was over. Like Washington's at Mount Vernon, his modest Rhode Island property was dependent on his own supervision and had not improved in value during his long absence, while his private resources had been consumed by the daily wartime necessities of himself and his family as his pay fell long overdue.

He was further relieved and gratified when Georgia followed the example of its sister state and also expressed its gratitude in terms of a substantial sum invested in a house called Mulberry Grove and several thousand acres of land on the river below Savannah. North Carolina followed, with a gift of 25,000 acres on the Cumberland River, which, though it was never occupied or even seen by Greene, brought useful funds to his descendants after his death.

Meanwhile the reinforcements from Yorktown under Wayne and St. Clair arrived and meant more mouths to feed, when the commissary was already in desperate straits. The Northern soldiers never considered rice anything but food for invalids and cattle and would not eat it, demanding meat instead, which often arrived as carrion not fit to eat at all. Their clothing was as usual in tatters; their tents and blankets were rotten with swamp water and the perpetual Low Country damp.

Mindful of the old rivalry between Wayne and St. Clair, Greene hastily detached Wayne to harass the British garrison at

Savannah and to "try by every means in your power," his instructions read, "to soften the malignancy and dreadful resentments subsisting between Whig and Tory; and put a stop, as much as possible, to that cruel custom of putting men to death after they surrender themselves as prisoners."

Wayne found Georgia "a desert" and even envied St. Clair his dull post in the ring enclosing the captive city of Charleston.

Chapter 30

With the spring of 1782, Kitty Greene arrived in camp, as she had so long desired to do. Accompanied by her eldest son, George—the Cambridge baby, now seven years old—and a Mrs. Kingston as companion, she had set out from Coventry at the end of the previous year and was detained at Philadelphia by a December snowstorm. As a guest of Greene's friends, the Pettits, she was made much of by Philadelphia society and thoroughly enjoyed herself as the wife of the Quaker general whose reputation had soared since she last saw him laboring under the unrewarding responsibilities of the quartermastership at Morristown in the dreadful winter of 1779–80.

During her visit at Philadelphia she was persuaded to leave George in the Pettits' care to continue his schooling, which was soon undertaken by the distinguished Patriot Dr. Witherspoon, president of Princeton, at whose home Greene had breakfasted with Washington on the morning after the battle in 1777. Escorted from Rhode Island by Greene's former aide, William Blodgett, now retired, Kitty and her companion were joined at Philadelphia by Major Burnett, who had been recovering his health on furlough and was pleased to act as their guide and protector southward.

At Salisbury, where they arrived in March, they met Colonel Williams, on his way home to Maryland in hopes of mending his health, damaged by the long campaign. From him they heard all the latest news of the South Carolina camp before traveling on through the High Hills and crossing the Wateree River at McCord's Ferry—familiar ground to Burnett, who was always able to provide hospitality from old friends along the way.

She reached the Dorchester neighborhood early in April, and her husband rode out to meet her with an escort of aides and guards who witnessed the roadside reunion with affectionate amusement. Leaving his horse to be led, Greene rode the rest of the way with Kitty in her phaeton drawn by two tired horses.

The arrival of the general's charming wife had much the same effect on camp morale as Mrs. Washington's annual visits to headquarters had had during the dreary Northern winters of the war. Kitty brought with her her constitutional social genius to enliven her husband's sober quarters at Skirving's and was soon a welcome guest among the war-worn ladies of the surrounding plantations. She found changes in the family at Greene's headquarters, not all of them for the best, though Greene was able to view his military household with his customary wry humor. "Our family is much as formerly," he wrote the absent Williams, who was sorely missed at the dinner table. "Pearce and Pendleton as polite as ever; Morris, as careless; Burnett, as cross; and Shubrick, as impudent. Morris is courting, but at a distance, too much so, I fear, to get the citadel. Washington is married, and fats upon the rice swamps."

William Washington's romance with Miss Jane Elliott, who nursed him as a prisoner after his Eutaw wound, was a wartime idyll that has been lost in the mists of time. Their acquaintance seems to have begun some time before the battle at Eutaw which disabled him, and he may have been a visitor at her plantation home outside Charleston in the intervals of campaigning against

Clinton. His cavalry troop being then without a flag, Miss Elliott made one for them out of a piece of crimson brocade cut from a window curtain. This flag still exists, in the keeping of the Washington Light Infantry at Charleston. Colonel Washington continued to live in South Carolina for the rest of his life, at a house in Charleston which still stands and a plantation home called Sandy Hill.

Under pressure from Wayne, Savannah was finally evacuated in July of 1782. The garrison was ordered to New York, where Sir Guy Carleton had arrived from Canada to succeed Clinton. Wayne then rejoined Greene at the Ashley River headquarters. There was talk of peace in the air now, but the change from Clinton to Carleton caused some uneasiness over a possible new flare-up in the North. So far it had occurred to no one that Yorktown would be the last real battle of the war.

Greene's army was as usual naked and hungry. Now they were idle as well, with plenty of time to contemplate their physical distress. "The sickly season" of midsummer brought additional anxiety to Greene as fever spread rapidly through the camp. The hospitals were crowded, and deaths became so frequent that funeral services were omitted. By late August the Low Country climate was beginning to tell on Kitty's Northern constitution, and Greene wrote Pettit that she had gone to one of the Sea Islands with a party of friends to enjoy the fresh air and fruit and vegetables which were abundant there. "The people are very friendly, and strive to render this country agreeable to her, but the fevers fill her with apprehensions," he added. "She is a very great favorite, even with the ladies, and has almost rivalled me where I least expected it; her flowing tongue and cheerful countenance quite triumph over my grave face. I bear it with great philosophy, as I gain on one hand what I lose on the other."

During August Greene received word of a British foraging party working southward from Charleston toward the Combahee district, where a quantity of precious army stores had been collected. General Gist, who like Wayne had been sent down from Yorktown, undertook to intercept the British force and drive it off without calling in Lee and Laurens from their respective posts nearer headquarters.

Laurens, who was known to be "laboring under an ague," was

so poorly that he had been confined to bed at his quarters. But when he got wind of an "enterprise" going forward without him, he left his bed for the saddle and overtook Gist on the march at the ferry on the north bank of the Combahee. The enemy was just across the river. Gist gave Laurens command of some works being thrown up to hamper the British retreat, and the young colonel spent the evening very agreeably at a nearby plantation, where he was much pampered by the young ladies.

After an evening's hospitality which did not break up until two hours before his detachment was due to be put in motion to prevent the British from crossing the river, Laurens rode out at dawn, perhaps a little lightheadedly, and led his small company straight into an ambuscade set by a British party who had left their boats hidden in the tall grass beside the road. Once aware of his danger, Laurens characteristically gave the order to charge instead of surrendering and fell fatally wounded after the first British volley. Gist rushed to his support too late, and the British retired without losses, though the American casualties were serious indeed. Greene was much afflicted when he heard of Laurens's quite unnecessary death, which took place at the same house where he had been entertained the night before.

The work of Greene's army was nearly done, and everyone was sick of it and longing to go home, himself not least. There were little mutinies and little plots, all discovered in time and severely suppressed. In September he was stricken with a severe bout of fever, and Kitty rushed back from her island holiday to nurse him, though by the time she could arrive he was again at his desk writing his endless appeals for food, clothing, and a bare subsistence for his suffering men. Wayne, too, had succumbed to an attack of fever, which he professed to dread more than the devil or British bullets.

Leslie, now commandant at Charleston, had received orders to prepare for its evacuation, and he asked Greene for a formal truce until his transports could arrive. Greene was constrained to refuse, pending permission from Congress, and Leslie's foraging parties continued to harass the neighborhood and entertain Greene's outposts.

Greene wrote Williams that Kitty had already set her heart on a grand ball in Charleston to celebrate the evacuation when it came. "You know I am not much in this way," he remarked with his usual good-natured acquiescence in Kitty's whims.

When Admiral Hood finally arrived off Charleston with the transports for Leslie's troops, it was late September. Another three months went by before Charleston saw the last of the British, and conditions in Greene's army were worsening daily. Wayne, a new broom in the Southern scene, convinced Greene that Charleston merchants would compete for military bids to supply the American army with surplus British goods, especially since everybody knew that when the city was evacuated valuable stores would have to be abandoned or sold at a loss. Greene advertised for bids to supply his commissary and received only one reply, from a man named Banks who claimed to be a Virginian with a partnership in Fredericksburg.

There are several versions of the notorious Banks affair, some of them laboriously incomprehensible now, some of them snap judgments designed to reflect discredit on Greene, who had conducted his own quartermastership stint in the North with a minimum of the profitable sidelines which are likely to accompany that service. Apparently Banks represented that he had connections in Charleston and was able to feed and clothe the army through these channels if Greene would provide him with $1,500 cash—the sum varies according to the source consulted— and offered to bill the Superintendent of Finance in Philadelphia for the balance as it fell due.

Greene's commissary department was by this time in such a low state that he had no choice between providing for his men through Banks or turning them loose to forage for themselves, a course which was not to be contemplated.

His past experience with men and army contractors in particular seems to have failed to enable him to recognize in Banks the typical purveyor-peculator who talks smoothly with his hand in the till. In his daily harassment over his starving, naked troops who were again approaching the point of mutiny, Greene undertook an obligation that was to hang a cloud of debt and calumny over the rest of his conscientious life. Banks appears to have been either a complete scoundrel or a very inept wheeler-dealer who wound himself up in the same net he spread for Greene. He had connections in South Carolina, it was true—one of them Greene's own aide, Burnett, and a Mr. Waties of Charleston, who had already had dealings with Banks and reported him "upright and obliging."

Obliging he certainly was, as soon as Greene raised the cash for him, and the promised goods began to come in promptly. But Banks had overextended himself in other directions as well, in a colossal private gamble, and his creditors in Charleston began to press him for payment, while Philadelphia looked with suspicion on his bills. If Banks's sources of supply dried up, the army would stop eating again. His Charleston creditors suggested to Banks that Greene should personally become surety for Banks and endorse his bills on Philadelphia. Wrought upon by his daily knowledge of the army's desperate needs, Greene pledged as collateral for Banks's debts the little personal independence represented by the grants of the grateful Southern Legislatures.

Then something went wrong. Rumors of Greene's involvement with Banks's shaky credit, rumors even of a partnership in Banks's private deals, leaked out through Banks's rash correspondence—if not his misrepresentation—with his Virginia associates. Phrases in his letters to them were capable of misinterpretation to indicate Greene's complicity in Banks's speculations for his private profit, or the letters had been cunningly designed by Banks to read that way. The matter finally came to the attention of Governor Harrison of Virginia, who wrote a friendly warning to Greene against "a dangerous partnership" while assuring him that Banks's "insinuations" had won no credence from him or his council.

Greene was horrified and angry. He sent for Banks and in front of witnesses confronted him with the incriminating correspondence and the governor's letter. Banks insisted that he had meant no harm but could not explain the ambiguous allusions to Greene, who in his determination to preserve his soldiers from further hardship had actually put his small personal fortune and his family's future in jeopardy. A handbill was published exonerating him from participation in the commercial part of Banks's transactions. Greene himself had once written that "no man was without his enemies but a fool." He now found that he had enemies, indeed, eager to repeat the unfounded calumny which his innocent association with Banks had bred.

Chapter 31

General Leslie was a temperate, decent man, and he made careful preparations to evacuate Charleston—dispersing his Tories to other havens as far as he was able and allowing citizens who were "well affected" to the American cause to leave the town and rejoin their friends in the ravaged countryside. When he opened communications with Greene on the subject of his peaceable departure to Hood's transports in the harbor, it was agreed that the Americans should take possession of the city as the British rear guard left it, that no hostilities should occur as the latter marched to the docks, and that no injury should be done to the city by the enemy before their departure.

Gist had been taken ill, St. Clair had returned to his Pennsylvania home, and Williams, Lee, and Howard had all left the army to resume civilian life. Wayne, always a problem when idle, was assigned to complete the arrangements for the reoccupation of Charleston and to lead the American troops into the recovered city.

On December 14, 1782, the British morning gun boomed for the last time over Charleston, as Leslie's forces left their advance positions three miles outside the city to march to the harbor where the wharves were already crowded with Tory refugees waiting to board the ships. It was Boston, Philadelphia, 96, and Savannah all over again—weeping families abandoning their homes and possessions to follow the British drums, not so much from loyalty now as from fear of the consequences to themselves when British protection was withdrawn. Some were bound for St. Augustine, some for the West Indies, and some all the way to England. Farewells were forever.

Behind this tragic company came the British troops, marching to the music of their fifes and drums toward the transports that would carry them away from the war at last. Behind them came Wayne's light infantry, colors flying, drums beating, heads up, like sheep dogs herding the red-coated enemy down King's Street and around the right-hand turn to Gadsden's wharf where the ships lay. It was sometimes necessary for the British rear to call back over their shoulders to slow down the relentless pace of the high-stepping Americans, whose ill-shod feet that day were as light as their hearts.

Houses newly emptied of their British cuckoos had flung out flags and decorations on balconies and windowsills. Patriots who for years had had to suppress their feelings shouted a welcome to Wayne's ragged ranks. By three o'clock that afternoon, when Greene escorted Rutledge's successor, Governor Mathews, into the regained capital, the streets were lined with a colorful pageant of delirious celebration, cheering crowds, flags, and hastily contrived banners of all kinds.

Riding alongside the convalescent Gist in the procession behind Greene and the governor was the unsung hero of the 1776 battle for Charleston—old General Moultrie. He had been a prisoner of war since the surrender in 1780 until he was exchanged for Burgoyne in February of 1782 and had joined Greene at the Ashley River headquarters in September. "I can never forget," he wrote in his memoirs, "the happy day when we marched into Charleston with the American troops. Both citizens and soldiers shed tears of mutual joy. It was an ample reward for the triumphal soldier, after all the hazards and fatigues of war he had gone through, to be the instrument of releasing his friends and fellow-citizens and restoring them to their liberties and the possession of their city and country again."

It has been alleged that the partisan corps under Marion and Sumter were excluded from the parade at Charleston because they were too shabby to make a smart appearance—"not too ragged to *fight*, only too ragged for *show!*" This appears to have been deliberate misrepresentation, as was also the account which says that some of Greene's men were attired only in loincloths because of the destitution prevailing in the army. By the end of 1782 the clothing supplied by Banks had been issued and the troops were better off than they had been for months. The partisans were never dependent on the army commissary but received homemade clothing and even food from their secret friends in the swamp country.

Marion and Sumter did not appear in the parade because they had left the field some time before the evacuation of Charleston took place. In a simple ceremony under the cedars at Wadboo near Fairlawn plantation Marion had held his last muster, thanked and praised the hard-bitten men who had followed him through years of privation and hazard, took each of them by the hand, and saw them disperse to their homes. The Senate of South Carolina, of which he was a member, voted him its thanks for his services and a gold medal, which he probably never received. A more appropriate gesture would have been to bestow on him a fraction of the financial reward it had already voted for Greene.

Sumter, difficult and sulky always, had wound up his command at Orangeburg before taking his seat in the Assembly at Jacksonboro. He too was almost overlooked in the encomiums heaped on Greene. Both he and Marion returned home to plantations stripped of cattle, horses, tools, slaves, and personal effects, and began the laborious, patient rebuilding of the comfort and security they had sacrificed to the war.

Kitty Greene had her evacuation ball at Charleston, attended by citizens and soldiers smartened up as far as was possible for their first gala occasion after dreary months of captivity and campaigning. Kosciuszko decorated the long Assembly room with garlands of magnolia leaves and festoons of paper flowers and bunting put together by the ladies. The army minstrels played minuets and country reels, assisted by resident Charleston musicians. Greene looked on indulgently while his pretty wife danced with Wayne—who still carried a musket ball in his thigh from Yorktown—and all the field and staff officers who had been able to satisfy themselves that they were presentable enough to attend.

The refreshments may have been negligible—they had to be supplied from depleted Charleston larders and by heavy-handed army cooks—but nobody minded that. Tomorrow the same old problems of forage and commissary would resume, for although the British fleet of three hundred sail lay at anchor in a curved line offshore waiting for the tide, Carleton was still in New York and it was still not the end of the war.

When the candles burned down and the morning light extinguished them, many revelers trooped down to the waterfront to watch the British squadron disappear over the horizon, while the American flag was ceremoniously raised over Charleston.

At the Congress in Philadelphia speeches were made in praise of General Greene, and a suggestion of promotion to lieutenant general was offered but not acted upon. At the same time it was resolved that he should remain in South Carolina with the remnants of his army until the peace treaty was ratified at Paris, which meant another winter under arms. Washington had established a new winter headquarters at Newburgh on the Hudson while awaiting his release from duty, as negotiations for the evacuation of New York City began.

Wayne took the bulk of Greene's army across the Ashley River to James Island, where a pine forest and sandy soil were supposed to provide a healthful site. While civilian government was being restored in the state, the army had still to act as police, and there was the usual scrimmage about its food—fresh, stringy beef without enough salt, and rice and corn were brought in. But rice, the Pennsylvanians said, was "washy food for duty men."

Greene accepted Rutledge's offer of his handsome house in Broad Street as headquarters, and Kitty entertained her new friends there, for she had been cordially received into the Charleston circles. Wayne was a frequent guest in Broad Street, and his admiration for Kitty was undisguised. But Greene was used to Kitty's conquests, and Wayne was not the only one.

The spring of 1783 came early, and the troops encamped on James Island found it "a little paradise" of exotic bloom and balmy air. They had fashioned a rough abatis of brush and tree-tops around the camp, with only a few openings, which reduced the guard duty. Although they were kept busy with routine daily drill and work parties for sanitation, the deterioration of idle duty without the stimulus of combat gained on them, and they finally even got bored with the unaccustomed leisure to hunt and fish.

News that the peace treaty had been signed at Paris arrived at Charleston in April, 1783, and again there were great celebrations. The city was illuminated, and there was a *feu de joie* on James Island which half of Charleston crossed the river to attend—but neither rice nor bread was issued to the army that day because the commissary had none. Washington at Newburgh on the Hudson was coping with something near mutiny, and bands of insurgent deserters descended on Philadelphia demanding back pay and furloughs. An inept Congress fled to Princeton, where it made itself fairly comfortable in summer exile.

The spirit of unrest in the army was understandable. The work was done, yet nobody was free to go home. At last Greene received his orders to dismiss the troops, with a fraction of their overdue pay advanced. The North Carolina and Virginia men marched away first, anxious to escape the constant summer menace of the Low Country fevers and dysentery. The regiments from Pennsylvania and Maryland were promised transport by sea, but it was July before enough ships could be gathered to embark them.

Kitty Greene had been away from the children more than a year now, and she was pregnant again. Accompanied by Pearce and Kosciuszko, she sailed in July in the first transport of troops bound for Pennsylvania. She waited a month in Philadelphia while a new phaeton was built for her under Pettit's supervision, "pestered to death with ceremony and civility," Pearce reported to the general.

After a shopping spree which drew a rebuke from her husband, she picked up young George from Witherspoon's household at Princeton and drove on in the new phaeton to Rhode Island, retrieving little Nat and the two girls from their Uncle Jacob's care.

With the departure of his wife and the last ships full of troops, Greene wrote Pettit that he "felt like Samson after Delilah cut his locks." He soon lost another companion when Wayne went north on furlough. In acknowledgment of his services at Savannah, the Georgia Legislature had bestowed on Wayne a plantation called Richmond, which overlooked the river twelve miles above the city. Although he grumbled that it was not as handsome a gift as Greene's Mulberry Grove nearer the coast, Wayne was enthusiastic over the prospect of becoming a planter after the war and rode out to view his new property. He found it run-down and overgrown, plundered of its slaves and conveniences by Tory and British raiders. The land was fertile and with some expenditure could be cultivated to yield a substantial income.

Wayne went back to Philadelphia hoping to sell some of his Pennsylvania holdings and thus raise capital for the purpose of stocking Richmond with slaves and equipment so that he could start a prosperous new career in Georgia. He anticipated that his estranged wife Polly would prefer to remain at their Waynesborough home nursing her customary bad health, and although he was devoted to his children, the marriage had long been nothing but an outworn obligation to his vital, energetic spirit.

Kitty Greene was still in Philadelphia when Wayne arrived there, disabled by a violent fever which had attacked him during the voyage from Charleston. He was confined to bed at the home of a friend, while all his old associates flocked around him as his health began to improve in his native air. After a lively series of balls and stag parties at the City Tavern, he was stricken again with his old enemy the gout, but this too was overcome by his ebullient anticipation of a new life in the South near his friends the Greenes.

Congress voted him a long-overdue promotion in rank, albeit by brevet only. He was elected again to the Assembly in the Federalist party and failed to put through a bill to permit the theaters of Philadelphia to reopen with a repertoire by his friend, the actor Hallam. Disappointed in his legislative prospects, he looked increasingly toward Richmond and a planter's life, convinced that a fortune was to be made out of growing rice in Georgia.

Homesick as he was himself, Greene delayed at Charleston to put his Southern grants in order by renting out his Georgia rice lands "for a song" and finding an overseer to take charge of the plantation on the Pon Pon. Although as a Quaker he was opposed to slavery, without which no plantation could be worked at all, he determined to devise a plan whereby his slaves could become free workers on the land.

To provide the place on the Pon Pon with livestock, seeds, tools, and labor for immediate planting under a competent overseer put a heavy drain on his depleted resources, but at last he was able to leave its reconstruction in the hands of his man Saunders and begin his own homeward journey. Instead of making a comfortable sea trip all the way to New York or Newport, he elected to travel overland in the summer heat, probably for some reason connected with the still unresolved Banks affair in Virginia, or a desire to see General Washington on the way. He had a new heavy carriage, sent down from Philadelphia by Pettit, and he was accompanied by two aides, Hyrne and Edwards, when he left Charleston on August 11, 1783.

Crossing the Brandywine northward, he reflected that he had traveled down the same road in the opposite direction nearly three years before, on his way to take command of Gates's army. Word of his approach had spread into Philadelphia, and officers and citizens drove out to meet him and escort him to the door of his tavern, when a shout of "Long life to Greene!" rang out as he left his carriage, much moved by his reception.

Chapter 32

At Philadelphia Greene renewed old wartime acquaintance with the Pettits, Morrises, and others, all of whom had seen Kitty since he had. He learned from Pettit that Banks had speculated with the bills on Congress which Greene had endorsed for the army contracts at Charleston and that he would be held responsible for those that bore his signature. Robert Morris, as a gesture of confidence in Greene's integrity, offered to lend him money with which to put his Southern property into immediate operation, on the expectation that his plantations would soon pay handsome dividends.

His private financial situation was perpetually his first concern. At the beginning of the war his resources were all invested in the forges at Potowomut and Coventry, the business being entrusted to the firm of brothers in whose care he had left his family. Jacob, the eldest, lived at Coventry during his absence and had recklessly extended his interests to the pursuit of privateering—the polite name for the piracy which armed private vessels to prey on enemy ships at sea. It was a risky venture, though authorized by Congress early in 1776 in lieu of an American navy. By the end of the war American privateers had accounted for some six hundred British ships with their cargoes.

The brothers Greene were not the most successful among these venturers but continued to hold shares in several vessels engaged in the trade. During his quartermastership Greene had formed a business partnership with Cox and Pettit, both merchants deserving of his confidence, but he had always taken less than the customary advantage of the prerogatives of his office, while his daily expenses and irregular pay made heavy inroads on his small resources.

Congress was still at the "temporary capital" at Princeton, where it had fled from the army mutineers the previous June. Washington had been summoned to Princeton from his Newburgh headquarters and with his wife was established at a house called Rocky Hill, with his Lifeguards encamped around him.

Greene's formal announcement to Congress of his arrival at Princeton was dated October 7. His outspoken correspondence with that muddle-headed body had not endeared him to its members, and no formal reception was accorded by them to the officer who, next to Washington, had done the most in the field to achieve independence. Greene was not surprised at this seeming discourtesy, having written to a friend the year before that Congress employed him but did not love him.

His welcome from the Washingtons and his former comrades was as warm as he could have wished. He lingered at Princeton, hearing all the Northern news and bringing Washington up to date on the state of the country as revealed by his recent journey from Charleston through North Carolina and Virginia. A Congressional committee, of which James Madison was an inconspicuous member, voted Greene the gift of two pieces of field ordnance taken from the British, to be presented to him by the commander in chief, "as a public testimonial to the wisdom, fortitude, and military skill which distinguished his command in the Southern department"—a tardy and somewhat less practical reward than the real estate already bestowed on him by the Southern Legislatures.

When Greene finally set his face homeward to Rhode Island in November, Mrs. Washington had already departed from Princeton for Mount Vernon, and the general was preparing to ride to West Point, from where he would lead an imposing cavalcade to occupy New York City as the British left it. Neither he nor Greene had any reason to suspect that their farewell at Princeton would be their last.

Greene's homeward journey through New England to join Kitty at a residence prepared for him at Newport was a long parade, studded with addresses of welcome and congratulation and offers of hospitality. He reached Newport on November 27, 1783, and for the first time saw all four of his children together around his own hearth. Kitty was in poor health, awaiting the birth of another child.

The house he had built at Coventry was now in the possession of his brother Jacob, and except for a run-down farm at Westerly, which was his share of his father's estate, he and Kitty no longer owned a home in Rhode Island. Because of the state of Kitty's health, he felt compelled to spend the winter of 1783 at Newport, instead of returning to his new enterprises in the South. He rented the stately Crary house in Mill Street across from the old stone tower, and here he was visited by the friends of his youth and some of his wartime comrades.

Public service was offered to him and was steadfastly refused in his desire to withdraw into family life on his Southern acres and become a planter. At the same time he declined to attend the general meeting at Philadelphia of the Cincinnati Society, which had been formed by the surviving officers of the Revolution while they were encamped on the banks of the Hudson. It was named for the Roman patrician who had resigned a military dictatorship to return to the plow on his own estates. The society was described as an expedient, sanctioned by the commander in chief, "to perpetuate their friendship and to raise a fund for relieving the widows and orphans of those who had fallen during the war." It was organized with a president (Washington), a treasurer (MacDougall), and a secretary (Knox). Its badge (designed by L'Enfant) was a bald eagle in gold, worn suspended from a dark-blue ribbon, and was presented to each member with a parchment diploma inscribed with the name and rank of the recipient. As membership was to be hereditary, the Cincinnati were at first viewed with some alarm by an over-Republican faction as "constituting an incipient order of nobility," but it was pointed out that no political, military, or social prerogative was claimed.

Greene never took an active part in the society, probably more from conflicting obligations than from disinclination, though he was named president of the State Society for Rhode Island and possessed the insignia, which has also been held by his descendants.

After the birth of the child, named Louisa Catherine, Kitty was slow to regain her usual strength and spirits, and in July of 1784 Greene sailed alone for Charleston to look into his new possessions and bring back funds. He found the same ferment in South Carolina that existed in the North as the young nation tried to find its feet and salvage its finances and devise a lasting form of government. It would be 1789 before the convention at Philadelphia would wrangle out and get ratified a Constitution that would stand up to the wars and internal crises of another two hundred years.

The gratitude of the Carolinas and Georgia was designed to make him comfortable for the rest of his life, except that the properties bestowed on him were profitless without the slave labor he still abhorred. A further handicap was the sudden death of Banks, leaving his complicated affairs in a hopeless state of bankruptcy. Greene, as Banks's unwilling guarantor, was now more than ever involved, for Banks's creditors came down on him for payment, even while acknowledging that Greene had had no self-interest in Banks's original contracts.

These additional obligations, and a lack of adequate funds in the Greene brothers' firm, compelled him to sell the plantation on the Pon Pon and confine his hopes to the Georgia estate called Mulberry Grove, which lay below Savannah on the river. It was a heart-breaking come-down, damaging his family's future security and his own peace of mind in the retirement he had hoped to enjoy into a prosperous old age.

He signed new notes to keep Banks's creditors at bay, while he tried to build up his resources in the South. He entered a claim in Congress for his debts incurred on behalf of the army—which was not settled until after his death. A hurricane ruined his first rice crop. He went into further debt in order to purchase several thousand acres on Cumberland Island off the lower coast of Georgia. This proved to be a valuable investment, since his land was covered with a magnificent stand of live oak and pine which he arranged to market.

He was back and forth between Newport and Charleston during 1785. Wayne was also going into debt to operate his own grant at Richmond. They were together at Mulberry Grove in March and jointly purchased a batch of new slaves, which were sent to Mulberry "to be well fed and clothed" in charge of the overseer there. Greene's onetime aide, Nat Pendleton, had married and established a prosperous law practice in Savannah, and they spent some convivial evenings at his home in the city. Greene also went down to Cumberland Island and sold off part of his land there at a profit to relieve his immediate debts, and then returned to Newport, this time to prepare his family for the voyage to Savannah.

Those old friends in Rhode Island who had suffered wrongs or injustice from the war came to him with their pleas for reimbursement or sympathy, and as always he was tireless in his efforts on behalf of those who claimed his help. Fairly large sums were consumed in scattered small amounts and loans which would never be repaid.

It was not until the autumn of 1785 that he was at last able to free himself of his Rhode Island commitments, make out his will, and find a ship to take him and his family to Savannah. He engaged a young man named Phineas Miller to accompany them as tutor to the children, agreeing to pay him thirty-five guineas a year and his keep. Miller was the son of a prosperous Connecticut family at Middlefield. He had recently graduated from Yale and was a protégé of its president, Ezra Stiles.

It was a "boisterous passage" of seventeen days, during which a man was lost overboard and the ship was more than once in danger. The Pendletons were waiting to welcome them, and Wayne was already there, having left his family behind in Pennsylvania with a light heart.

Viewed through Kitty's eyes, Mulberry Grove in its somewhat dilapidated condition may have left something to be desired, but it would not have been long before her housewifely talents made of it a comfortable and happy home. The estate had been confiscated ten years earlier from the Tory Governor Graham and had stood deserted since then, except for a few old slaves not carried off by the British raiders. Floods had wiped out the drainage system that had converted swamp acreage into rich rice fields, and the mulberry trees set out long ago to supply a silkworm project entertained by Graham had grown into an unkempt but imposing avenue leading to the pillared doorway.

The two-storied Georgian house had spacious fireplaces, requiring a large brick chimney at either end, built to warm and dry the rooms in the rainy riverside winters. Behind the house there were stables and a courtyard, a separate kitchen, as was usual in the South, and a poultry house which had a pigeon house on top with room for not less than a thousand birds. There were other outbuildings convenient for a large family, among them a fine smokehouse. The garden was admittedly in ruins, but a great variety of flowers and fruit trees still survived.

Greene's dinner table at Mulberry was seldom without guests, and he practiced no economy there. The Pendletons had a host of friends in Savannah who came to call and remained for refreshments, and Wayne brought in the more respectable of his many cronies, including some of the local Cincinnati. The Georgia young ladies, rebounding from the often unwelcome attentions of British and Tory suitors, were soon setting their caps for the famous and apparently unencumbered soldier of property at Richmond plantation, and more than one of them had already made an impression on Wayne's susceptible heart.

But his preference for the soothing hospitality of Mulberry was plain, and he was encouraged to make the most of it by both Kitty and her warmhearted husband—wrapped securely in his recovered domesticity and much occupied with his orchards, vegetable plot, and the timber cutting at Cumberland Island, where he had begun to build a new dwelling house at the site called Dungeness. It was not long before rumors, perhaps jealous ones, began in Savannah, and Greene was advised by several busybodies to warn Wayne off. Kitty described their relationship as "one between old and honest friends," and Wayne exclaimed in her defense, "Is no character, however perfect, out of reach of envy, malice, or destruction?" Greene seems to have taken no notice whatever, and comment soon subsided.

Happy as they were in their new surroundings, the Greenes seem always to have intended to divide their time between Mulberry and Rhode Island, perhaps to avoid the hot weather, though as time went by they might have been seduced by their Georgia Eden into abandoning the annual visit to the North. His youth came back to Greene in spite of his financial worries, and he was once caught playing "Puss-in-the-corner" with his wife amid the laughter of their children.

Between trips to Cumberland Island and even over the Florida border on his tireless money-making efforts, he kept up his correspondence with such distant friends as Kosciuszko and Lafayette and asked Knox's opinion about sending young George to be educated in France, as urged by Lafayette. The reply from Knox, now First Secretary at War in the national government at New York, has not survived. Greene found time now to read the books he had brought with him from his Coventry library and played with his children, who adored him; his youngest son in middle age recalled him as a tall man who used to take him on his knee and teach him to sing funny songs.

The evil aftermath of the Banks affair still hung over him and probably delayed his intended visit to the North in the summer of 1786. In June he was called to Savannah to meet one of the many creditors who still looked to him for payment on Banks's debts.

Kitty accompanied him, and after concluding the business conference they passed a pleasant evening with the Pendletons. They left Savannah early the following morning, in order to visit the rice fields of a neighbor along the river on their way home.

It was a hot summer day, but as an old campaigner he declined the loan of an umbrella to shelter him from the sun. After a long walk with his host around the rice fields in the humid midday heat, he rejoined Kitty at the house for the drive home to Mulberry Grove. By the time they reached their cool, shady rooms he had a violent headache. No one thought of sunstroke, after his years in the field with only whatever headgear happened to be available. The next day the pain lodged over his eyes, and a swelling of the forehead began.

Pendleton arrived toward evening, doubtless summoned by an anxious Kitty, and after one look at Greene he sent for a doctor. This man drew a little blood, as was customary for almost every ailment in those days, administered a few "common remedies," and went away. By the time a second physician could be called in, it was too late. The children were sent away to a neighboring plantation and retained all their lives a memory of the darkened house and their mother's tears. Wayne arrived in great anxiety to find his friend in a stupor from which he was never to be roused, and watched, weeping, by the bedside until the heavy breathing ceased. "I have seen a great and good man die," he wrote sadly to one of their former comrades.

Sunstroke, they said. But after all that campaigning in the summer heat of the war years, and considering a constitution that had withstood fever, bad food, and perpetual lack of sleep, a more likely diagnosis today would be a sudden heart failure brought on by the nervous aftereffects of Banks's perfidy, the ignorant public censure of his own motives and integrity, and the mounting pressures of his desperate effort to meet those debts which were not rightfully his, yet which threatened the peace and security of his family.

Savannah heard the news of his death with incredulity. His friends had seen him there, only a few days before, in perfect health. He was only forty-four years of age. He was beginning a new chapter in his life, like a bridegroom, with everything to live for. The country still needed men like him; there was much he could still have done, even in his Georgia retirement. Who could fill his place?

The body was taken by water to Major Pendleton's house in Bay Street in Savannah for the last honors—the same house he had left for the visit to Gibbons's rice plantation less than a week before. Minute guns were firing as the coffin was carried ashore, and a large crowd of citizens and militia were gathered to receive it. The streets were empty and silent, the shops were closed, the flags were all at half-mast. Troops with reversed arms and muffled drums led the procession from the Pendleton house to Christ Church while a band played the Dead March from *Saul*. A vault had been hastily opened. In the absence of a clergyman, Judge William Stephens read in a voice trembling with emotion the funeral service of the Church of England. The coffin was placed in the vault, the artillery fired thirteen rounds, and with trailed arms the troops withdrew slowly, followed by a silent, weeping crowd.

Kitty and the children spent that night at the Pendleton home, while Greene's former comrades retired to a coffeehouse and voted that his eldest son should be admitted to the Cincinnati at the age of eighteen. It was all they could think of to do in their shock and sorrow.

The news of Greene's death reached Mount Vernon through Harry Lee, who was then a member of Congress. "Universal grief reigns here," he wrote. "How hard is the fate of the United States, to lose such a man in the middle of life. Irreparable loss! But he is gone, and I am incapable to say more."

Washington said more, writing to one of Greene's friends who was a business partner in the Cumberland Island venture:

"Persuaded as I have always been of General Greene's integrity and worth, I spurned those reports which tended to calumniate his conduct in connection with Banks; being perfectly convinced that, whenever the matter should be investigated his motives for entering into it would prove pure and unimpeachable. I was not without my fears, however, that he might suffer in a pecuniary way by engagements with that man.

"I hope, however, that the case may ultimately be otherwise, and that upon a final settlement of his affairs there will be a handsome competency for Mrs. Greene and the children. But should it turn out differently, and should Mrs. Greene, yourself, and Mr. Rutledge think proper to entrust my namesake, G.W. Greene, to my care, I will give him as good an education as this country (I mean North America) will afford; and will bring him up to either of the genteel professions that his friends may choose or his own inclinations shall lead him to pursue, at my own cost and expense."

This from Washington, who had neglected his own affairs at Mount Vernon during the war and was already encumbered with several fatherless, penniless children in his own family of nieces and nephews, was an offer of true friendship and affection.

Afterward

And what became of Kitty Greene? She was still a young and attractive woman just turned thirty, left a widow with five small children, the eldest not yet twelve years old. The tutor, Phineas Miller, eleven years her junior, took charge of the shattered household at Mulberry Grove, dealing competently with the emergency and taking upon himself the distracting daily responsibilities and duties of running the plantation that had rested on Greene's shoulders. There is no portrait of Miller, but in all accounts of him the word "gentle" recurs, along with "cultivated" and often "conscientious." It was therefore to this gentle man that Kitty turned for comfort and companionship when the visits of condolence ended and her sorrowing neighbors returned to their own firesides and families.

Despite the rumored devotion of Anthony Wayne, whose nearby plantation was not flourishing, she soon sailed for New York, where she had many wartime friends in the Congressional circle. The children of course went with her, in the charge of Phineas Miller. She was again in New York in 1789, while it was briefly the capital of the new nation, and she dined then with the President and Mrs. Washington and attended the theater in their box.

She was back at Mulberry Grove in May of 1791 when the President interrupted his tour of the South to call on her there. After being feted and dined at Savannah by the local Cincinnati, Washington returned down the river to Mulberry for a family dinner and, with a due regard for *les convenances*, went on to a nearby tavern for that night's lodging before proceeding to Augusta the next day. It is probable that during the leisure of the second visit she confided to him as an old friend her doubts that she would be able to maintain the plantation in the straitened circumstances resulting from her husband's unexpected death after the drain already imposed on his resources by the Banks affair. And doubtless Washington's offer regarding young George's future was repeated and gratefully declined.

When she returned to Rhode Island for the following summer of 1792, she was again accompanied by the children and Miller, who had agreed to stay on at Mulberry as its manager or overseer, though his position was much more than that. He had become an indispensable member of the household. On the strength of his family background and Yale education and "gentle" manners, he was socially acceptable as an equal in the cultivated Southern society of Savannah which formed Kitty's immediate circle of friends and house guests, and he had by then probably taken his place as host during the Mulberry hospitality which remained undiminished, whatever her lack of funds. And it is probably due to his careful management that the plantation was able to support her and her family, possibly even with some assistance from his private funds.

Through Dr. Stiles of Yale, to whom Miller often paid his respects during his visits to the North, he became acquainted with another Yale man, recently graduated, who had had to work his way through college by tutoring and performing odd jobs of repair work which recommended him to the favorable notice of the faculty. Eli Whitney was looking for suitable employment, and Miller knew of a Carolina family in need of a tutor for the children. Since such an arrangement had worked out so well for himself, he suggested that Whitney might do worse than apply, and after some correspondence an understanding was reached with Miller's friends. When the Greene party sailed from New York for Savannah in the autumn of 1792, Whitney accompanied them.

Because of his belated start at the university, he and Miller were almost the same age, though Miller probably seemed to him a glamorous and sophisticated figure, with his comfortable Connecticut background and his present position in the employ of a charming, hospitable widow who spent money as though she had plenty of it. Whitney was wretchedly seasick on the voyage, his first, and Kitty's ready solicitude at once enveloped and enchanted him.

The intended job as tutor, when he got to it, proved to pay much less than he had been led to suppose, and another candidate had got there first. Whitney found himself at the age of twenty-eight stranded without funds a long way from home. Kitty was not in need of a tutor, but by now she and Miller had grown fond of their honest, somewhat Puritanical young protégé, while Whitney was enthralled by the to him luxurious and worldly life into which they had introduced him.

The widow Greene was something new in his experience—a self-confident, perhaps spoiled young matron with a natural gaiety of spirit and an outgoing friendliness that had enlivened even Valley Forge. The food at Mulberry was exotic and delicious to his New England palate—watermelons, sweet potatoes, seafood, rice and corn, cooked in the Southern style—and he tried to forget that the soft-voiced, smiling house servants who gave such prompt and willing attention to his comfort were slaves.

Mesmerized by this new experience, he accepted with some misgivings an invitation to stay on at Mulberry as a guest and read for the profession of law, probably with introductions from Kitty to men like Pendleton and Stephens at Savannah. In return, he insisted on doing little repairs on the plantation and invented for his hostess some household gadgets and devices—a tambour, or embroidery-frame, hairpins, and ingenious toys for the children.

While Kitty's guests sat around her dinner table sipping Madeira and discussing the postwar "depression" in the South, Whitney gained an unexpected insight into this new world. Tobacco prices had dropped, and its culture exhausted the soil; indigo was going into eclipse, and exports were off; the attempt to grow silk by importing the mulberry trees to feed the silkworms had failed for lack of skilled labor; slave prices were down, which represented a loss of capital to the owners. In 1794 Washington wrote: "Were it not that I am principled against selling Negroes, as you would cattle in a market, I would not in twelve months be possessed of a single one as a slave. I shall be happily mistaken if they are not found to be a very troublesome species of property ere many years have passed over our heads."

But there was a market for cotton, they said, if only production was not so slow. The green-seed cotton, which was all that would grow inland from the Sea Islands, had seeds that must be laboriously removed from the fiber by hand—a chore commonly done by Negro women at the rate of a pound of clean cotton a day. Someone remarked that there was a fortune waiting for the man who could invent a machine for separating the lint of the Up Country cotton from its seeds, and Kitty at once advised them to consult Whitney, who, she said, had even repaired her watch and could make anything.

At that time he had never seen raw cotton, but the idea of solving any handiwork problem was always a challenge to him. He got hold of some green-seed cotton and went to work in a little room they placed at his disposal. He had to make his own tools, because Savannah could provide nothing adaptable to his needs. Within a matter of days he had evolved a small table-model of the cotton gin that was the ancestor of the modern machine. Its simple mechanism provided a revolving cylinder with wire teeth which caught the lint and pulled it through a slotted wire grille too narrow for the seeds to pass, so they fell into a box beneath the roller. This was a clever improvement on a wooden roller system already in use which worked fairly well on the long-staple sea-island cotton with smooth black seeds. But in this existing device the tight-clinging seeds of the Up Country cotton broke, or were ground up and passed through with the lint.

When Miller and Mrs. Greene were finally admitted to the workshop for a demonstration, one problem remained unsolved. The lint stuck to the teeth of the cylinder and clogged its action. A persistent legend exists that Mrs. Greene picked up a clothes-brush—in some versions a hearth-brush—and applied it to the cylinder in the opposite direction, cleaning the teeth. A coarse brush was soon mounted by Whitney on a second revolving cylinder, with satisfactory results. Worked by hand, the machine would clean fifty pounds of cotton lint a day, and he at once began plans for a large machine that could be worked by a horse or by waterpower.

The essential features of the modern cotton gin, which so profoundly influenced American social and industrial history, are the same as this first hand-turned model—in which Kitty's clothes-brush played a part. Chief among the less fortunate results was the revival of the already unprofitable institution of slavery, by stimulating the cultivation of cotton, which demanded cheap unskilled field labor.

It was agreed among the three of them that they would keep the invention a secret until a patent could be secured. But by admitting a few acquaintances to view the model at Mulberry, they permitted news of it to escape, and because almost anyone could build a rough copy of so simple a mechanism, working imitations were soon in operation. Whitney was offered 100 guineas for the model on the spot but refused it in favor of applying for his own patent. The attempt to establish a monopoly was a mistake, for they were forced to wage a long and expensive battle against infringement of the patent that was finally granted the following year.

The revolutionary value of Whitney's achievement was apparent to the practical Phineas Miller. He was able to provide Whitney with sufficient funds to undertake the building of marketable machines, and they formed a partnership. Whitney returned to his native Connecticut to put up a factory at New Haven for the manufacture and distribution of machines, while Miller advertised for raw cotton to be ginned by the first machines installed at Mulberry and in the vicinity of Augusta where most of the green-seed cotton was grown. Since his capital was limited and Whitney had none at all, they would have done better to license their competitors to build and operate similar machines, but they were obstinately determined to hold a monopoly.

During one of the many lawsuits resulting from infringements, Whitney once appeared in court with a beautiful little model of the machine, and the judge so far unbent as to turn the crank "with obvious delight." But the patent laws at that time were weak, and a malicious rumor was spread that the Whitney gin damaged the fiber. Ill-luck dogged him. His New Haven factory burned down, with all his tools and materials. Though it was rebuilt—probably with Miller's money—rival machines were soon flooding the market.

Miller was meanwhile expending every cent he could command to buy raw cotton to feed their gins already operating in Georgia, and by 1795 he had sunk about $12,000 in the venture. Kitty rescued the partnership once by authorizing the use of estate funds to back up their credit. In 1796 she married Phineas Miller, after ten years of his daily companionship and mutual endeavor to save the children's inheritance. Even after Whitney gave up and turned to the manufacture of gun-parts at New Haven, Miller went on fighting for damages and patent rights until finally in 1799 he offered to sell or lease the existing gins for competitive manufacture. They sold Mulberry at auction—for $15,000—and moved the family to Dungeness on Cumberland Island, where the general had started to build a three-story mansion of about thirty rooms. Here they remained for the rest of their lives, while Whitney came and went, an always welcome guest. Kitty's half-motherly affection for him endured, in spite of distance, and her letters always urged him to return. "Come back to us and let me teach you, *by my own example*, how to enjoy the few fleeting years which anyone can count on," she wrote from Dungeness. "We are as gay as larks and really pass our time delightfully. Company enough you know we always have. We have a party of eighteen to eat turtle with us tomorrow. I wish you were the nineteenth!"

Whitney was there in 1802 and found the house without the "elegance" of Mulberry, but handsome, roomy, and stoutly built of the local concrete called tabby, made of lime and shells mixed with water. When he returned the following year, Miller was suddenly dead, exhausted before the age of forty by disappointment and the long legal struggle—just as the tide had begun to turn with the purchase by Tennessee of the patent rights to the gin.

The Greene children were all grown up and married, except George, who was drowned at the age of eighteen from an overturned canoe in the river. Martha married a man named Nightingale and named her son Phineas. Nat, Jr.'s, son, George Washington Greene, would write his grandfather's life in three scholarly volumes. Cornelia married Edward Littlefield—doubtless a Rhode Island cousin who bore her mother's maiden name—and went with him to live in Tennessee, accompanied by their children and their Negroes. Louisa, the youngest, was the last to marry and was said to exert "an unloving influence" over her mother as Kitty began at last to age. Louisa succeeded in coming between her mother and the rest of the family sufficiently to be named to inherit Dungeness.

She was apparently jealous of Whitney, who had not yet married. "I am prepared to love any woman who would make you happy," Kitty had written him impulsively during one of his long absences in the North. "I comfort myself sometimes in looking at your picture and mentally conversing with it—for it is true what Louisa says that I would *tell you* every thought of my soul—and I wish to consult you about finishing my house here. . . ."

Louisa's attempt to estrange Whitney by hinting of an intention on Kitty's part to bring a lawsuit against him over the partnership funds—obviously Louisa's own idea—was at least partially successful. He had not seen Kitty for seven years when she died of fever at Dungeness in 1814, at the age of fifty-nine.

Louisa herself eventually married a Mr. Shaw of Georgia and continued to live at Dungeness with the Nightingales. In 1818, when her nephew Phineas Nightingale was about fifteen years old, the boy was pottering around the shore near the Dungeness private wharf one day when a schooner put in from the West Indies and lowered a boat. Watching curiously from the wharf, Phineas saw the captain and the mate assisting a feeble old man ashore with his baggage, which consisted of one battered trunk and a case of Madeira wine.

When Phineas approached and gave his name, the aged visitor embraced him thankfully and to the boy's astonishment introduced himself as Colonel Lee. This elderly wreck was the fabulous Lighthorse Harry, hero of many a fireside tale of wartime gallantry and courage.

Lee's once charmed life, which had begun so brilliantly and after the war had led to a love match with his cousin Matilda Lee, heiress to the great house of Stratford on the Potomac, had crumbled into tragedy after the early death of Matilda in 1790. As governor of Virginia he married again in 1793, another heiress —Anne Hill Carter of Shirley on the James. The fifth child of this marriage, who would be known as Robert E., was born at Stratford in 1807.

After three terms as governor of Virginia, Colonel Lee became a member of Congress and was a revered and almost legendary figure in the new nation. But his income was small and his expenditures enormous, and like so many of his improvident, thoroughbred kind, he was wanting in all the qualities of a good businessman. He speculated in land, fell deeply into debt, and in 1811 was compelled to transfer possession of Stratford to his son Henry, then come of age, by Matilda, and remove his second family to live in Alexandria. There, except for Mrs. Lee's share in the Shirley estate, which went to her brother, they would have been in actual want.

By a series of unfortunate accidents Lee became involved in a political riot in Baltimore in 1812 and was brutally beaten up, along with several friends, by a mob. His injuries were permanent, and he became a penniless invalid at fifty-seven. His friends Madison and Monroe raised funds to send him to the West Indies in the hope of a cure, leaving his family in a small brick house in Alexandria.

But he did not improve, wandering from island to island for several years, until in a desperate effort to get home before he died, he sailed from Nassau on a schooner bound for Boston. Failing fast during the voyage, he prevailed upon the captain to set him ashore at Dungeness. He must have been unaware of Kitty's death in the year of his own collapse, but in any case he would have felt sure of shelter with the family of his old comrade at arms, General Greene.

He was too weak to walk from the wharf to the house, and Phineas ran on ahead to request his Aunt Shaw to send a carriage. Lee was warmly welcomed by the two sisters, who as children had often heard his name spoken with affection by their father, and he was promised comfort and security for as long as he cared to stay with them.

Several days later he found himself able to walk around the garden, leaning on young Phineas's shoulder, and received some visits from old comrades living in the neighborhood. Wayne, having failed as a Georgia planter, had returned North to conduct a distinguished campaign against the Indians in Ohio, which resulted in a lasting peace on that frontier. On his way back to Pennsylvania he died at Presque Isle, now Erie, during an attack of his old enemy the gout.

When the army and navy youngsters assisting at Andrew Jackson's campaign for possession of the posts along the Florida border heard that Lighthorse Harry Lee was ill at Dungeness, they begged the privilege of taking turns to sit at his bedside, day and night, just for the sake of bearing him company. On an afternoon in March a few weeks after his arrival at Dungeness he died, still sheltered by the memory of his beloved commander.

Selected Bibliography

A partial list of the chief sources consulted

Abbott, Wilbur. *New York in the American Revolution*. New York: Charles Scribner's Sons, 1929.

American Heritage. *Book of the Revolution*. New York: Simon & Schuster, 1958.

Appleton's *Cyclopedia of American Biography*. New York: D. Appleton & Co., 1898.

Arnold, S. G. *Rhode Island*. 2 vols. New York: Taylor, 1860.

Bass, Robert D. *The Gamecock*. New York: Holt, Rinehart and Winston, 1961.

———. *The Green Dragoon*. New York: Henry Holt & Co., 1937.

———. *The Swamp Fox*. New York: Henry Holt & Co., 1959.

Billias, George A. *Washington's Opponents*. New York: William Morrow & Co., 1969.

Bird, Harrison. *The March to Saratoga*. New York: Oxford University Press, 1963.

Boyd, Thomas. *Lighthorse Harry Lee*. New York: Charles Scribner's Sons, 1931.

Callahan, North. *Henry Knox*. New York: Rinehart & Co., 1958.

Carrington, Henry. *Battles of the American Revolution*. New York: 1877.

Chinard, Gilbert. *Washington as the French Knew Him*. Princeton, N.J.: Princeton University Press, 1940.

Cohn, D. L. *Life and Times of King Cotton*. New York: Oxford University Press, 1956.

Commager, Henry Steele, and Morris, Richard. *The Spirit of '76*. 2 vols. New York: The Bobbs-Merrill Co., 1958.

Cutter, William. *General Israel Putnam.* 1857.

Drake, Francis. *Henry Knox.* Boston: Samuel Drake, 1873.

Draper, Lyman. *King's Mountain and its Heroes.* 1881.

Forbes, Allen, and Cadman, Paul. *France and New England.* New York: State Street Trust Co., 1925.

Freeman, Douglas Southall. *Washington and His Generals.* 7 vols. New York: Charles Scribner's Sons. 1951-57.

Gibbes, R. W. *Documentary History of the American Revolution.* Columbia, S.C.: Banner Steam-Power Press, 1853.

Greene, Francis Vinton. *Nathanael Greene.* New York: Appleton, 1893.

Greene, George Washington. *Nathanael Greene.* 3 vols. Boston: Houghton Mifflin, 1900.

Gregorie, Anne King. *Thomas Sumter.* Columbia, S.C.: R. L. Bryan Co., 1931.

Headley, J. T. *Washington and His Generals.* 2 vols. New York: Baker and Scribner, 1847.

Heath, William. *Memoirs.* Thomas and Andrews, 1798.

Humphreys, David. *Israel Putnam.* 1804.

James, William. *Francis Marion.* Marietta, Ga.: Continental Book Co., 1948.

Laurens, John. *Correspondence.* New York: Arno Press, 1969.

Lee, Henry. *Memoirs of the War in the Southern Department.* New York: University Publishing Co., 1870.

Lossing, Benson. *Field-book of the American Revolution.* 2 vols. New York: Harper, 1850.

McCrady, Edward. *History of South Carolina in the Revolution.* 2 vols. New York: The Macmillan Company, 1901.

Martin, Charles. *Life of Artemus Ward.*

Mirsky, Jeannette. *The World of Eli Whitney.* New York: The Macmillan Company, 1952.

Montross, Lynn. *Ragtag and Bobtail.* New York: Harper, 1952.

Morris, Robert. *Encyclopedia of American History.* New York: Harper, 1953.

Moultrie, William. *Memoirs.* New York: Longworth, 1802.

New York State Archives. University of the State of New York, 1926.

Partridge, Bellamy. *Sir Billy Howe.* New York: Longmans Green, 1932.

Peterson, E. *Rhode Island.* New York: Taylor, 1853.

Ramsay, David. *History of South Carolina.* 2 vols. Newberry, S.C.: W. J. Duffie, 1858.

Reed, Joseph. *Life and Correspondence.* 2 vols. Philadelphia: 1847.

Sellers, C. C. *Benedict Arnold.* New York: Minton, Balch, 1930.

Sheer, George, and Rankin, Hugh. *Rebels and Redcoats.* New York: World Publishing Co., 1957.

Simms, William Gilmore. *Francis Marion.* New York: J. C. Derby, 1854.

———. *Nathanael Greene.* New York: Derby & Jackson, 1858.

———. *The Partisan.* New York: Lovell, Coryell, & Co., 1850.

Sparks, Jared. *John Sullivan.* Little, Brown: 1848.

Stryker, William. *Battles of Trenton and Princeton.* Boston: Houghton Mifflin, 1898.

Thayer, Theodore. *Nathanael Greene.* New York: Twayne, 1960.

Tuckerman, Bayard. *Lafayette.* 2 vols. New York: Dodd, Mead, 1889.

Valentine, Alan. *Lord Stirling.* New York: Oxford University Press, 1969.

Wallace, Willard. *Appeal to Arms.* New York: Harper, 1951.

Weigley, Russell. *The Partisans' War.* South Carolina Tricentennial Commission, 1970.

Whiteley, Emily Stone. *Washington and His Aides.* New York: The Macmillan Company, 1936.

Whitlock, Brand. *Lafayette.* 2 vols. New York: Appleton, 1929.

Wickwire, Franklin and Mary. *Cornwallis.* Boston: Houghton Mifflin, 1970.

Willcox, William. *Portrait of a General* (Clinton). New York: Knopf, 1964.

WPA Guides to Georgia, New Jersey, Rhode Island, Virginia, and South Carolina.

Index